ZED BOOKS TITLES ON CONFLICT AND CONFLICT RESOLUTION

The hope that conflicts within societies might decrease markedly with the demise of the Cold War have been cruelly disappointed. Zed Books has published a number of titles which deal specifically with the diverse forms of modern conflict, their complex causes, and some of the ways in which we may realistically look forward to prevention, mediation and resolution.

Adedeji, A. (ed.), *Comprehending and Mastering African Conflicts: The Search for Sustainable Peace and Good Governance*

Allen, T. and J. Seaton (eds), *The Media of Conflict: War Reporting and Representations of Ethnic Violence*

Bishara, M., *Palestine/Israel: Peace or Apartheid*

Cockburn, C., *The Space Between Us: Negotiating Gender and National Identities in Conflict*

Cristalis, I., *Bitter Dawn: East Timor – A People's Story*

Duffield, M., *Global Governance and the New Wars: The Merging of Development and Security*

Evans, G., J. Goodman and N. Lansbury (eds), *Moving Mountains: Communities Confront Mining and Globalization*

Fink, C., *Living Silence: Burma under Military Rule*

Fisher, S. *et al.*, *Working with Conflict: Skills and Strategies for Action*

Gopal, S., *Anatomy of a Confrontation: Ayodhya and the Rise of Communal Politics in India*

Guyatt, N., *The Absence of Peace: Understanding the Israeli–Palestinian Conflict*

Jacobs, S., R. Jacobson and J. Marchbank (eds), *States of Conflict: Gender, Violence and Resistance*

Kapadia, K. (ed.), *The Violence of Development: The Political Economy of Gender*

Koonings, K. and D. Kruijt (eds), *Societies of Fear: The Legacy of Civil War, Violence and Terror in Latin America*

Koonings, K. and D. Kruijt (eds), *Political Armies: The Military and Nation Building in the Age of Democracy*

Lewer, N. and S. Schofield *Non-Lethal Weapons – Military Strategies and Technologies for 21ˢᵗ-Century Conflict*

Lumpe, L. (ed.), *Running Guns: The Black Market in Small Arms*

Macrae, J., *Aiding Recovery? The Crisis of Aid in Chronic Political Emergencies*

Mare, G., *Ethnicity and Politics in South Africa*

Meintjes, S., A. Pillay and M. Turshen (eds), *The Aftermath: Women in Post-conflict Transformation*

Melvern, L., *A People Betrayed: The Role of the West in Rwanda's Genocide*

Moser, C. and F. Clark (eds), *Victims, Perpetrators or Actors? Gender, Armed Conflict and Political Violence*

Nzongola-Ntalaja, G., *The Congo from Leopold to Kabila: A People's History*

Ohlsson, L., *Hydro Politics: Conflicts over Water as a Development Constraint*

Pirotte, C., B. Husson and F. Grunewald (eds), *Responding to Emergencies and Fostering Development – The Dilemmas of Humanitarian Aid*

Shiva, V., *The Violence of the Green Revolution*

Suliman, M. (ed.), *Ecology, Politics and Violent Conflict*

Turshen, M. and C. Twagiramariya (eds), *What Women Do in Wartime: Gender and Conflict in Africa*

Vickers, J., *Women and War*

For full details of this list and Zed's other subject and general catalogues, please write to: The Marketing Department, Zed Books, 7 Cynthia Street, London NI 9JF, UK or email:

sales@zedbooks.demon.co.uk

Visit our website at: http://www.zedbooks.demon.co.uk

FRAGILE PEACE

State Failure, Violence and Development in Crisis Regions

EDITED BY TOBIAS DEBIEL
WITH AXEL KLEIN

Zed Books

LONDON · NEW YORK

in association with

The Development and Peace
Foundation
BONN

Fragile Peace: State Failure, Violence and Development in Crisis Regions was first published in English by Zed Books Ltd, 7 Cynthia Street, London N1 9JF, UK and Room 400, 175 Fifth Avenue, New York, NY 10010, USA in 2002 in association with The Development and Peace Foundation, Bonn.

www.zedbooks.demon.co.uk

Published with the support of the German Ministry for Economic Cooperation and Development.

First published in German as *Der zerbrechliche frieden. Krisenregionen zwischen Staatsversagen, Gewalt und Entwicklung*, Verlag J.H.W. Dietz Nachf. GMbH Bonn.

Cover designed by Andrew Corbett
Set in Monotype Fournier by Ewan Smith, London
Printed and bound in the United Kingdom by Bookcraft Ltd, Midsomer Norton

Distributed in the USA exclusively by Palgrave, a division of St Martin's Press, LLC, 175 Fifth Avenue, New York, NY 10010.

A catalogue record for this book is available from the British Library

ISBN 1 84277 170 1 cased
ISBN 1 84277 171 X limp

Contents

Boxes, Tables and Maps

The Development and Peace Foundation

Notes on the Contributors

Bernardo Arévalo de León is director of WSP (War-torn Societies Project), International Office for Latin America, and coordinator of the Programme on Security and Defence Studies at the Facultad Latinoamericana de Ciencias Sociales (FLACSO). His publications include (together with Edelberto Torres-Rivas) *From Conflict to Dialogue: The WSP Guatemala Way*, Geneva and Guatemala City (1999); 'Demilitarization and democracy: implications of the popular referendum for the Agreement on the Strengthening of Civilian Power and the Role of the Army in a Democracy', in *The Popular Referendum (Consulta Popular) and the Future of the Peace Process in Guatemala*, Washington, DC: Woodrow Wilson International Center for Scholars (November 1999; Working Paper 241), pp. 43–50; *Sobre Arenas Movedizas: Sociedad, Estado y Ejercito en Guatemala*, Guatemala: FLACSO (1998).

Nicole Ball is senior fellow at the Center for International Policy in Washington, DC and visiting senior research fellow at the Center for International Development and Conflict Management at the University of Maryland. Current projects include editing a handbook on security sector governance for African practitioners written by African security and development specialists and developing a security sector institutional assessment tool. She has also co-authored a background paper on accountability in the security sector for the UNDP *Human Development Report 2002*. Her recent publications include 'Transforming security sectors: the IMF and World Bank approaches', *Conflict, Security, Development*, 1 (1) (2001): 45–66; 'The challenge of rebuilding war-torn societies', in Chester A. Crocker, Fen Osler Hampson and Pamela Aall (eds), *Turbulent Peace: The Challenges of Managing International Conflict*, Washington, DC: US Institute of Peace Press (2001); 'Off-budget military expenditure and revenue: issues and policy perspectives for donors', CSDG Occasional Papers No. 1, King's College, London, January 2002 (with Dylan Hendrickson).

David Darchiashvili is head of the Research Department of the Georgian Parliament and coordinator of the Security and Civil–Military Relations programme at the Caucasian Institute for Peace, Democracy and Development (CIPDD) in Tbilisi, Georgia. His publications include *Georgia: The Search for State Security*, Stanford University, Center for International Security and Arms Control, Caucasus Working Papers (1997); 'Trends of strategic thinking in Georgia: achievements, problems and prospects', in G. K. Cassady Craft, S. A. Jones and M. Beck, *Crossroads and Conflict: Security and Foreign Policy in the Caucasus and Central Asia*, London and New York: Routledge (2000), pp. 66–74.

Tobias Debiel is a political scientist and a research associate at the Development and Peace Foundation (Stiftung Entwicklung und Frieden, SEF) in Bonn. He is active in several non-governmental organizations, among them the World Economy, Ecology and Development Association (WEED) and the German Platform for Peaceful Conflict Management. He is co-editor of books on the peaceful settlement of conflicts, the new interventionism and the privatization of global policy. He has published more than eighty articles in distinguished journals, readers, handbooks, occasional papers series and newspapers. Recent publications include 'Strengthening the UN as an effective world authority: cooperative security versus hegemonic crisis management', *Global Governance*, 6 (1) (January–March 2000) Boulder and Cologne: 25–41; (together with Martina Fischer) *Crisis Prevention and Conflict Management by the European Union: Concepts, Capacities and Problems of Coherence* (Berghof Report, No. 4, September 2000), Berlin: Berghof Research Centre for Constructive Conflict Management.

Rainer Freitag-Wirminghaus is research fellow at the German Institute for Middle East Studies, Hamburg. He has carried out numerous research projects on geo and security policy in the Caucasus and Central Asia as well as on the oil problems in the Caspian Sea. His publications include 'Politische Konstellationen im Südkaukasus', in *Aus Politik und Zeitgeschichte* (15 October 1999, B 42/99): 21–31; 'Südkaukasien und die Erdöl-Problematik am Kaspischen Meer', in Gerhard Mangott (ed.), *Brennpunkt Südkaukasus*, Vienna: Braumuller (1999), pp. 247–82.

Hans-Joachim Heintze is associate professor at the Institute for International Law of Peace and Armed Conflicts, University of Bochum. He has carried out numerous research and training projects in the areas of human rights as well as general and humanitarian international law. His publications include 'On legal understanding of autonomy', in Markku Suski (ed.), *Autonomy: Applications and Implications*, The Hague: Kluwer (1998), pp. 7–32; 'The status of German minorities in bilateral agreements of the Federal Republic', in Stefan Wolf (ed.), *German Minorities in Europe*, New York: Berghahn (2000), pp. 205–18; 'New direction in the approach of the OSCE High Commissioner on national minorities', *Netherlands Quarterly of Human Rights* 19 (2001): 101–12.

Uwe Holtz is professor and honorary lecturer in political science at the University of Bonn; president of the European Association of Former MPs; member of the governing body of the Development and Peace Foundation. From 1974 to 1994 he was chairman of the German Parliamentary Committee for Economic Cooperation. His publications include (as editor) *50 Jahre Europarat*, Baden-Baden: Nomos (2000); 'Entwicklungspolitik – Bilanz und Herausforderungen', in Karl Kaiser and Hans-Peter Schwarz (eds), *Weltpolitik im neuen Jahrhundert*, Bonn: Nomos (2000), pp. 481–508; 'A preliminary assessment of the EU–ACP Agreement', *D+C (Development and Cooperation)* 2 (2000): S. 8–12.

Axel Klein is head of research at DrugScope and the Institute for African Alternatives (IFAA) in London. He has carried out research projects in the Horn of Africa, Nigeria and the Caribbean on conflict, society and culture and the politics of drug control. His recent publications include (together with Mohamed Suliman) 'Die Inversion der Ethnizität: Von Wahrnehmung zur Konfliktursache. Die Fur- und Nubakonflikte im Westsudan', in *Friedensbericht 1998*, Chur, Zurich: Swiss Peace Foundation (1998), pp. 257–76; 'Between the death penalty and decriminalisation: new directions for drug control in the Commonwealth Caribbean', in *New West India Guide*, Leiden, Holland, 75 (4) (2001): 193–228.

Sabine Kurtenbach is senior research assistant at the Institute of Ibero-American Studies attached to the German Overseas Institute Hamburg. She is also co-editor of *Jahrbuch Menschenrechte*, Frankfurt/Main: Suhrkamp. Her publications include 'Costa Rica – intelligentes Konfliktmanagement als Basis friedlicher Entwicklung', in *Die Friedens-Warte*, Bd. 75 (2000, H. 3–4): 371–87; 'Zivilgesellschaft und zivile Konfliktregelung. Der Beitrag der Zivilgesellschaft zur Beendigung bewaffneter

Konflikte', in P. Hengstenberg, K. Kohut and G. Maihold (eds), *Zivil-gesellschaft in Lateinamerika. Interessenvertretung und Regierbarkeit*, Frankfurt/Main: Vervuert (2000), pp. 221–34.

Andreas Mehler is director of the Institute for African Affairs in Hamburg and a former senior researcher for the Conflict Prevention Network (SWP-CPN) at the Stiftung Wissenschaft und Politik (SWP) in Berlin. His publications include (as an editor with Ulf Engel) *Gewaltsame Konflikte und ihre Prävention in Afrika. Hintergründe, Analysen und Strategien für die entwicklungspolitische Praxis*, Hamburg: Institute für Africa-Kunde (1998); (with Claude André Ribaux) *Crisis Prevention and Conflict Management in Technical Cooperation: An Overview of the National and International Debate*, Wiesbaden: Universum *GTZ* series, No. 270 (2000).

James Oporia-Ekwaro is originally from Uganda and is currently director of the Centre for Information and Research on Africa Policy Alternatives (CIRAPA), London. In the 1970s he served as associate secretary for Africa of the World Student Christian Federation (WSCF), Nairobi, and later in Geneva as associate general secretary at the international office. From 1977 to 1979 he served at the All Africa Conference of Churches (AACC), Nairobi, Kenya, first as executive secretary for international affairs and later as deputy general secretary. He served as ambassador of Uganda to China, North Korea, Cambodia and Vietnam, based in Beijing in 1979–82. From 1991 to 1998 he worked at Christian Aid in London, first as head of department for Africa and later as senior policy adviser on conflict. He is currently working on his doctorate in international relations, specializing in African security.

Siegfried Pausewang is senior research fellow at the Chr. Michelsen Institute of Research on Development and Human Rights in Bergen, Norway. He has been carrying out social research work in Africa, especially in Ethiopia, for over thirty years. His publications include the chapter 'Ethiopia', in *Human Rights in Developing Countries Yearbook 1996*, The Hague, Holland, pp. 195–247; (together with Kjetil Tronvoll et al.) *The Ethiopian 2000 Elections: Democracy Advanced or Restricted?* Oslo: Norwegian Institute of Human Rights (2000); *Peasants, Land and Society*, Munich and London: Weltforum Verlag (1983); as an editor, *Ethiopia: Rural Development Options*, London: Zed Books (1990).

Abbreviations

CIS	Community of Independent States
CSCE	Conference on Security and Cooperation in Europe
DfID	Department for International Development (UK)
ECOSOC	Economic and Social Council (of the UN)
EHRCO	Ethiopian Human Rights Council
EPRDF	Ethiopian People's Liberation Front
EU	European Union
GUUAM	Georgia, Ukraine, Uzbekistan, Azerbaijan, Moldova
ICCPR	International Covenant on Civil and Political Rights
ICTR	International Criminal Tribunal for Rwanda
ICTY	International Criminal Tribunal for the former Yugoslavia
IMF	International Monetary Fund
MINUGUA	Misión de Naciones Unidas para Guatemala
NGO	non-governmental organization
OAS	Organization of American States
OAU	Organization of African Unity
OECD	Organization for Economic Cooperation and Development
OLF	Oromo Liberation Front
OSCE	Organization for Security and Cooperation in Europe
PFDJ	People's Front for Democracy and Justice (Eritrea)
RRA	Rahanwein Resistance Army
SNM	Somali National Movement
SPLA	Sudanese People's Liberation Army
TPLF	Tigray People's Liberation Front
UNDP	United Nations Development Programme
URNG	Unidad Revolucionaria Nacional Guatemalteca, National Revolutionary Unit of Guatemala
WIDER	World Institute for Development Economics Research
WTO	World Trade Organization

Foreword

UWE HOLTZ

The Development and Peace Foundation (Stiftung Entwicklung und Frieden) presents this publication to examine different crisis regions and conflict scenarios under three aspects: state failure, violence and development. Coming out exactly four years after the publication of *Successful Peace* (*Der gelungene Frieden*), in the ONE World (EINE Welt) series, this is an important contribution to the field.

Gustav Heinemann, Germany's president from 1969 to 1974, urged that peace must be made anew on a daily basis. Today – in view of the global reach of terrorism, and strife in the Balkans, the Caucasus, the Near and Middle East as well as in other developing regions – we understand this imperative better then ever.

Events during the 1990s, such as the genocide in Rwanda as well as many other crises and wars, made it plain that our existing conflict-prevention capacities are woefully insufficient. New types of armed conflict are emerging that are de-linked from the state and are often conducted in the name of religious, ethnic or clan-related identities. They have further increased the challenge to politics: guerrillas, mercenaries, warlords or fanatical terrorists respect neither the formality of boundaries nor the sanctity of peace accords.

The barbaric acts of terror perpetrated in the United States on 11 September 2001 were a challenge to the international community as a whole. As the UN Security Council unanimously voted, they were a belligerent attack on one country and have to be combated as a threat to world peace and international security, with all the means consistent with the UN Charter. This unanimous vote is 'historic in scope' because in addition to the NATO partners, old and new rivals such as Russia and China have also rallied around the USA:

> They have all understood that what is at stake here is a good as precious as it is fragile: whether we will be able to enjoy the security that

guarantees our freedom; whether we will be able to open our borders, universities, and workshops to outsiders; whether we will be able to protect the spaces of freedom that we have won in bloody contests, spaces in which religions and ideologies can subsist side by side in a reasonably peaceful fashion. (Josef Joffe)[1]

It is in this sense that September 11 forces us to reflect on, and make sure of, the innermost mechanisms that hold our societies together. These forces of cohesion, including democracy and human rights, individual and economic freedom, equal rights for men and women, material prosperity, social responsibility and solidarity, the rule of law and acknowledgement of the state's monopoly of the use of force, the 'light' of enlightenment and reason, the separation of Church and state, a future that is not predetermined, and respect for life, nature and the generations to come, have a universal formative power. In Europe, too, these values have been under threat time and again.

September 11 is one more reason for the 'West' to think about what we owe to our ONE World. In view of universally acknowledged values such as freedom, solidarity and shared responsibility, the heads of the world's states and governments, including those from the wealthier countries, gathered at the United Nations Millennium Summit in New York in September 2000 and took an oath to shape the world in the new century so as to make it a more humane and just place in which to live. In concrete terms, they committed themselves to reducing the share of the poor among the world's population by one half by 2015. In the first report presented by the North–South Commission in 1980, Commission Chairman Willy Brandt called on the world to understand the efforts aimed at balancing the interests of industrialized and developing countries as a new 'historic dimension for the active pursuit of peace': 'While hunger rules peace cannot prevail. He who wants to ban war must also ban mass poverty.' Are we now, finally, making proactive efforts to translate this insight into practice – not as the one and only element, but as one of the important components of a new sustainable peace policy?

In the post-September 11 world, both Germany and Europe are in fact faced, more clearly than ever, with a range of challenges, both new and old. The development towards a peace-dedicated responsibility of Europeans in their own territory, for neighbouring regions and beyond, has accelerated – albeit in conjunction with the concern that war could assume the role of a dominant expedient, forcing politics into the background. Karl von Clausewitz, though often misunderstood, had, in his theoretical treatise *On War*, accorded priority to politics in determining the objectives to be achieved by means of war. Politics, he noted, determined the aims of its military instrument, for which reason the former will always run like a red thread through the acts of war, never relinquishing its influence on it. All else, in particular the conduct of war as an end in itself, he went on, must be seen as bloodthirsty.

The use of military means is invariably a double-edged affair and can be no more than *ultima ratio*. What, then, is *prima ratio*? Seen in terms of the tensions and frustrations to which the gulf between poor and rich gives rise, it is to bring together development and peace, an objective that has found expression in the Foundation's name: to engage in a new kind of *détente* consisting of economic, social and ecological components. Above all, development, in the sense of UNCED's *Agenda 21*, is the new name for peace. The chief task of development policy is to contribute to a development that is at once economically sustainable, socially equitable, humane, democratic and peaceful.

The ONE World volume *Successful Peace*, edited by Professor Volker Matthies in 1997, imparted the message that peace is possible and feasible even in the face of adverse conditions. The task is now to determine what institutional material, normative and emotional causes are responsible for the fragility of peace and how to create the conditions needed for a more stable and more durable peace.

In his introduction to this volume, the editor, Tobias Debiel, presents some interesting reflections on the complex issues at hand: the crisis of the state, but also the arrogance of ruling cliques as central causes of armed conflict and impediments to development; the structures, inherent dynamics and formal transformation of violence that increasingly characterize countries in conflict and further complicate peace-making; and the transformation of war-torn countries. These theoretical observations are interwoven with an overview of the different contributions organized by geographical region: the South Caucasus, including a case study on Georgia; Central America, with a case study on Guatemala; the Horn of Africa, with a case study on Ethiopia. The editor concludes the volume with a contribution of his own on the challenge presented by September 11, pleading in favour of a reorientation of foreign, security and development policies.

All the contributions are rooted in scholarship and present strong analyses and concrete policy recommendations geared towards practical politics. The contributors cast light on the manifold reasons for the fragility of peace, inferring from their diagnoses both conditions and measures needed for a stable peace.

Since 1998 Germany's Red–Green government coalition has developed its own overall strategy for civil crisis prevention, conflict resolution and peace consolidation, forging ahead with a policy of disarmament and arms control in the sense of a forward-looking peace policy. As a result, Germany's entire development policy has been redirected towards crisis prevention and peace policy. Specific measures include the development of a civil peace service, the Cologne debt-relief initiative, and the German contributions to international programmes geared to fighting poverty, malnutrition and the spread of AIDS. Crisis prevention has become an integral element of all of Germany's development cooperation programmes. Germany took the UN proclamation of 2001 as the 'international year of dialogue between cultures' as an occasion to enlarge its contributions aimed at harnessing intensified intercultural communication in the service of effective conflict prevention. The German government's increased worldwide support for human rights, democracy and the rule of law not only aims to promote successful, sustainable development, but also seeks to create the conditions needed for durable stability and peace.

Development cooperation is a cross-cutting field where the question of survival brings different policy areas together. Effective overall policy coherence as well as coordination of objectives and action at the national, European and international levels and between these levels are the *sine qua non* of greater success in the field of development policy. In Germany, political coherence at the national level could best be achieved by instituting a development cabinet at the federal level. This cabinet would be responsible for defining and overseeing the foreign trade- and security-related aims of German policy. The development impact assessments for proposed legislation that have been instituted by the German government are an important step on the road to policy coherence.

One stated objective of the German government is to move the European Union to develop further its Common Foreign and Security Policy into a comprehensive security strategy. Embracing political, military, economic, social and ecological elements, this strategy would interlock with Europe's foreign, security, defence and development policies and strengthen the EU conflict-prevention capacity.

The United Nations, the World Bank, the International Monetary Fund and the World Trade Organization are actors crucial to the balance of forces in our world as well as to a fair accommodation of national interests. The creation of legal structures for international relations, including clearly defined avenues of appeal, is the appropriate response to the global trend towards the privatization of the use of force and the ruthless application of violent means in pursuit of particularistic interests. Should the fair accommodation of interests based on due process become the rule in international politics as well, the preachers of violence would see their chances of recruitment considerably reduced.

As the examples of Guatemala, Rwanda and Afghanistan illustrate, it is not only more humane but also far less costly to prevent armed conflicts than to clean up and reconstruct afterwards. Reasonable and effective development cooperation contributes not only to improving people's living conditions but also to creating a framework favourable to peace and security. Development cooperation does, however, run the risk of being pressed into a Procrustes' bed of conflicting geopolitical, economic and foreign policy interests, jeopardizing its potential positive impacts. In future all cooperation programmes involving technical, financial and personnel assistance must contain elements contributing to conflict prevention.

Development policy can draw upon a wide range of experience in dealing with conflicts and their causes and can make fundamental contributions to coming to terms with these factors. The task of dealing effectively with conflicts must focus above all on four levels: on conflict prevention, in particular by addressing causes of conflicts such as poverty, persecution, insufficient political participation and exploitation of the environment; on mediation and de-escalation of conflicts; on post-conflict management; and on promotion of inter-ethnic and intercultural dialogue. All of these measures contribute significantly to undercutting the support for international terrorism. In institutional, financial and personnel terms, German international policy must be placed in a better position to contribute effectively to international civil crisis prevention, conflict regulation and peace consolidation. This should include the use of new forms of cooperation between governmental, non-governmental, international and multilateral actors.

Where must the significance of development cooperation be sought? It can – appropriately used – defuse emergency situations and provide meaningful contributions to and impulses for development in a developing country as well as helping to prevent violent conflicts, and to this extent it can become a hallmark of good practice. It can provide impulses and incentives for improving the situation of people in developing countries, play a role subsidiary and complementary to efforts undertaken in these countries, and serve as a catalyst in solving problems there.

The heads of state and government attending the UN Millennium Summit set themselves the goal of halving, by 2015, the figure of 1.2 billion of the world's population living in absolute poverty. Intensified efforts are essential if this goal is to be reached: on the part of developing countries, industrialized countries and inter-governmental organizations, at governmental and non-governmental levels alike. The German government is supporting this ambitious goal through the national action plan adopted on 4 April 2001, which is binding for all German ministries and agencies. The German government has committed itself to working towards coherence between all policy fields in pursuit of the primary goal of poverty reduction and to using its influence at the European level and in the framework of the OECD towards this end. It has also pledged to continue all efforts aimed at improving the quality and increasing the sustainable effectiveness of development cooperation. The attainment of these goals calls for the necessary political will and for mobilization of greater development-related resources.

Peace and conflict prevention are constitutive elements for the survival capacity of our ONE World. 'So the question is no longer', the philosopher Immanuel Kant wrote, 'whether perpetual peace is a thing or a chimera, and whether we are not deceiving ourselves in our judgement if we assume the former; but we must act as if the thing existed.' Securing this fragile 'thing' is part of the high art of politics and a worthwhile objective of scientific advisory services. May the present volume prove to be of use to the policy of peace.

(Translation: Paul Knowlton)

NOTE

1. Josef Joffe is co-editor of the German weekly *Die Zeit* and an international writer and broadcaster. His essays and reviews have appeared in periodicals including the *New York Review of Books*, *New York Times Magazine*, *New Republic* and *Prospect* (London). He is a regular contributor to major US and British dailies and a commentator on US, British and German television and radio. Among his recent publications is *The Great Powers*, London: Phoenix (1998).

Do Crisis Regions Have a Chance of Lasting Peace? The Difficult Transformation from Structures of Violence

TOBIAS DEBIEL

§ The past decade has been marked by a large number of intra-state wars. The situation has been characterized by the massive use of violence with scant regard for civilians, by humanitarian disasters, and by repeated ceasefire agreements and violations. All regions of the world have been affected: sub-Saharan Africa with its numerous conflict systems (Horn of Africa, the Great Lakes region, Southern Africa, West Africa), Latin America (with the focus on Columbia, Peru and Central America), the Caucasus, Central and Southern Asia (especially Afghanistan, Tajikistan and Sri Lanka) as well as East and South-East Asia (in particular Indonesia and the Philippines). Most of the conflicts were aimed at overthrowing the regime currently in power. Of similar importance was striving for autonomy or secession.

Following a rapid increase in the frequency of war in the late 1980s and early 1990s, things have quietened down to a certain extent since the mid-1990s, although a permanent settlement has still not been found in a large number of conflicts (Wallensteen and Sollenberg 2000). The situation in numerous countries could be referred to as a 'fragile peace'; that is to say, even though a temporary settlement has been found to blatant warlike clashes, the economy, state and society remain shaped and influenced by structures of violence. Indeed, in some cases, the situation is so fragile that we could speak of a latent war – even though a return to armed struggle is not always directly imminent. The option of violence is deeply embedded in the collective memory and often influences (consciously or unconsciously) the present thinking and actions of the political players locally. Examples of such situations include Georgia, Azerbaijan (Nagorno Karabakh), El Salvador, Guatemala, Peru, Mozambique, Ethiopia and Eritrea (which were involved in an inter-state war from 1998 to 2000), Liberia, the Philippines, Tajikistan and certainly also Afghanistan following the overthrow of the Taliban regime.

Although inter-state wars have played only a secondary role in the last decades, it is extremely rare that warlike clashes are of an exclusively intra-state nature. They become understandable only when placed in the context of the respective regional 'conflict system' (Mwagiru 1997) and when their geopolitical status is taken into account. Regional neighbours and interested powers from outside the region exert direct and indirect influence on initially internal conflicts. They support rebel organizations and offer them refuge or bases. In other cases, they assist governments in fighting insurgencies. Refugee camps then become the starting point for and the target of transnational violence. Direct intervention using government troops is not ruled out, either. In particular, great powers are willing to interfere militarily in their 'back yard', as the Americans call Central America, or in 'nearby foreign countries' (the Russian equivalent for the South Caucasus and Central Asia).

What start out as local conflicts can therefore easily spread to bordering states by 'spillover' effects and embroil the entire sub-region. At the geopolitical level, categories such as 'rogue states' form the political-ideological basis for hegemonic intervention. The majority of wars worldwide follow these patterns and can be defined as 'regionalized' or even 'internationalized civil wars'.

In certain regions of the globe, intractable constellations have become consolidated that encourage war and prevent a lasting peace. A sweeping crisis of authority in state institutions leads to the emergence of 'markets of violence' (Elwert 1999) in which legally established relations and procedures no longer apply and, instead, weapons, valuable cultivated products and raw materials, protection money and forced levies serve as currencies beyond the law. Refugee communities are often involved in operating these markets and under these conditions may become *refugee warrior communities*. This causes civil war economies to spread beyond national frontiers, forming a network of, among other things, arms procurement, recruitment of mercenaries and illegal trading in drugs, diamonds and tropical timber in the entire sub-region. Organized crime determines everyday life.

Do such crisis regions have a chance of lasting peace? Can deep-rooted structures of violence be transformed in such a way as to enable a successful and forward-looking development to take off, which will facilitate socio-economic welfare and political participation, as well as the unfolding and realization of cultural identity for broad sections of the population? These are the central questions posed in this book. As an introduction to the detailed contributions, I would like to present a number of basic observations as well as brief summaries of the individual chapters.

First, I shall identify the lack of consolidation of the state as well as the arrogance of ruling cliques as central causes of war and obstacles to development. It is this state crisis that leaves spheres open for corruption, self-enrichment, tyranny and violence. Second, I shall examine the structures and momentum of the violence that is increasingly influencing countries involved in war and compromising their transformation into peaceful states. In the third section I will deal with the main topic of this book, the transformation of war-torn countries. In doing so, I shall present the conceptual contributions from Part One and discuss three stages on the difficult path to lasting peace: 1) reform of the security sector (military and paramilitary forces, police and secret services); 2) promoting an independent judiciary; 3) possibilities and dangers of decentralization and separation of powers.

The fourth section relates to the fundamental considerations of experience gathered in the selected crisis regions, with examples from the South Caucasus, Central America and the Horn of Africa. In these regions, previously 'hot' conflicts have been formally settled (Central America), 'frozen' (South Caucasus) or waged in new constellations (Horn of Africa). What the sub-regions have in common is that the transition to structures for peace is proving to be extremely difficult, and violence – sometimes in different forms – continues to exist. In conclusion, I shall take a brief look at the consequences of September 11 for the perspectives and prospects of regional conflict management – a subject that is examined in detail by a separate contribution (Chapter 10).

THE CRISIS OF THE STATE AS A CAUSE OF WAR AND AN OBSTACLE TO DEVELOPMENT

The structures of the state adopted by Europe exist, at best, only in formal terms in a large number of crisis regions. In many cases, power cliques have appropriated the state machinery, financing themselves mainly from the revenues that can be creamed off from the value added of the agricultural sector, the earnings of the export sector, and trading in valuable raw materials or even drugs. Frequently, they also survive through the external support provided by aid donors or through humanitarian NGOs performing state functions (especially in sub-Saharan Africa and Central/Southern Asia). In some cases, there is even evidence that power élites behave rationally in not encouraging development or combating poverty in their countries – otherwise they would jeopardize the continuing influx of external assistance.

A large number of states in the South (sub-Saharan Africa, the Arab region, South, South-East and East Asia, Latin America) and the East (the Balkans, the Caucasus, Central Asia, parts of the Russian Federation) display distortions in this respect. In crisis countries, the state proves, to a certain extent, to be strong and weak at the same time[1] and can be described in terms of the 'lame Leviathan' paradox (Khadiagala 1995: 35). This means that, on the one hand, it is quite able to keep social relations under control temporarily and appropriate resources in selected areas. On the other hand, however, it is ineffective and distended in the performance of its welfare and security functions and thus not in a position to implement coherent policy concepts beyond certain urban core centres or to regulate social relations in a comprehensive manner (Migdal 1988: 8). Indispensable public functions, such as maintaining social peace and the rule of law, providing infrastructure and services for basic needs, ensuring a minimum level of management in agricultural and industrial production and distribution, and establishing access to affordable foodstuffs and basic goods, are not fulfilled.

The hardly consolidated state in crisis countries is, as a rule, characterized by a high degree of centralization and a lack of legally guaranteed autonomy at the local level. The political class is recruited extensively from urban élites and business people, who then secure access to the value added via the state machinery. In some cases, so-called 'strong men' establish themselves as a parallel structure at local level, with the urban state class unable to take effective action against them (Migdal 1988: 136–7). State failure is the pivotal issue for explaining intra-state conflicts, the vulnerability of crisis countries to external destabilization and continued obstacles to development. In Europe, state-building is a process that has taken place over several centuries. Crisis countries in the South and East of the globe are required to make the transition to consolidated nation-states within a far shorter period (Ayoob 1995: 32–3, 39–40). This time pressure leads to the overburdening of the political, administrative and, in part, also military capacities, which erodes the legitimacy of the states. In contrast to the corresponding phases of the European state-building process, today's politicians and state leaders in Southern and Eastern countries are faced with high demands concerning greater prosperity, economic redistribution, political control and social participation, which they cannot meet. The legitimation of the mostly authoritarian or dictatorially led systems therefore remains brittle. This legitimation is – to use Weber's terminology – founded on an extremely inconsistent mixture of traditional, charismatic and rational elements.

Attempts to catch up on the consolidation of the state harbour a considerable potential for violent conflict. However, these attempts are necessary for Southern and Eastern countries in order to be able to exist in a modern system of states. On the other hand, they do run into a sort of paradox: the endeavour to establish an efficient system of institutions, increase social welfare and integrate the different groups of the population through developing a common identity comes in a phase of world history in which the nation-state's capacities for shaping policies have diminished substantially in the face of global pressure, even in the consolidated industrialized states.

The widespread clientelistic method of safeguarding power in crisis countries has led many researchers to speak of the 'neopatrimonial state'. Patrimonial rule can be understood in this context as relating to the social and economic interrelations between the patron and the client, which are based on the reciprocity of favour and loyalty between persons equipped with unequal resources and which can adopt extremely differing forms (for instance, nepotism, clanism and regionalism). Neopatrimonial rule adapts this fundamental principle embedded in traditional societies to the modern state, which should be characterized by bureaucratic-rational procedures. While the classic patron is himself in possession of natural resources, especially land, the modern patron operates as a mixture of 'broker' and 'political entrepreneur', distinguishing himself more through access to the disposal of public resources. The political entrepreneur appropriates resources through occupying public offices. These he uses for the purpose of self-enrichment (through which he procures considerable private property for his 'close family' over time). At the same time, he needs them to satisfy his respective clientele (in the logic of an 'extended family') (Schlichte 1996: 96–9).

In terms of conflict theory, it is interesting to note that clientelistic rule can bring about the temporary stabilization of a country. This is, however, a deceptive and precarious form of stability, which is very much at risk especially over the medium and long terms, since clientelism represents the counter-model to competition and is characterized by a high level of inefficiency. This means that it is not able to sustain the resources needed for it to function and is, instead, essentially based on creaming off profits from the export of raw materials or on channelling international financial support to loyal power groups and sections of the population. As soon as these financial resources cease to materialize because of economic crises or declining willingness on the part of donors to grant support, a collapse is inevitable, and can occur suddenly and violently. To a certain extent, neopatrimonialism thus harbours the seed of self-destruction within itself. In order to maintain a well-thought-out ethno-regional balance and satisfy the growing needs of those favoured by it, the requirement for resources grows constantly, thus undermining the state's efficiency internally and preventing social transformation (Migdal 1988: 223, 225).

The role of development aid has to be viewed in critical terms in this context. In the past, it could – despite the many undisputed successes in the area of securing basic needs – be interpreted in numerous cases as an infusion required for the survival of clientelism. Governments in the South (and, since the cessation of bipolarity, also of the East) attached greater importance to continual financing through external donors than to their responsibility for satisfying the needs of their own populations. When aid payments to numerous regimes were suspended in the early 1990s through the introduction of human rights and democratic conditionality, this promptly led to a far-reaching crisis of legitimation, especially in African countries. This legitimacy crisis was of a twofold nature: internally, it was no longer possible to serve and maintain the many diverse clientelistic loyalties; outwardly, the basis for doing business had changed, with the ruling regime then being measured according to standards that it could not fulfil.

STRUCTURES AND THE CHANGING FORM OF VIOLENCE

War and crisis countries are characterized by intractable structures of violence that stand in the way of prospects for peace. In view of the lack of socio-economic perspectives, young men, in particular, form an ideal base for organized violence. A further factor is the extensive and cheap availability of weapons, especially small arms, which makes it easy to organize gangs, militias and small armies. Although the wide circulation of small arms is not a cause of conflicts in the narrower sense, it does indirectly influence the course of conflicts, the splintering of warring parties and shifts in the balance of power among them. In the early 1990s, Karp (1993: 9) estimated that a well-equipped militia of around ten thousand soldiers could be maintained in times of war for approximately $75 million per year, of which around $40 million would be needed for weapons, accommodation, food and clothing, with the rest going on pay. The costs rise substantially where a militia is also to be armed with heavier weapon systems such as armoured vehicles, artillery or anti-tank missiles. However, such amounts can certainly also be raised through recourse to war economy structures and with regional support (Karp 1993: 11–12).

As the state is not able to curb crime, or is sometimes even directly involved in it, it extensively fails as a guarantor of law and order in many countries. Seen against this background, prosperous individuals increasingly avail themselves of private security services. Companies as well as governments and rebel groups hire growing numbers of mercenaries, with the result that we can speak of a 'privatization of security' analogous to the 'privatization of violence' by rebels, organized crime and terror organizations. Private 'service providers', including mercenaries for combat operations, private guard and security services, and security consultancy companies, assume military and police functions. Outstanding examples can be found in Africa, especially in Sierra Leone and Angola (Cilliers and Mason 1999). The trend towards privatization in the security sector is particularly relevant as it concerns the core domain of state sovereignty. Virtually all regions of the globe are affected by this phenomenon, although it does vary in form and extent.

In large urban centres, the privatization of security fosters the ever-increasing division between the rich and poor sections of society, which results in different security zones and ghettoization into so-called *gated communities*. In the crisis regions of Africa, Latin America and Asia, private companies such as Executive Outcomes (since dissolved), Gurkha Security Ltd and Military Professional Resources Inc. protect production exclaves or operate as military advisers or combat units in civil wars beside national armies, UN peace-keeping troops, rebel groups and mafia-type gangs.

THE DIFFICULT TRANSFORMATION OF COUNTRIES RAVAGED BY WAR

Societies with experience of force and violence are faced with many diverse tasks. In many cases, the economy is ruined, the political system has lost its legitimacy and warlords exert huge influence. At the same time, ex-combatants, refugees and internally displaced persons have to be integrated into society. In such situations, moral and cultural values can be the subject of considerable dispute. In post-war societies it is seldom clear, for example, what is to constitute the social identity. Furthermore, the differentiation between victims and perpetrators can be difficult if virtually all sides are committing human rights violations. In a fragmented society, competing groups sometimes consider themselves to be the backbone of the 'new order' and run the risk of entering into a destructive struggle for power and positions.

The challenges for reconstruction are correspondingly great, as Nicole Ball illustrates in Chapter 1. Wars not only cause material damage, but also result in social and psycho-social breakdowns and, not least, unresolved power conflicts normally continue to exist after wars have ended. In such a situation, *peace-building*, according to Ball, aims at creating 'human security' – a comprehensive concept that focuses on the welfare, participation possibilities and fears of the individual citizens.

A large number of war-torn or war-prone countries are dysfunctional because their government has little legitimacy and the state apparatus is overcentralized, and cannot guarantee its citizens either security or prosperity. Power is being abused rather than being used responsibly. Given this background, Ball is of the view that attention must be centred on reforming political institutions. But how can those providing development aid contribute towards achieving this? According to Ball, it is not just a case of offering material and technical assistance. She feels that it is more important for local players to become 'informed consumers'. They should be aware of 'what they need, who can provide it for them and how to get value for money'. In her opinion, the conditions and regulations imposed by international players up to now have, however, been far from adequately adapted to local conditions and have lacked the necessary flexibility. This, she maintains, concerns the processes and terms of financing mechanisms for development and emergency aid, the (frequently short-term and short-sighted) mandates of UN peace missions, and the procedures for recruiting international personnel.

Ball emphazises that focusing on more effective governance can present aid donors with a dilemma, since supporting state institutions – which often do not have democratic legitimation – has a direct effect on the power struggle between the government and opposition parties. At the same time, she says, waiting for possible elections or concentrating on non-governmental organizations also harbours risks because valuable time is lost in this way. Ball therefore asks that a joint vision be developed as early as possible for the country in question, with close cooperation between a variety of players from politics and civil society.

The core issue of consolidating the state comprises three aspects, which I will now look at in detail: first, the deprivatization of violence through reforming the security sector; second, supporting an independent judiciary as part of the development of the rule of law; third, the opportunities and dangers of a vertical division of power, that is to say the decentralization of competencies and decision-making powers. The first two criteria, in particular – the reform of the security sector and justice – have received greater attention in very recent times, especially through the Brahimi Report (2000) on the reform of UN peace operations.[2]

Security sector reform The security sector represents what is probably the most sensitive area within the *institution-building* process, as Nicole Ball emphasizes. On the initiative of Great Britain, in particular, the Development Assistance Committee of the Organization for Economic Co-operation and Development recently developed orientation points for reforms in this domain (OECD/DAC 2001; see also Chalmers

2000).[3] The security sector (military, paramilitary security forces, police, secret services) is of crucial importance in times of political crisis and for overcoming post-war situations; it is, for example, a decisive factor in the success of a peace agreement whether the so-called security forces support or sabotage such an agreement. At the same time, however, the so-called security sector often represents more of an 'insecurity sector' for the population since it is often substantially responsible for repression and human rights violations.

A clear division of responsibilities between the security forces is of central importance, as are their subordination, accountability and responsibility *vis-à-vis* civil authorities.[4] The military in particular has a tendency to assume ever more new responsibilities and gain autonomy *vis-à-vis* the government. Civil authorities do not set sufficient limits for the military – be it because they fear resistance, or because they want to be able to call on the military for assistance if their power is threatened.

Problems in the division of competencies between the different sections of the security apparatus are typical in developing and transforming countries. The army, supplied with modern equipment and major arms for national defence, is often also in charge of certain aspects of internal security, while the authority and equipment of police work tend to be weaker. In view of this, it is advisable to prepare the police better for internal state functions that have previously been performed by the military, with the provision of equipment and resources following clearly defined criteria. Furthermore, there must also be clearly determined hierarchies within the security forces that are controlled and supervised by equally clearly defined civil structures. Transparency through public control is the only way to prevent hidden benefits, financial allocations and functions that are outside the bounds of legality. Of crucial importance is a functioning parliament that, not least, exerts control and decision-making rights with regard to its budgetary powers. Finally, an independent judiciary and free media are indispensable institutions for punishing and preventing human rights violations committed by the armed forces.

Promoting an independent judiciary   Besides the security sector, the judiciary forms a core element of the state. The rule of law is the central prerequisite for dealing with conflicts in an institutionalized manner and, thus, the best guarantee within the state for excluding recourse to violence. What are the distinctive features of a well-functioning legal system? Three elements can be listed: an independent and impartial judiciary, the right to a defence and a fair trial, and the establishment of the constitutional principles of a state under the rule of law, such as the presumption of innocence of the accused.

These criteria are not met in a large number of countries. The judiciary is 'effective' only where it concerns arresting journalists critical of the government or opposition politicians. Private law disputes and criminal law matters are rarely heard or tried in an appropriate manner because of a lack of qualifications and resources. If the state fails in prosecuting flagrant and blatant crimes, this results in people taking the law into their own hands and even in lynch-law – a phenomenon that has increased to an appalling degree over the past few years in Guatemala, for example. For post-war societies and those between wars, the central criteria for consolidating the legal system focus mainly on matters of establishing the truth, the documentation of acts of violence, the accountability of perpetrators and, in many cases, also restructuring the judicial apparatus.

The shortcomings of the judiciary in crisis countries are frequently so grave that the population regards it as being non-existent. Inadequate training, clandestine structures, a lack of coordination between investigating authorities and the police, plus the inextricability of political, military and judicial élites prevent criminals from being convicted. This leads to the emergence of ignominious traditions of lawlessness and impunity. How can reform of the judiciary be supported from outside? Various strategies are possible:

- a critical political dialogue that encourages and presses the government to give way to the judiciary to control the monopoly on the use of violence;
- technical support in decentralizing the judiciary so as to make the law and statutes effective and enforceable at local level;
- basic and in-service training courses for judges, state prosecutors, defending counsel and judicial officers;
- the introduction of procedures to ensure that top positions in the judiciary are appointed according to the quality of the applicants and not their political affiliations; and
- strengthening the media and human rights organizations in their role

as watchdogs and 'the fourth power' beyond the state triangle of the executive, the legislature and the judiciary.

It is noticeable that international organizations and federations of states are increasingly debating the deployment of judicial experts as part of international peace operations. In addition to the Brahimi Report on the reform of UN peace-keeping operations already referred to, the resolutions adopted by the EU summit held in Helsinki in December 1999 and the follow-up process are also significant in this context. These measures are aimed at making instruments in the area of non-military crisis management more effective and establishing a civil *rapid-reaction capability*. The EU commissioner charged with this responsibility, Christopher Patten, declared that the EU needs to take initiatives in a large number of areas, such as humanitarian aid and rescue services, mine clearing and disarmament, and, not least, the dispatching of police personnel. Of particular interest for our topic is the fact that he also referred to the provision of administrative and legal support for democratization as well as the observation of elections and human rights in crisis regions (Debiel and Fischer 2000).

This is precisely the point taken up in the contribution by Hans-Joachim Heintze in Chapter 2. To begin with, he identifies the independence of the judiciary as being the central feature of the modern constitutional state – a bastion of enlightenment against despotic rule, so to speak. He demonstrates that, through international law, the members of the modern state system have increasingly committed themselves to democracy and the rule of law since the founding of the United Nations. Article 9 of the International Covenant on Civil and Political Rights of 16 December 1966, which provides for protection against arbitrary arrest and stipulates that arrested persons must be brought before a judge, plays a special role in this regard. Just how much importance the United Nations now attaches to an independent judiciary and the primacy of constitutionality under the rule of law is illustrated, according to Heintze, by the fact that the UN Human Rights Commission, with the adoption of Resolution 1995/36, appointed a special rapporteur for this domain to analyse the practice of states as well as the impact of international aid in this context.

What can be done in crisis situations characterized by state failure, the destruction of social conditions or even the absence of the state's monopoly on the use of violence? In the case of failure on the part of the state, Heintze maintains, gradual state-building from the bottom up can constitute the focal point for a new beginning. In the 1990s, the UN was involved to this end in numerous peace-keeping missions, for instance in Namibia, Cambodia and Somalia. Besides forming representative bodies at the local level, the mandate also included observing and assisting in elections as well as human rights education. However, it certainly should not be forgotten, Heintze points out, that the credibility of the world organization suffered severely when UN and US troops themselves committed grave human rights violations in 1993 at the height of the clashes with General Aidid and other warlords. For the most part, international involvement in UN civil administration actions has been in Kosovo (UNMIK) as well as in Bosnia-Herzegovina, where the establishment of a new court system and the setting up of a Human Rights Chamber had been approved under the Dayton Agreement.

In Heintze's view, the acceptance of a legal order by the population at large is decisive for the success or failure of international endeavours. Such acceptance, he says, can be enhanced by taking into account local traditions, although it is sometimes also important for international players to dissociate themselves from previous legal systems – for example, where these are perceived as having been repressive, as was the case in Kosovo. Finally, he concludes, it must be realized that the creation of an independent judiciary is always a factor associated with power politics. The findings and recommendations of truth commissions (as in El Salvador and Guatemala) have, for example, directly questioned the legitimacy of (former) rulers and the military.

An important but also politically very delicate issue addressed by Heintze concerns the international criminal courts. States affected usually see such tribunals as restricting their sovereignty, and question their legitimacy or sometimes even their legal bases. The Cambodian government, for example, allowed international experts only a consultative role in relation to the prosecution of the genocide committed under Pol Pot. The situation is different for the *ad hoc* tribunals for the former Yugoslavia and for Rwanda, where the Security Council acted under Chapter VII of the United Nations Charter (*enforcement measures*). Using the example of the International Criminal Tribunal for the former Yugoslavia (ICTY), Heintze shows that even international criminal courts are dependent upon local support – for example, for the extradition of accused persons, the preservation of evidence, or the protection of witnesses. The same argument applies to the Rwanda Tribunal, which is based in Arusha (Tanzania) and cooperates with the authorities in Kigali. There is also a national jurisdiction in Rwanda as well as the (questionable) revitalization of traditional procedures for the settlement of conflicts (the so-called Gacaca system)[5] – institutions that are partly competing with and partly complementing the International Criminal Tribunal for Rwanda (ICTR).

Decentralization and the division of power Where attention is focused on the consolidation of the state, the division of power has to be considered besides *institution-building*. This is especially the case in multi-ethnic states. There are, in principle, two approaches: group autonomy and decentralization (Sisk 1996). Division of power through group autonomy is directed at granting the minorities extensive self-determination rights and involving them as proportionately as possible in the political structures of the state as a whole. This can entail both territorial and non-territorial forms of group autonomy. Non-territorial group autonomy includes forms of limited self-administration by ethnic groups (for instance, on cultural matters), which are independent of the place of domicile. Further instruments are the joint exercising of executive power through group coalitions, veto rights for minorities, proportionality rules for appointments to public office, and the allocation of state funds, to mention just a few.

The division of power through decentralization focuses on shifting political decision-making from the centralized state to the regional and local levels, usually in the form of a federal state structure, and on strengthening of municipal self-administration. In Chapter 3 Andreas Mehler examines decentralization processes – especially in relation to Africa – paying detailed attention to the features that exacerbate conflicts. Mehler dents high-flying expectations of greater participation and the rule of law arising from decentralization *per se*. His bone of contention is that it is not only the centralized state that abuses power: 'local despotism' also exists. Furthermore, shifts of power could, as a result of a transfer of competencies or municipal elections, lead to disturbances and unrest – especially where there is an atmosphere of distrust and enmity – thus intensifying existing conflicts between majorities and minorities, or between 'locals' and 'strangers' in a region. Mehler argues that, in this case, a defeated group, which possibly has a majority within the national context, could even call for intervention by the security forces. He also points to the scenario that a central power could lose its previous function of mitigating or settling conflicts if competence is transferred on a 'top-down' basis.

Mehler is not fundamentally opposed to the decentralization of competencies. Like Heintze, he feels that the local level might be the starting point for development and human security in situations where the state has broken down, as the recent examples of Somaliland and Puntland (Horn of Africa) have demonstrated. Nevertheless, he also refers to the still unresolved problem of integrating such very individual local institutions at a superordinate level.

Mehler concedes, however, that the concept of decentralization does open up opportunities for more problem-oriented solutions. He adds that a well-functioning overall system with different vertical levels of exercising power and decision-making can also best deal with the challenge of political and socio-economic change. Competition between élitist groups can be defused, he contends, if power issues are decided not only in the national arena but also where counterbalances can be formed at regional and local level. In particular – and this is a central argument – the risks of a decentralization process must be weighed against the risks that could be incurred in the case of political standstill, in other words against 'the cost of doing nothing'.

EXPERIENCES FROM SELECTED CRISIS REGIONS

What experiences can be observed in the endeavour to overcome structures of violence and manage the transition to peaceful development? Three sub-regions are examined in this book as examples: the South Caucasus, Central America and the Horn of Africa. A case study is also presented for each of these conflict systems, relating to Georgia, Guatemala and Ethiopia respectively. Thus an overview of the regional and international dimensions of conflicts is provided, while at the same time the specific characteristics at national and local levels are taken into account.

In the South Caucasus and Central America the situation calmed down to a certain extent in the mid-1990s following years or decades of warlike violence, though without the underlying causes of the conflicts having been resolved. In the Horn of Africa, there were hopes in the early 1990s following the overthrow of the military dictatorship in Ethiopia (the 'Derg regime') and the independence of Eritrea that the new political leaders would be able to open the door to lasting peace and new development opportunities for their peoples after three decades of war. However, the war between Eritrea and Ethiopia from 1998 to 2000 soon showed that the 'fragile peace' was exactly that. Besides the great suffering that the so-called border war[6] caused, one further aspect is also of significance: the war was instrumentalized for internal power issues by both sides and served as a diversion from the difficulties involved in transforming the state, economy and society. Whether and how this problem can be overcome is now more topical than ever.

South Caucasus: geopolitics, consolidation of the state and the power of nationalism The Caucasus is a multi-faceted and geopolitically explosive flash-point, where complex historical causes of the conflicts combine with the Soviet legacy. The problem of state-building is closely linked to the violence-prone processes of forming national and ethnic identities, which tend towards violence. Furthermore, the territorial integrity of many states is questioned from both the inside and the outside, with socio-economic development characterized by a mixture of state, market-oriented and subsistence economies. In some cases, illegal mafia-type and violence-based economies have formed, which constitute the basis of striving for political power.

In Chapter 4 Rainer Freitag-Wirminghaus puts his finger on the importance of the Caucasus when he says that: 'The interaction of transformation-related structures, conflicts surrounding pipeline routes and geostrategic ambitions in the power struggle resulting from the so-called *great game* for the prize of the oil in the Caspian Sea have turned the region into a trouble spot that is unique in the world.' The collapse of the Soviet Union triggered power struggles as well as the struggle for autonomy and secession. Besides the particularly brutal Chechnya war, the clashes between Ossetians and Ingushetians (Russian Federation) are of particular significance in the North Caucasus. In the South Caucasus, Georgia is being rocked by ethno-territorial conflicts in Abkhazia and South Ossetia. The Nagorno Karabakh conflict, which led to a war between Armenia and Azerbaijan and has been 'frozen' by a ceasefire since 1994, plays a key role in the latter region.

The Caucasus was troubled by a wave of nationalist movements after 1988, some of which were rooted in traumatic experiences from the past. However, the resulting national independence movements were not able to hold on to power for very long because of their lack of political experience and their ideological orientation. Instead, the old élites returned, personified by Haidar Aliyev (Azerbaijan) and Edward Shevardnadze (Georgia). They were able to take advantage of their experience gained from power struggles as well as their clientelistic patronage networks from the Soviet era. Even though they presumably had little interest in real democratization, they were successful in counteracting a total collapse of security and order.

Freitag-Wirminghaus identifies the weakness of state structures as the central cause of the conflicts. However, he also warns against the misapprehension of equating a weak state that fails as an institution with the absence of power structures: 'Chaos and authoritarianism are not mutually exclusive, rather, chaotic states often strengthen the tendency towards an authoritarian system.' In his view, presidential rule with an overwhelming executive is confronted with a dilemma: although a certain degree of stabilization is feasible through the combination of personality cult, patronage and corruption, establishing a modern state according to the Western model is not. The advantage of a strong executive, according to Freitag-Wirminghaus, can be a more extensive scope for action in the area of foreign policy. In the Nagorno Karabakh conflict, in particular, the presidents proved at times to be more prepared to compromise and more realistic than the respective public at large in their individual countries. However, the authoritarian system reached its limits at the same time, he argues, because negotiation and peace processes operating exclusively at presidential level could no longer be conveyed to the oppositional factions of the élite and the population.

In Chapter 5 David Darchiashvili examines the state crisis and the conflicts in Georgia from a very interesting angle by focusing the analysis on the characteristics of the political system. According to this approach, national and state security in Georgia are affected not only by ethno-territorial conflicts and outside interference but also to a substantial extent by an inadequate legal system, the inefficient use of personnel and material resources, the absence of a culture of civil and democratic control of the executive, the state's political and economic vulnerability and, not least, rampant corruption that can hardly be distinguished from organized crime and represents a serious national threat. In Darchiashvili's view, the crisis of national security and the state is expressed in the insecurity of many citizens who are left to the mercy of arbitrary state rule and everyday crime. However, it also expresses itself in the conflicts that have shaken Georgia since the collapse of Soviet rule, such as the civil war that took place in 1992/ 93 between the supporters of President Zwiad Gamsachurdia (1990– 91), who came to power and was subsequently removed from office, and an alliance built around his successor, the current state president Edward Shevardnadze (since 1992), plus the autonomy and secession conflicts concerning South Ossetia and Abkhazia, which led to open armed clashes in 1991–92 and 1992–94 respectively.

Darchiashvili stresses that a stable peace can be achieved only within the framework of a liberal, constitutional democracy. He attaches particular importance to parliamentary, judicial and public control of the security sector in this regard. Darchiashvili takes a critical view of the popular argument that Georgia's greatest threat emanates from external powers – especially from Russia. He urges that the undisputed negative consequences of external interference should not be overemphasized and that there should be a greater awareness of the significant space for political manoeuvring, even in a small country such as Georgia. Darchiashvili maintains that the key to a well-functioning security policy, in both the domestic and the foreign policy realm, lies in the loyalty of the citizens to the state. The domain of Georgian politics is characterized by serious failings in this regard, he adds, and must develop greater consistency in the area of security policy, in relation to both the relevant constitutional provisions and foreign policy objectives.

In an illuminating look at concepts of nationalism, Darchiashvili finally discusses the power of nationalism in Georgia. In doing so, he makes it clear that although 'civic' nationalism is more rational and reconcilable with democracy compared with 'ethnic' nationalism, it cannot be effective without relating back to a number of ethnic features (language, religion, a common heritage and other cultural character-istics). He sums up the situation in the following terms: 'The complete transformation of ethnic nationalism into civic nationalism, that is to say reconciling the instinctive inclination towards an ethnic heritage and one's own language, appears to be impossible. It is better to modify the rhetoric and politics of liberal-democratic forces favouring civil nationalism in transitional democracies and direct these towards "civilizing and pacifying" ethnic nationalism.' With regard to the solution of ethno-territorial conflicts Darchiashvili proposes that modern methods of a territorially or culturally based division of power should be considered.

Central America: regional pacification, change of violence and stalled transformation   Central America was rocked by numerous wars in the 1980s in particular. In Nicaragua, the Sandinistas had overthrown the Somoza regime in 1979, and from 1981 on had to defend themselves against the Contras, who were supported by the USA. In El Salvador, a well-organized guerrilla force developed, which was, however, prevented from becoming victorious through massive intervention by the USA. The war in Guatemala lasted 30 years and cost the lives of 30,000 people. The roots of the war lay in the discrimination against the indigenous majority of the population (principally the Maya) by the so-called Ladinos (the élite, originally of Spanish origin, who 'blended' with the indigenous population over the course of centuries). In the 1970s, the indigenous population became the social base for a guerrilla war, during which the government army and the paramilitaries had no qualms about committing massacres and even genocide.

It proved possible to stop these wars between 1990 and 1996, as a result of a regional peace treaty drawn up in August 1987. The United Nations also played an important role in the finalization and implementation of the peace treaties for El Salvador and Guatemala. Was this the prelude to a development towards democracy and peace? In Chapter 6, Sabine Kurtenbach points out that progress has been made with regard to democratization, although the lives of many people are still marked by repression, gang and everyday crime, crimes of survival and the most varied forms of social violence (against street children, beggars, petty criminals). As she puts it: 'In the second half of the 1990s ... more people died by violent means in El Salvador than during a war there. Viewed in terms of murders per 100,000 of its population, El Salvador has at times ranked ahead even of Colombia as the world's most violent country.' Kurtenbach thus takes up a central problem that is also evident in relation to other countries and regions (Southern Africa, West Africa, South-East Asia, the Caucasus): the virtually seamless transformation of the violence of civil war into violent crime. According to Kurtenbach, poverty and the marginalization of large sections of the population likewise form a breeding ground for old and new forms of violence. The widespread availability of weapons, grim living conditions and the growing drug trade do the rest, she adds.

Kurtenbach views international support for more extensive *peace-building* in critical terms, pointing out the shortcomings also referred to by Ball. She regards it as particularly counterproductive that the International Monetary Fund (IMF) and the World Bank have, with their structural adjustment policy, undermined the social dimensions of post-conflict peace-building pursued by UN agencies. Kurtenbach points out – again in agreement with Ball – that in the final analysis, 'the individual state ... still remained the central player in the peace-building process' and that a 'national project' needs to be agreed upon in the countries concerned. She argues that although the efficiency of government institutions and opposition forces has increased over the years, personalism and clientelism continue to exist, with the military, in particular, able to block far-reaching changes. Kurtenbach does, however, find it positive that the municipal level has been upgraded in political and economic terms in Central America. This decision-making level, she says, is closer to crucial challenges such as satisfying basic needs (living accommodation, food, work), overcoming social violence and crime, and, finally, enhancing participation. She does not confirm the risks of decentralization put forward by Mehler using the example of Africa, although she does agree with his basic thesis that state-building at local and regional levels can be successful only in close association with the overall state level.

In Guatemala, the government and the guerrillas agreed a peace treaty on 29 December 1996. As in El Salvador and Nicaragua, there were two issues at the centre of the agreement: first, the arrangements for demobilizing and reintegrating the armed opposition, plus the monitoring of the process by international organizations; second, opening up the political systems of the countries, as well as redefining civil–military relations. In Guatemala, a further special agreement was concluded on the rights of the indigenous peoples, in which the government of the country – where the Maya do, after all, make up around 50 per cent of the population – took up the rights of the majority for the first time.

The peace treaties between the Guatemalan government and the guerrilla URNG (Unidad Revolucionaria Nacional Guatemalteca – National Revolutionary Unit of Guatemala) established a type of minimum consensus, which has so far been implemented only to an inadequate extent. Although the guerrilla fighters handed over their weapons and the armed forces in the region considerably reduced their troop numbers, far-reaching changes that would have an effect on the prevailing structures of violence failed to materialize – for instance, improving the living conditions for broad sections of the population, establishing an efficient tax system, greater socio-economic and political participation for the indigenous population, a functioning party system, and creating a situation of constitutional law and order. Although, in contrast to earlier times, the military no longer dominates the political system, the armed forces are not under the control of the politicians, either. There are no clear definitions or allocation of responsibilities for the military and the police, and there is no plan for a coherent military conversion. As a result, the state is hardly existent as a guarantor of human security.

Chapter 7, by Bernardo Arévalo de León, analyses the stalled transformation of Guatemala towards a democracy against this background and demonstrates how the military has been able – not least through the weakness of civil institutions – to secure relative autonomy in the political system. According to Arévalo de León, the democratic opening-up process (*apertura*) began as far back as 1985, when part of the army was successful in having the leadership of the government returned to civilian hands – not least in their own interests, the intention being to make the fight against rebellion even more effective under the 'Thesis of National Stability'. Political élites and civil-society groups did, however, take advantage of the opportunity to make some progress in the democratization process. With the support of the 'modernizers' within the military, it was even possible to commence peace negotiations.

Nevertheless, Arévalo de León, like Kurtenbach, still sees considerable problems, such as the fear and insecurity still widespread among broad sections of the population. He points out that the political élite has not developed its own 'national project' and that democracy exists more in formal than substantial terms. He illustrates the situation succinctly as follows: 'We have the hardware of democracy, but the software of authoritarianism.' In particular, there has, in Arévalo de León's view, been a failure to subordinate the Guatemalan army to the constitutional order – a situation that has been reinforced by the defeat of a constitutional referendum in May 1999. He sees the main responsibility for this as lying with the civil authorities, which left the armed forces their 'relative autonomy' and even kept the option open for themselves to call in the military in times of crisis. What conclusions can be drawn? Arévalo de León pins his hopes on a critical public comprising non-state institutions (research centres, universities, non-governmental organizations) and the media. These should, he argues, acquire analytical and technical capacities for reshaping civil–military relations and elaborate policy-oriented proposals in close cooperation with political parties and state institutions.

The Horn of Africa: chronic conflicts, failed states and human insecurity The Horn of Africa has been one of the most fragile crisis regions in the world over the past decades, displaying a chronic mixture of war, the breakdown of states, poverty, hunger and human misery. The characteristics of 'regionalized civil wars', that is to say the reciprocal destabilization of neighbouring countries through the support of rebel groups and the supply of arms, can all be found in the Horn region. In addition, lower-intensity types of conflict, such as cattle rustling, spread beyond national borders. Hopes of Ethiopia and Eritrea being able to become pillars of more stable development after the fall of the 'Derg Regime' (1991) did not materialize, and the state of Somalia has for more than a decade existed only in fictional terms. There is an effective though predominantly repressive state apparatus in northern Sudan, which is under Arab-Muslim influence. However, in relation to the southern regions it is used principally for a war against the African-Christian and animistic population that has lasted nearly fifty years.

Developments in the different countries are very closely intertwined, as Axel Klein points out in Chapter 8 on the Horn of Africa. Nobody in the Horn region can shield himself from the trials and tribulations of his immediate neighbour. With the reasoned exception of Somalia, all the countries in the Horn are characterized by cultural diversity and common ethnic, religious and cultural elements. The situation favours, he argues, the rapid spread of conflicts, as fighters and weapons can switch from one flash-point to another without any hindrance. Where do the roots of the conflicts lie? According to Axel Klein, any model suitable for explaining the crises in the Horn region must consider various factors, such as the exhaustion of renewable natural resources, stagnating development, divergent ethnicity and the crisis of the state. In Klein's view, conventional diplomacy can achieve some level of success in inter-state conflicts, as it finally did in the war between Eritrea and Ethiopia – admittedly, only after tens of thousands of people had been killed. The ending of such wars, however, does not settle internal struggles for power, autonomy or secession, which is why alternative instruments were tried out for this purpose in the 1990s. It is precisely traditional structures, he contends, that can become crucial for the acceptance and implementation of political principles such as the division of powers, federalism and constitutional matters. In Somaliland and Puntland, for example, clan elders were successful in elaborating basic rules for a reasonably stable coexistence, disarming the militias and establishing government institutions, thus setting off the 'bottom-up state-building' process advocated by Heintze where the state has failed. A similar approach was adopted at the national level between May and August 2000 in the city of Arte (Djibouti) through the mediation of Djibouti's President Omar Guelleh. According to Klein, it is, however, evident that the relationship between the clans in this case is much more delicate than the clan structure at the decentralized level, with this peace process being sabotaged by influential warlords.

Klein concludes that in local conflicts – for instance, those concerning resources – traditional mechanisms could help towards a settlement, as can be proved for Ethiopia and Sudan. However, he adds, it must also be taken into consideration at all times – precisely as Mehler warns – that local government representatives could misuse such decentralized procedures for securing their own power. Klein's final point is that social change is taking place in many regions of the Horn by virtue of growing urbanization, which is weakening the influence of traditional authorities. For this reason, he says, the real challenge lies in promoting new intermediary institutions, whose task must be to build bridges between state structures and the different (urban and traditional) social structures.

Ethiopia occupies a special position in the Horn of Africa. On the one hand, it is the regional hegemony and, on the other hand, it has not been subjected to external colonization. Nevertheless, the country has been partly influenced by the age of colonization. In Chapter 9, Siegfried Pausewang looks at the arrogance of state power as well as the failure relating to democracy and the rule of law in Ethiopia. His finding is a realistic one: 'Ten years after the overthrow of the "Derg" – the military dictatorship (1974–91) that, following the overthrow of Emperor Haile Selassie, was led from 1977 onwards by Colonel Mengistu Haile Mariam – Ethiopia is once again in deep crisis.' Pausewang sees a blatant contradiction between the wording and the reality of the constitution. He points out that although the Tigray People's Liberation Front (TPLF), the political force dominant since 1991, initially adopted a transitional constitution with strongly federal elements in cooperation with other ethnic groups, the conflicts with the Oromo people, which accounts for between one-third and one-half of the Ethiopian population, and its liberation front, the OLF, soon intensified.

The constitution that came into force in 1995 was modern and almost exemplary with its catalogue of civil rights. Furthermore, it cannot be denied that the regime of Meles Zenawi did produce distinct improvements compared with the brutal repression of the Derg dictatorship. Nevertheless, Pausewang contends that neither democracy nor the rule of law has been able to gain a foothold as yet. Human rights violations are still widespread and the elections over the past few years (the last being in 2000 and 2001) have not led to any real democratization. He goes on to say that minimum constitutional guarantees are infringed upon as soon as the dominant party, which equates its own interests with those of the state, fears for its power. Pausewang presents a number of informative examples to illustrate how power is maintained by the use of what are sometimes cunning instruments. One of these is pseudo-decentralization: 'The administration is decentralized but the party tightly controls it. Moreover it has become standard practice that when complaints are lodged, the central government refers to the decentralized responsibility of the regions and zones. However, where its own political interests are concerned it intervenes swiftly and without scruples.'

The judiciary, which had few qualified personnel following the replacement of élites in 1991, is currently in the midst of a deep-seated crisis. Although there are courageous judges in Addis Ababa who also rule against state authorities on occasions, the government can annul such judgments by referring difficult cases to the local level, over which it has greater control. In view of the experiences in Africa, and especially in Ethiopia, Pausewang assesses the role of the state in fundamentally critical terms. In his view, there can be no talk of a weak state or 'state failure': he sees the core problem of crisis countries in the *modus operandi* and exercising of power practised by the state itself, with the army constituting a decisive instrument of support where internal control and repression are concerned. In conclusion, Pausewang demonstrates that reforming the military does not necessarily lead to a lesser degree of militarized rule. He points out that the disarming of the Mengistu army, for example, was used by the government of Meles Zenawi to expand local police and special operations forces. The case study can, therefore, be read as a reminder to external players not to be over-hasty in approving reforms in the security sector but, rather, first to examine them very closely indeed.

REGIONAL CONFLICT MANAGEMENT IN THE LIGHT OF SEPTEMBER 11

The completion of this publication project comes at a time when far-reaching changes have been triggered by the terror attacks of September 11 and the reaction of the USA, the only remaining superpower. These events suddenly made the vulnerability of the complex industrial societies of the North – already existent for some time but recognized by only a few – abundantly clear. The setting up of a global, so-called anti-terror coalition does also have consequences for the perception of regional conflicts, their geopolitical status and the possibilities for settling them. For example, it focuses attention on the significant role played by privatized violence – something long neglected in the political, scientific and public domains – be it in the form of organized crime, warlordism or transnational terrorism. Privatized violence is a phenomenon that contributes substantially to the protracted consolidation of structures of violence.

Against this background, I discuss in Chapter 10 how the new security policy coordinates impact on regional conflict management. Four points are highlighted: first, Western states (and their new allies) now apprehend the term 'extended security', which incorporates the dimensions of threats beyond the security dilemma and stresses the interdependence of the regions of the world, in a very tangible manner against the backdrop of a real threat to themselves. They have to respond to the increasing and transnational role of privatized violence. This redefinition of security goes hand in hand with redefining the right to self-defence, something that was carried out by the UN Security

Council in Resolutions 1368 and 1373 adopted immediately after the terror attacks.

Second, September 11 is of substantial significance for global security policy. Even though the precise consequences can be discussed only in speculative terms at the moment, it is patently clear that the terror attacks and the response of the only remaining and, at the same time, 'wounded world power' are having repercussions on the West's priorities and commitment in all regions of the globe, resulting in a reassessment of international organizations as instruments and fora for building alliances and obtaining legitimation. There is, in this regard, evidence of a (seemingly) paradoxical trend in US foreign policy, namely the renaissance of geopolitical patterns of thought and action with simultaneous recourse to (selective and hegemonic) multilateralism.

Third, a consequence can be predicted: conflict constellations in the different regions of the world will be re-evaluated and reinterpreted by globally oriented players. Although this applies in particular to Central and Southern Asia, the Islamic World and the Middle East, it also concerns the regions examined in this volume. The Caucasus is likely to be most affected by virtue of its forming a bridge between Europe and Central Asia, its being imbued with organized crime, and the fact that both the USA and Russia have geostrategic interests in this Eurasian interface. Eastern Africa (the Horn of Africa and East Africa) will experience increased attention, given that this region has increasingly grown as a turntable for the drugs trade and, in parts, has also become a refuge for terrorist networks. The governments of Central America, finally, are under pressure to adapt their relationship with the USA in view of the officially declared 'war against terrorism' – an undertaking that will certainly meet with scepticism among sections of the population and opposition if this turns out to mean unconditional subordination to US interests.

My fourth point is that foreign, security and development policy has so far reacted according to very conventional lines and not responded adequately to the new challenges. Effective formulas against the new threats posed by privatized violence will not lie in massive military strikes or undifferentiated measures for increasing 'internal security', nor in a development-policy offensive to combat poverty, as important as this would be for overcoming unjust social structures, everyday violence and gang crime. What are needed, rather, are militarily organized police actions externally, selective protective measures internally and a change in the way the intelligence services operate. In global economic and development policy terms, it is essential first and foremost to drain the financial bases of markets of violence and open up alternatives to criminal economic sectors (drug cultivation and illegal trade networks, to mention just two). Furthermore, the consolidation of state institutions is important in situations of fragile peace. Strengthening the ability to govern through such a development policy will, however, help overcome structures of violence only if it is accompanied at the same time by the courageous commitment of external players to establish constitutional and public control of state power.

(*Translation: Barry Stone*)

NOTES

This anthology follows on from debates conducted in the course of five international workshops between November 1999 and November 2000 within the context of the SEF Policy Forum on Regional Conflict Management. The Development and Peace Foundation (SEF) arranged this series of events with the generous support of the German Federal Ministry for Economic Cooperation and Development (BMZ); for documentation and conference contribution see <http://sef-bonn.org>. I should like to express my sincere thanks to Jonathan Cohen, Kiflemariam Gebrewold, Hartwig Hummel, Uwe Kerkow, Burkhard Könitzer, Sabine Kurtenbach, Volker Matthies, Gudrun Molkentin, Michèle Roth, Christiane Schulz, Angelika Spelten and Bernhard J. Trautner for their numerous ideas and suggestions on the content of the workshops and the book.

1. The controversy surrounding the term 'soft state' (Myrdal 1968) can thus be resolved briefly and to the point in Nuscheler's words (1988: 112): 'As a general rule, the "development state" proved strong only in its repressive capacity but soft in this planning, guiding and implementing capability.'

2. The report was submitted in August 2000 by the Independent Panel on United Nations Peace Operations under the direction of former Algerian Foreign Minister Lakhdar Brahimi, who was appointed UN special envoy to Afghanistan in October 2001 (a position that, incidentally, he had previously occupied up to 1999). The Brahimi Commission stresses that multidimensional peace-keeping operations should be oriented more in the future towards supporting *good governance*, strengthening the rule of law, and *institution-building* (cf. Brahimi Report 2000: ix). The Commission points the way by referring, in particular, to the deployment of civilian policemen, as well as administration and legal experts. It calls for 'a doctrinal shift in the use of civilian police and related rule of law elements in peace operations that emphasizes a team approach to upholding the

rule of law and respect for human rights and helping communities coming out of a conflict to achieve national reconciliation' (para. 119).

3. An animated debate on this issue is now also taking place in Germany; see for example Wulf 2000.

4. In contrast to the conventions common in the Anglo-American discussion, I regard justice and the civil structures responsible for monitoring and controlling the security sector as independent areas.

5. The government has pushed ahead with the setting up of such local tribunals over the past few years. A significant measure was the appointment of 200,000 lay judges on 4 October 2001 (cf. Human Rights Watch Press Release, 4 October 2001, 'Rwanda: elections may speed genocide trials. But new system lacks guarantees of rights'), <http://hrw.org/press/2001/10/rwanda1004.htm> (access on 5 October 2001).

6. See Negash and Tronvoll 2000 concerning the more complex causes of the war.

REFERENCES

Ayoob, M. (1995) *The Third World Security Predicament: State Making, Regional Conflict, and the International System*, Boulder, CO, Cologne and London: Lynne Rienner.

Brahimi Report (2000) *Report of the Panel on United Nations Peace Operations: Comprehensive Review of the Whole Question of Peacekeeping Operations in All Their Aspects*, New York, NY, United Nations (A/44/305, S/2000/809, 21 August), <http://www.un.org/peace/reports/peace_operations/report.htm> (access on 15 May 2001).

Chalmers, M. (2000) *Security Sector Reform in Developing Countries: An EU Perspective*, London and Brussels: Saferworld and Stiftung Wissenschaft und Politik/Conflict Prevention Network.

Cilliers, J. and P. Mason (eds) (1999) *Peace, Profit or Plunder? The Privatisation of Security in War-Torn African Societies*, Halfway House, South Africa: Institute for Security Studies (in cooperation with the Canadian Council for International Peace and Security, Ottawa).

Debiel, T. and M. Fischer (2000) *Crisis Prevention and Conflict Management by the European Union. Concepts, Capacities and Problems of Coherence*, Berlin: Berghof Research Center for Constructive Conflict Management (Berghof Report, No. 4; September 2000).

Elwert, G. (1999) 'Markets of violence', in G. Elwert, S. Feuchtwang and D. Neubert (eds), *Dynamics of Violence: Processes of Escalation and De-Escalation in Violent Group Conflicts*, Berlin: Duncker and Humblot, pp. 85–102.

Karp, A. (1993) 'Arming ethnic conflict', in *Arms Control Today*, 23 (7) (September): 8–13.

Khadiagala, G. M. (1995) 'State collapse and reconstruction in Uganda', in

I. William Zartman (ed.), *Collapsed States: The Disintegration and Restoration of Legitimate Authority*, Boulder, CO, and London: Lynne Rienner, pp. 33–48.

Migdal, J. S. (1988) *Strong Societies and Weak States: State–Society Relations and State Capabilities in the Third World*, Princeton, NJ: Princeton University Press.

Mwagiru, M. (1997) 'The causes of war and chain reactions: linkages of the conflicts in East Africa', presentation made at the Development and Peace Foundation International Symposium, 1–2 December 1997, Berlin, <http://sef-bonn.org/sef/veranst/1997/symposium/mwagiru.html> (access on 30 November 2001).

Myrdal, Gunnar (1968) *Asian Drama: An Inquiry into the Poverty of Nations* (3 vols), New York: Twentieth Century Fund.

Negash, T. and K. Tronvoll (2000) *Brothers at War: Making Sense of the Eritrean–Ethiopian War*, Oxford: James Currey.

Nuscheler, F. (1988) 'Learning from experience or preaching ideologies? Rethinking development theory', in *Law and State, a Biannual Collection of Recent German Contributions to these Fields*, Tübingen, Vol. 38, pp. 104–25. The original appeared in *Dokkyo International Review*, 1, Soka, Japan: Dokkyo University.

OECD/DAC (2001) 'Helping prevent violent conflict. Orientations for external partners', supplement to the DAC *Guidelines on Conflict, Peace and Development Co-operation on the Threshold of the 21st Century*, Paris, <http://www.oecd.org/dac/pdf/G-con-e.pdf> (access on 5 November 2001).

Schlichte, K. (1996) *Krieg und Vergesellschaftung in Afrika. Ein Beitrag zur Theorie des Krieges*, Münster/Hamburg: Lit.

Sisk, T. (1996) *Power Sharing and International Mediation in Ethnic Conflicts*, Washington, DC: United States Institute of Peace Press.

Wallensteen, P. and M. Sollenberg (2000) 'Armed Conflict 1989–99', *Journal of Peace Research*, 37 (5): 635ff.

Wulf, H. (2000) *Security-Sector Reform in Developing Countries: An Analysis of the International Debate and Potentials for Implementing Reforms with Recommendations for Technical Cooperation*, Eschborn: GTZ (October).

PART ONE

State Failure and the Transformation of War-torn Societies

PART ONE

Some Failure and the Transformation
of Western Sciences

ONE

The Reconstruction and Transformation of War-torn Societies and State Institutions: How Can External Actors Contribute?

NICOLE BALL

§ In the last half of the twentieth century, an average of nearly one million people perished each year as a result of armed conflict. The cost of these wars in terms of missed developmental opportunities is substantial. Although socio-economic development may not come to a halt during conflict, what is possible to accomplish under conditions of war tends to be both very limited and constantly under threat of reversal. What is more, the growing trend of the warring parties to use natural resources to sustain war seemingly indefinitely is further reducing some countries' long-term development potential.

Armed conflict both retards the development process and erodes a country's development foundation as people are killed, abandon their homes, their education and their livelihoods, or flee their countries; as infrastructure is damaged or destroyed; as resources are diverted from the routine maintenance of existing social and economic infrastructure; and as a country's resource base is depleted. War-related damages are difficult to quantify, but estimates typically run into billions of dollars. Fundamental requirements for sustainable, poverty-reducing development such as a state capable of furnishing public goods, of impartially protecting property rights and personal safety, and of providing a predictable, equitable legal framework for investment are often beyond the capacity of post-conflict governments.[1]

Beyond the physical destruction, armed conflict that arises out of internal power imbalances gravely complicates efforts to create an environment conducive to sustainable development. Although many of the wars fought since 1945 have become regionalized, their roots have been in local conditions, and it is likely that this pattern will continue in the twenty-first century. Internal disputes that have degenerated into violent conflict have been caused by a complex combination of political, economic and social cleavages, with struggles over access to the levers of power being paramount. An extensive study of the causes of violent conflict undertaken by the UN University's World Institute for Development Economics Research (WIDER) has concluded:

> the causes of conflict are to be found in the interactions of power-seeking with group identity and inequalities ... The violence is not, at least purportedly, the objective, rather it is *instrumental*, used in order to achieve other ends. Usually, the declared objective is political – to secure or sustain power – while power is wanted for the advantages it offers, especially the possibilities of economic gains.
>
> ... As Cohen (1974: 94) points out, 'men may and do certainly joke about or ridicule the strange and bizarre customs of men from other ethnic groups, because these customs are different from their own. But they do not fight over such differences alone. When men *do*, on the other hand, fight across ethnic lines it is nearly always the case that they fight over some fundamental issues concerning the distribution and exercise of power, whether economic, political, or both.' (Stewart 2000)

The institutions in both the public sector and civil society that should be capable of mediating these disputes in many non-OECD countries are typically weak or non-existent. What is more, in countries such as apartheid-era South Africa, Yugoslavia under Slobodan Milosevic, Rwanda in 1994 or Zimbabwe at the beginning of the twenty-first century, civilian leaders have exploited the relative lack of countervailing democratic processes by fomenting violence or otherwise creating the conditions necessary to justify repressive actions against their populations to prevent fundamental political and economic reforms. In other countries, such as Indonesia, security forces have played a more autonomous role in preventing peaceful change. For these reasons, improving economic and political governance is the key to conflict transformation and prevention, and hence to reconstituting war-torn societies, or peace-building.

DEFINING PEACE-BUILDING

In the early 1990s, peace-building was generally viewed as a series of activities intended to help countries recover from violent conflict (Boutros-Ghali 1992, 1995). By the end of the 1990s, however, it was becoming increasingly common to view peace-building as a means of preventing and mitigating violent conflict within societies as well as helping them recover from such conflicts. This more comprehensive view of peace-building is exemplified by the definition employed by the Canadian government:

Peace-building is the effort to strengthen the prospects for internal peace and decrease the likelihood of violent conflict. The overarching goal of peace-building is to enhance the indigenous capacity of a society to manage conflict without violence. Ultimately, peace-building aims at building human security, a concept that includes democratic governance, human rights, rule of law, sustainable development, equitable access to resources, and environmental security. The pursuit of this goal in countries torn by internal conflict poses special and complex challenges.

Peace-building may involve conflict prevention, conflict resolution, as well as various kinds of post-conflict activities. It focuses on the political and socio-economic context of conflict, rather than on the military or humanitarian aspects. It seeks to address this challenge by finding means to institutionalize the peaceful resolution of conflicts. External support for peace-building should supplement, not substitute, local efforts to achieve a sustainable peace.[2]

While peace-building can help forestall state disintegration and civil war, there is no doubt that peace-building is most challenging in countries that have experienced significant violence. There are at least three types of challenges facing countries seeking to make a war-to-peace transition:

• strengthening political institutions,
• providing a safe and secure environment for poverty-reducing development, and
• promoting economic and social revitalization.

Because violent conflicts invariably increase the number of poor in countries that, for the most part, had high rates of poverty prior to the outbreak of violence, it is important to give attention to economic development activities that will help reduce the incidence of poverty. And while it is generally not the poor who cause violent conflicts, however desperate their situation, serious economic disparities and a lack of employment opportunities that pay a living wage do make people more vulnerable to those who seek to foment violence. There can be no sustainable, poverty-reducing economic and social development, however, without political development that has as one of its objectives a reasonably equitable distribution of economic and political power and the reasonably equitable sharing of the fruits of development. There can be no such political development without security of individuals, social groups, and society as a whole – as opposed to security for a specific government or security of particular ruling groups, which is prevalent in many war-torn societies. In short, sustainable, poverty-reducing development requires due attention to both economic and political governance (Ball 1998a: 4–5; Chalmers 2000: 6–7).

The centrality of good governance to the achievement of economic development has become increasingly clear to the development community over the last decade. Development agencies, including the World Bank, the United Nations Development Programme (UNDP) and the International Monetary Fund (IMF), have consequently been seeking to define for themselves what the promotion of good governance entails. Although the World Bank and the IMF still tend to view governance primarily as an economic issue, most donors would agree with the UNDP definition of governance:

> the exercise of economic, political and administrative authority to manage a country's affairs at all levels, comprising the mechanisms, process and institutions through which that authority is directed. Good governance is, among other things, participatory, transparent, accountable and efficient. It also recognises that governance is exercised by the private sector and civil society, as well as the state, all of which have important roles to play in promoting sustainable human development.[3]

PRIORITY PEACE-BUILDING TASKS

In a country attempting to overcome the effects of civil war, strengthening political institutions and supporting a transformation of the security sector are simultaneously critically important and even more

Table 1.1 Major characteristics of war-affected countries

Political institutions	• Lack of government legitimacy • Weak state incapable of fulfilling basic functions of government • High degree of centralization • Minimal experience with participatory government • Considerable disaffection with political leaders • Weak political parties, poorly developed concept of 'loyal opposition' • Predominance of power politics; lack of consensus on national direction; insufficiently developed 'rules of the game'; polarized society • In situations with no clear victor, perception of all parties that their side has won, leading to unrealistic assessments of political strength • Absence of mechanisms to mediate societal disputes • Weak civil society organizations
Security sector	• Bloated state security forces that must be reduced; armed opposition forces and informal paramilitary forces that must be disbanded/disarmed • Armed forces control over internal security function • Lack of accountability of security forces to democratically elected civil authorities • Lack of transparency on security issues • Lack of civilian capacity to manage and monitor security forces, both public sector and civil society • Lack of mechanisms to evaluate true security needs • Lack of personal security for citizens, due to proliferation of small arms and light weapons, increased criminality, culture of impunity • Involvement of security forces in political system and economy • Regionalized conflict that may persist

Table 1.1 continued

Economy and society	• Extensive damage to economic/social infra-structure • High levels of debt; mortgaging of assets for war • Unsustainable levels of security expenditure • Skewed distribution of income, wealth and assets • Multiple claims to land and assets • High levels of corruption • Substantial numbers of war-affected populations • Severely weakened social fabric (destruction of communities, creation of culture of violence, fostering a sense of impermanence, mistrust) • Abysmal indicators of human well-being

difficult to achieve than in countries that have not experienced civil war. Their importance lies in the close link between the causes of war and inadequate political governance. Their difficulty lies in the enormous pressures that exist to achieve short-term goals in the early stages of a peace process.

Thus a major challenge confronting both the societies emerging from violent conflict and the international development community seeking to assist them in this process is to identify ways to incorporate the longer-term objectives of institution-building into short-term rehabilitation and reconstruction efforts. Difficult as it may be, the effort must be made. The termination of civil war offers a unique opportunity to address fundamental imbalances in political institutions, including those existing between the security forces and the rest of society, that contribute to violent conflict and make sustainable, poverty-reducing economic and social development more difficult to achieve.

Table 1.1 summarizes the main characteristics of countries making the war-to-peace transition. Many of these are governance-related. Some have been explicitly enshrined in peace agreements, but often the longer-term tasks associated with strengthening economic and political governance are not mandated by the peace accords. Even more serious, they are frequently not included in efforts to consolidate the peace at the end of formal peace processes.

DONOR ROLES AND RESPONSIBILITIES IN SUPPORTING THE REBUILDING OF WAR-TORN SOCIETIES

Experience indicates that three factors are especially important to efforts to rebuild war-torn societies. These are:

- The national leadership must be committed to a significant transformation and reform process.[4]
- The principles, policies, laws and structures developed during the reform process must be rooted in the reforming country's history, culture, legal framework and institutions. Part of the peace process may, however, involve implementing negotiated changes in legal frameworks and constitutions.
- The reform process should ensure that those within government who have the right and responsibility to participate are involved and that there is consultation between government and civil and political society.

Whether or not these conditions exist depends to a very large degree on domestic vision and political commitment to a process of reform and transformation. The development of this vision and commitment can be fostered by public–private partnerships, where experienced members of civil society encourage the government to engage in reform and are invited to participate in reform processes. In countries emerging from periods of internal conflict, commitment, vision, strong civil society and other prerequisites are often weak. Where they are not entirely lacking, however, it may be possible for the international community to foster an environment conducive to their development.

Experience from around the world suggests that appropriately designed and delivered external support can significantly benefit efforts to make the war-to-peace transition. As the characteristics of war-torn countries suggest, creating a durable peace and promoting sustainable, poverty-reducing development in such environments requires action on a wide variety of fronts. The local stakeholders' capacity to meet these demands is, however, severely constrained by the legacies of war: institutional weaknesses, limited human and financial resources, pro-

BOX I.I EXTERNAL SUPPORT FOR SMALL ARMS
COLLECTION PROGRAMMES

Civil wars lead to a proliferation of small arms in society. In order to redress this problem in countries such as Albania, Cambodia and Mozambique, programmes have been developed to remove these weapons from society. Such programmes cannot succeed in isolation. They need to be undertaken in conjunction with efforts to address the underlying causes of conflict. They also need to be well designed and run. In most post-conflict societies, this has meant technical and financial assistance from abroad.

Operation Rachel, a joint South Africa–Mozambique programme begun in 1995, has succeeded in finding and destroying weapons and ammunition hidden during the country's civil war, which ended in 1992. It involved collaboration between the South African Police Service and the Police of the Republic of Mozambique, and most of the technical expertise and financial and material resources were provided by South Africa. In view of the contribution of weapons from Mozambique to South Africa's burgeoning violent crime problem, it was an investment that had clear benefits for South Africa. For Mozambique, the elimination of arms caches supported that country's peace-building efforts. According to a recent assessment of Operation Rachel, 'This successful collaboration between the two police forces and the two governments has been widely noted and is considered a useful precedent for similar efforts elsewhere.'

A Tools for Arms project supported by the Christian Council of Mozambique, which collected a smaller number of arms in exchange for tools and machinery, received funding from the Canadian International Development Agency.

Source: Sami Faltas, Glenn McDonald, and Camilla Waszink (2001), *Removing Small Arms from Society: A Review of Weapons Collection and Destruction Programmes*, Geneva: Small Arms Survey, 2001, <www.smallarmssurvey.org> and Canadian International Development Agency, *CIDA Peace-building Fund Approved Projects*, <www.acdi-cida.cg.ca>

found mistrust and animosity generated by civil war, and economic fragility. This has encouraged the local stakeholders to turn to the international community for technical assistance, financial advice and political support. For these same reasons, repairing the ravages of war is an arduous, complex and lengthy process.

While there are international actors that can provide useful assistance to countries seeking to recover from violent conflict, it does not automatically follow that reforming countries will always receive appropriate assistance. Nor does it automatically follow that reforming countries will make the best use of assistance provided.

Stakeholders in reforming countries need to become informed consumers of the external assistance offered. Informed consumers are characterized by the ability to identify what they need, who can provide it for them, and how to get value for money. In order to use external assistance as effectively as possible in building democratic societies that have sustainable, poverty-reducing development as a major objective, there are three questions that local stakeholders should consider:

• What is necessary for our country to recover from the war?
• What sort of assistance do we require to accomplish these tasks?
• Who can provide that assistance to us in the most cost-effective manner?

For its part, the international community has made progress over the last decade in understanding the needs of post-conflict environments and in its ability to deliver what is needed. Nevertheless, considerable work remains to be done. In order to improve the quality of external assistance to conflict-affected countries, the donors of this assistance need to prioritize the following objectives:

• First, build on what exists locally and take local ownership seriously.
• Second, create sustained partnerships among international agencies.
• Third, enhance the effectiveness of the assistance provided.
• Fourth, help restart government.

BUILDING ON LOCAL NEEDS AND CAPACITIES

External stakeholders experience a greater degree of success to the extent that they avoid imposing specific organizational structures and modes of operation. They must accept that there are different ways to achieve many of the ends that they seek – responsible, accountable, transparent governments; strong civil societies; accountable security forces; poverty-reducing development. The objectives of their assistance should be to empower a) governments to discover what will work best for them in order to achieve the desired end states and b) civil society to participate effectively in the process.

Operationally, external actors can provide technical assistance in a wide range of areas, including consultative methods, planning complex processes, and confidence-building mechanisms. If technical assistance is provided, continuity is highly important. Local stakeholders are extremely pressed for time to reflect. Conflict-affected countries in particular face many urgent problems that are very difficult to prioritize, and have a limited number of people with the requisite interest and skills. Therefore, it is desirable to provide such countries with on-site personnel who can act as mentors to local stakeholders – both in the public sector and in civil society.

As far as possible, technical assistance should also incorporate the experience of other countries that have gone through war-to-peace transitions. There are several advantages to 'peer-based' technical assistance. For one thing, lessons learned may be more readily accepted when they are imparted by someone who has confronted similar challenges. For another, people from other war-torn societies, particularly those who come from the same geographic region and/or share similar historical backgrounds, may have insights that are more appropriate to the country in question than someone whose frame of reference is North America or Western Europe. In both cases it is important, however, to stress the word 'may'. Inappropriate advice can come from many quarters, and it is important to find high-quality advisers, rather than 'politically correct' ones.

CREATING SUSTAINED PARTNERSHIPS

One lesson that is progressively being incorporated into the policies and programmes of international actors relates to the importance of sustained assistance from the entire international community throughout a peace process. At the beginning of the 1990s, there was a tendency to assume that diplomatic and military efforts should be concentrated in the early part of the peace process, including the negotiation phase, while financial and technical assistance should come into play once the peace agreement was signed and hostilities had ceased.[5]

As experience accumulated, development actors came to realize that they needed to devote a relatively modest amount of resources to planning for post-war activities and building collaborative relationships with the parties to the conflict during the negotiation phase. Among the earliest instances of donor engagement in the negotiation phase were the Dayton negotiations regarding Bosnia and the UN-brokered discussions in Guatemala.

The speed with which events occur once peace agreements are signed argues very strongly in favour of donor involvement at the earliest possible moment in a peace process. Furthermore, early engagement by the development community can help the parties to the conflict address relevant socio-economic issues in a realistic manner and facilitate the process of developing mechanisms for tackling crucial socio-economic

---

BOX 1.2 WORLD BANK POLICY FOR OPERATING
IN CONFLICT AREAS

7. If the Bank determines that continued assistance in the conflict-affected country is not possible, it may initiate a watching brief for all or a part of the country, in order to develop an understanding of the context, dynamics, needs, and institutions of the area to position the Bank to support an appropriate investment portfolio when conditions permit. This activity normally involves consultations with the Bank's partners. The nature of the watching brief in any given country depends on such factors as the presence or absence of a government in power, access of potential partners, and the ability of Bank staff to visit the country or access specific areas. In the context of a watching brief, the Bank may support additional activities, at the country's request. All such additional activities are subject to the prior approval of the Board.

Source: World Bank (2001), 'Operational Policy 2.30: Development Cooperation and Conflict', *World Bank Operational Manual*, January.

issues that are likely to become politicized or ignored once the peace agreement is signed. All of this places a premium on donors developing methods of keeping their knowledge base about conditions in individual conflict-affected countries as up to date as possible during the conflict and the peace negotiation phase.

Donors have undertaken institutional reforms to enhance their capacity for early action. The World Bank, for example, has developed a watching brief methodology to enable it to keep abreast of developments in countries where the Bank has had to suspend operations due to civil war (World Bank 1998: 42–3). Previously, when the Bank ceased operations, it also ceased collecting information, primarily because staff salaries were largely tied to lending programmes. Few managers were willing to dip into their budgets for non-lending activities in order to finance work on a country that might not have an active lending portfolio for many years.

As far as peace-keeping operations are concerned, it has been evident from the outcome of several early post-Cold War peace processes such as those in Cambodia, El Salvador and Mozambique that a two-year, or less, mandate often requires peace missions to be shut down before the accords have been fully implemented. There is still variation, however, in the extent to which this knowledge is being incorporated into the next generation of peace-keeping mandates. While a lengthy international peace-keeping presence has been accepted for Bosnia and Kosovo, the UN mission in Sierra Leone is working on rolling six-month mandates. The missions in East Timor and the Democratic Republic of the Congo were authorized for approximately fifteen months each in the first instance.

Restrictions on the length of mandates often arise because of resource constraints. Peace operations are costly and the UN has been in financial crisis for some years. Efforts have been made to use resources more efficiently and accountably within the UN as a whole, but such reforms could not by themselves resolve the problem of non-payment of dues. In additional to financial constraints, there are political ones. Many UN members are also wary of what may appear to be a significant open-ended commitment in very troubled countries or regions.

In addition to the problem of missions not being able to oversee the complete implementation of peace accords, very short mandates, even if the intention is to renew, create significant problems in recruiting and retraining-high quality staff (Ball and Campbell 1998: 56–67), as well as giving the impression to parties seeking to avoid complying with peace agreements that they can 'wait out' the international community. The IFOR mission in Bosnia-Herzegovina offers a prime example of this latter point.

In some cases, notably Bosnia, East Timor, Kosovo and Sierra Leone, maintaining a proactive and flexible military and police presence is critical to the creation of a durable peace. The conflicts in the Balkans have shown, for example, that sustaining the peace process can require peace-keeping troops to engage in what might be termed non-military activities, such as arresting indicted war criminals and combating organized crime syndicates that have their roots in the war economy. Similarly,

---

BOX 1.3 SECRETARY-GENERAL'S RESPONSE TO
THE BRAHIMI REPORT

21. Virtually every part of the United Nations system, including the Bretton Woods institutions, is currently engaged in one form of peace-building or another ...

22. It makes sense that so many parts of the system are engaged in peace-building, because it embraces multiple sectors of activity including political, military, diplomatic, development, human rights, child protection, gender issues, humanitarian and many others. However, a clear division of labour has not yet emerged within the system, neither in the formulation of comprehensive peace-building strategies, nor in their implementation. As a result of this lack of clarity, the Panel implied that there were risks of competing demands on limited donor resources, potential duplication of efforts, and/or gaps in key areas that needed to be addressed.

23. ... I ... concur with the Panel's recommendation, and have instructed the Executive Committee on Peace and Security, in consultation with the other Executive Committees, to formulate a plan to address these issues, by the end of March 2001.

Source: UN, GA (2000), Report of the Secretary-General on the implementation of the report of the Panel on United Nations Peace Operations, A/55/502, 20 October.

in countries where 'negotiated' settlements have essentially been imposed on warring parties – Angola, Bosnia, Kosovo and Sierra Leone – events have demonstrated that peace-keepers must be prepared actively to keep the peace in order to promote the rule of law in post-conflict societies. These issues are under discussion within the peace-keeping community, but have by no means been fully resolved. Some UN member governments are unwilling to allow their units to engage in peace-enforcement activities, and some national units have shown themselves to be more effective fighting forces than others. This underscores the importance of being able to choose among troop-contributing countries.

ENHANCING THE EFFECTIVENESS OF PEACE-BUILDING ASSISTANCE

Donors have made a conscious effort to improve the effectiveness of the assistance they provide to war-torn countries. They have had mixed results in these efforts.

One of the earliest lessons identified was the need for flexible, fast-disbursing funds that donors could utilize during the transition period. Development assistance funds are slow-disbursing while faster-disbursing humanitarian or emergency funds tend to have restrictions on the types of activities they can support that render them unavailable for development-type transition activities. Fast-disbursing windows now exist in most donor agencies, and most donor agencies have also created peace-building or transition units. Some of these units operate only in post-conflict environments; others have a preventive mandate as well.

The creation of special funding windows and units for peace-building activities is one indication of the seriousness with which the donors are now approaching post-conflict assistance. At the same time, it is important that the activities funded meet the needs of war-torn countries. Donors have made significant efforts to learn from the past and incorporate those lessons into ongoing programmes. The World Bank, for example, conducted an evaluation of its experience with post-conflict reconstruction and a major 'lessons learned' study on demobilization and reintegration of former combatants.[6] Other donors have conducted numerous country- and issue-specific 'lessons learned' studies and programme evaluations. Operational staff involved with peace-building activities in nearly twenty donor agencies have been meeting twice a year since late 1997, and have recently undertaken a survey of good practices in a number of peace-building-related areas. Important as lessons learned and assessment work are, it is essential that the lessons and good practices are put in context. There is a tendency within the development community as a whole, not merely that section dealing with post-conflict situations, to seek 'solutions' to problems that can be applied more or less universally. Although there are many similarities between post-conflict countries, wholesale application of approaches that have proven successful in one post-conflict environment to another post-conflict environment may well be ineffective or even counter-productive (Ball 1998b).

In addition to contextualizing lessons learned and good practices work, dissemination of good practices is critically dependent on the quality and motivation of staff. Donors have increasingly sought to strengthen staff assigned to post-conflict countries. In some cases, staff with previous experience in one post-conflict transition country have been assigned to other war-torn countries, especially within the same region. Staff from El Salvador have transferred to Guatemala; staff from Mozambique have transferred to Angola; staff from Bosnia have transferred to Kosovo. The UNDP has recognized the importance of recruiting resident coordinators from outside its own bureaucracy and in some cases outside the UN. Once again, however, it is important that staff are aware of the differences that exist between countries and do

---

BOX 1.4 DONOR EFFORTS TO IMPROVE
OPERATIONAL CAPACITY

The Global Peace-building Network, managed by the World Bank Post-Conflict Unit, provides access to the Conflict Prevention and Post-Conflict Reconstruction Network (CPR). The CPR's focus is to improve operational capacity of the main multilateral and bilateral actors in helping to prevent conflict and engage in reconstruction, rehabilitation, reconciliation, reintegration, and peace-building in countries that have experienced internal conflicts. The Global Peace-building Network's website is located at: <wblnoo18.worldbank. org/ESSD/pci.nsf/Home?OpenView>

not attempt to re-create exactly the same programmes that worked well in other countries.

One way of overcoming problems associated with staff without adequate experience in war-torn countries and the tendency to apply one-size-fits-all approaches is to ensure that the local stakeholders are included from the beginning. That said, the weakness of human capacity and the extreme politicization and polarization that characterize war-torn societies are important limitations on efforts to include local stakeholders in programme design and implementation. An equally serious limitation, however, is the unwillingness of many donor representatives to promote genuine participation by local stakeholders. This is a problem that afflicts non-governmental actors as well as official actors, and appears to derive from a fear of loss of control. Despite considerable rhetoric about 'empowerment' and 'ownership', donor agencies and their representatives frequently insist on defining what is to be done, how it is to be done, and who is to do it.

BOX 1.5 STAKEHOLDER INVOLVEMENT IN
BOSNIA

Research sponsored by the United States Institute of Peace on peace-building in Bosnia demonstrates the importance of local stakeholder involvement. 'Virtually every initiative represented in this report, be it policy research, training, or a grassroots initiative, notes the importance of early and substantial involvement by Bosnians in the conception, design, and implementation of reconciliation and reconstruction activities, from the provision of aid to the development of conflict resolution training curricula.'

Source: Steven M. Riskin (ed.) (1999) 'Three dimensions of peace-building in Bosnia. Findings from USIP-sponsored research and field projects', Peaceworks, 32: 2, Washington, DC, United States Institute of Peace, December.

RESTARTING GOVERNMENT

One priority area that has generally not received the attention it deserves is that of strengthening governmental capacity. When wars end, governments are typically seriously overextended, lack capable staff, and are unable to fulfil key functions and deliver critical services.[7] The armed opposition – which retains control of its weapons throughout a portion of the transition phase – remains highly wary of the government. Opposition leaders frequently believe that the government will fail to deliver benefits in an equitable fashion and may seek to limit the government's role in peace-building, particularly in areas formerly controlled by the armed opposition. At the same time, there is significant pressure to implement peace-building programmes rapidly to keep the peace process on track.

These conditions present donors with a dilemma. In order to implement peace-building activities, resources can be channelled either through the government or through non-governmental bodies and international organizations. The sitting government is simultaneously the government and one of the factions contesting for political power in the period prior to any elections mandated under the peace accords. It aspires to fulfil all the functions of government, but lacks adequate capacity and may have ceded certain responsibilities to a peace-keeping mission under the terms of a peace agreement. Consequently, donors may view bypassing the government as the desirable course to follow in the name of efficiency and impartiality, at least until new elections have been held.

This short-term strategy may, however, create significant problems in the medium to long term. If the donors postpone substantially strengthening institutions and building human resource capacity until a new government is elected, or if they turn preferentially to non-governmental bodies to design and execute peace-building programmes, there is a strong probability that the post-election government will be no more prepared to carry out key tasks than was the pre-election government. Indeed, its capacity for independent action could be severely weakened. Cambodia offers an excellent example of the hazards of this approach.

As urged by the US and France, both UNTAC [the United Nations Transitional Authority Cambodia] and the bilateral donor agencies adhered to a restrictive definition of political 'neutrality' prior to the elections, when it came to dealing with the existing bureaucracy, apart from activities to facilitate the election. Accepting the argument that this bureaucracy was beholden to the SOC faction [State of Cambodia, that is the ruling Cambodian People's Party], and potentially a SOC instrument for influencing the vote, the donors beginning to be active inside Cambodia severely constrained UNTAC's rehabilitation component and refused to provide financial support that would have enabled the SOC to restore its collapsed capacity to pay civil servant salaries ... One cannot know what effects on the election outcome might have resulted if the 'neutrality' policy had allowed for budget support during the UNTAC period ... It is clear, however, that the more than two years between a) the collapse of Soviet aid and the budget support that had entailed and b) the start of IFI [International Financial Institution] aid for the RCG [Royal Cambodian Government] budget had significant negative consequence for the post-May 1993 reconstruction and reconciliation processes that were designed to dovetail with legitimation. (Brown and Muscat 1995: 66–7)

Yet, as El Salvador demonstrates, making the government the main vehicle of peace-building assistance can be equally problematic. The USA, which had been a major player in the Salvadoran civil war on the side of the sitting government, channelled its economic assistance through the government's National Secretariat for Reconstruction (SRN). The SRN had its roots in the National Commission for the Restoration of Areas, the agency that implemented the US-backed counter-insurgency programme during the war. The government was able to gain electoral advantage by controlling the distribution of funds through the SRN. Thus the agency that was meant to provide peace agreement-mandated assistance to the areas most affected by the war in fact was used by the government to perpetuate its rule, fostering a political environment inimical to reconciliation.

The increased emphasis among those involved with development on the importance of governance has made the donors more aware of the general need to strengthen government institutions, but there are still numerous problems inherent in donor approaches. What is necessary – although extremely difficult to achieve in practice – is a nuanced approach that progressively strengthens the central government's capacity to carry out key activities while minimizing its ability to use resources for partisan political purposes. For the most part, however, donors appear to have taken the easier route of avoiding a concerted effort to enhance state capacity.

Some Palestinian line ministries, municipalities, and agencies continued to approach donors on an individual basis, rather than operating through MOPIC [Ministry of Planning and International Cooperation] or any other centralized mechanism. Some donors complained about this. Most, however, continued to pursue the path of least resistance, arranging whatever projects seemed easiest with whatever level or branch of Palestinian authority or society seemed most amenable ... Some donors responded by citing the need to disburse funds expeditiously. The effect, however, was that donors committed their assistance in those sectors where Palestinian counterpart institutions were strong (for example, education and health), rather than those where institutional capacity or competence was weak (for example, agriculture or tourism). This pattern, of course, exacerbated uneven institutional development and hindered effective economic planning. (Brynen et al. 2000: 231)

A notable exception involves the institutions responsible for administering justice – the police and, to a lesser extent, the judiciary and the penal system. Police reform programmes are now part of many peace-building efforts. While such reforms take a very long time to implement and frequently have to overcome numerous obstacles, the

---

BOX 1.6 SECURITY AS A VITAL BASE FOR DEVELOPMENT

The security of persons, property and assets and the protection of human rights are fundamental to sustainable development and preconditions for people to improve their lives, particularly the poor ...

In a 'post-conflict' country, security is widely seen as one of the crucial elements for any reconciliation and long-term development. It requires both ending the insecurity resulting from war, and new forms of (criminal) insecurity that so often hit countries that have been in conflict for a long time. Insecurity limits the likelihood of reconciliation, undermines the legitimacy of institutions of the state, and hampers any possible recovery and economic development. It has become a widening area for donor involvement, with specific activities in training and capacity building.

Source: OECD 2001: 22.

donor community has understood the critical importance of providing security for individuals in post-conflict environments.[8] It has been far less aware of the importance of developing the capacity of the civil authorities to monitor and manage the defence and intelligence services (DfID 2000). As of early 2002, there was only one donor, the UK Department for International Development, that had a policy of support for reforming the defence sector, although other donors were considering their policies in this area and the OECD Development Assistance Committee had issued some general guidance to its members on supporting reforms in the entire security sector (DfID 1999a, 1999b; OECD 2001).[9]

CONCLUSION

The international community has gained valuable experience since the beginning of the 1990s in addressing the needs of post-conflict countries, and has begun to implement important changes in the content of its assistance and its operating procedures in order to maximize the value of the assistance it provides to war-torn countries. At the same time, many of the problems that plagued the earliest peace-keeping missions and peace-building efforts remain in evidence nearly a decade later. In March 2000, a joint report on the Balkans from the European Union's foreign policy representative, Javier Solana, and the European Commission noted that 'The effectiveness of the EU's policies is affected by the plethora of actors involved. Division of labour is too ad hoc and there is a high degree of duplication ... The effectiveness of our policies suffers from the multiplicity of institutions and frameworks in the region, from complex and lengthy procedures for policy formulation' (World Bank 2000). In Kosovo, the three largest donors – the UNHCR, the US Office for Foreign Disaster Relief and the DfID – gradually evolved methods of coordinating the activities of the foreign donors. But one of the participants in this process observed that: 'It isn't clear whether this system will outlive the departure of the individuals who set it up and made it work.'

Thus we are confronted by a paradox. High-calibre, experienced individuals are crucial for the success of peace-building. The right people can often overcome significant institutional and organizational deficits. At the same time, too much continues to depend on individuals. The failure to institutionalize good practice is undermining the international community's efforts to support the transition from war to peace in many parts of the world. The slow and difficult process of institutionalizing an approach to post-conflict recovery that puts the local stakeholders – including those who have been the victims as well as those who have been the perpetrators of war – at the centre of external support for rebuilding must not only continue; it must be accelerated.

NOTES

1. Of course, many post-conflict governments were unable to fulfil these functions satisfactorily prior to the war, but it is none the less clear that their capacity is further eroded by lengthy wars.

2. Government of Canada (2000), 'Peace-building Initiative Strategic Framework', <http://www.acdi-cida.gc.ca/cida_ind.nsf/vLUallDocByIDEn/5E976E2 DCE2DEE1F8525698B00605DA2>. By 2001, the United Nations had also adopted a more comprehensive definition of peace-building: 'The Security Council recognizes that peace-building is aimed at preventing the outbreak, the recurrence or continuation of armed conflict and therefore encompasses a wide range of political, developmental, humanitarian, and human rights programmes and mechanisms ... These actions should focus on fostering sustainable institutions and processes in areas such as sustainable development, the eradication of poverty and inequalities, transparent and accountable governance, the promotion of democracy, respect for human rights and the rule of law and the promotion of a culture of peace and non-violence' (United Nations, Security Council 2001, S/PRST/2001/5).

3. UNDP, <http://magnet.undp.org/Docs/crisis/Default.htm>

4. According to the *Oxford Encyclopedic English Dictionary* (Hawkins and Allen 1991), 'reform' means 'to make or become better by the removal of faults and errors', and 'transform' means 'to make a thorough, dramatic change in the form, outward appearance, character, etc. of'.

5. Development assistance agencies and the international financial institutions are by no means the only source of financial and technical assistance. Other actors, such as ministries of finance, foreign ministries, ministries of justice, national police forces, private enterprise and civil society, also have a role to play.

6. Field studies for the post-conflict evaluation were conducted of Bosnia and Herzegovina, El Salvador and Uganda. Desk studies were conducted of Cambodia, Eritrea, Haiti, Lebanon, Rwanda and Sri Lanka (World Bank 1998).

7. On the critical tasks facing conflict-affected countries, see Addison 2000: 18. Additionally, Addison argues: 'a development state is unlikely to arise without investment in democracy' (p. 5). On the linkage between weak governance and slow economic development, see Kaufmann, Kraay and Zoido-Lobatón 2000.

8. Examples of the growing literature on police reform and associated judicial system reform include Call 1997; Oakley et al. 1998; Byrne et al. 2000.

9. On the role that donors might play, see Ball 2000, 2001.

REFERENCES

Addison, T. (2000) 'Reconstruction from war in Africa: communities, entrepreneurs, and states', Helsinki: World Institute for Development Economics Research, United Nations University.

Ball, N. (1998a) *Spreading Good Practices in Security Sector Reform: Policy Options for the British Government*, London: Saferworld.

— (1998b) *Managing Conflict: Lessons from the South African Peace Committees*, USAID Evaluation Special Study Report No. 78, Washington, DC: USAID/Center for Development Information and Evaluation, <www.dec.org/usaid_eval> (under the heading 'USAID Evaluation Special Study Reports').

— (2000) 'Good practices in security sector reform', in Herbert Wulf (ed.), *Security Sector Reform*, BICC Brief No. 15, Bonn, Bonn International Centre for Conversion, <www.bicc.de> (under the heading 'Publications', then 'Briefs').

— (2001) 'Transforming security sectors: the IMF and World Bank approaches', *Conflict, Security, Development*, 1 (1): 45–66.

Ball, N. and K. Campbell (1998) *Complex Crisis and Complex Peace: Humanitarian Coordination in Angola*, New York: Office for the Coordination of Humanitarian Affairs, United Nations.

Boutros-Ghali, B. (1992) *An Agenda for Peace*, New York: United Nations.

— (1995) *An Agenda for Peace, 1995*, 2nd edn, New York: United Nations.

Brown, F. Z. and R. J. Muscat (1995) 'The transition from war to peace: the case of Cambodia', paper prepared for the Overseas Development Council Program on Enhancing Security and Development, Washington, DC.

Brynen, R., H. Awartani and C. Woodcraft (2000) 'The Palestinian territories', in Shepard Forman and Stewart Patrick (eds), *Good Intentions: Pledges of Aid for Postconflict Recovery*, Boulder, CO: Lynne Rienner.

Byrne, H., W. Stanley and R. Garst (2000) *Rescuing Police Reform: A Challenge for the New Guatemalan Government*, Washington, DC: Washington Office on Latin America.

Call, C. (1997): 'Police reform, human rights, and democratization in post-conflict settings: lessons from El Salvador', in *After the War is Over What Comes Next? Promoting Democracy, Human Rights, and Reintegration in Post-conflict Societies*, Washington, DC: USAID, Center for Development Information and Evaluation.

Chalmers, M. (2000) *Security Sector Reform in Developing Countries: An EU Perspective*, London and Brussels: Saferworld and Stiftung Wissenschaft und Politik, Conflict Prevention Network.

Cohen, A. (1974) *Two Dimensional Man: An Essay on the Anthropology of Power and Symbolism in Complex Society*, Berkeley: University of California Press.

DfID (1999a): 'Poverty and the security sector', policy statement, London: DfID.

— (1999b) 'Security sector reform and the elimination of poverty', a speech by Clare Short, Secretary of State for International Development, Centre for Defence Studies, King's College, University of London, 9 March 1999, London, <www.dfid.gov.uk>.

— (2001) 'Annex 4: supporting security sector reform: review of the role of external actors', in *Security Sector Reform and the Management of Military Expenditure: High Risks for Donors, High Returns for Development. Report on an International Symposium Sponsored by the UK Department for International Development*, London, June.

Government of Canada (2000) 'Peace-building initiative strategic framework', <www.acdi-cida.gc.ca/cida_ind.nsf/vLUallDocByIDEn/5E976E2DCE2DEE 1F8525698B00605DA2>.

Hawkins, J. M. and R. Allen (eds) (1991) *Oxford Encyclopedic English Dictionary*, UK: Clarendon Press.

Kaufmann, D., A. Kraay and P. Zoido-Lobatón (2000) 'Governance matters: from measurement to action', *Finance & Development*, 37 (2) (June), <www.imf.org/ external/pubs/ft/fandd/2000/06/kauf.htm>.

Oakley, R. B., M. J. Dziedzic and E. M. Goldberg (eds) (1998) *Policing the New World Disorder: Peace Operations and Public Security*, Washington, DC: National Defense University Press.

OECD (2001) *Helping Prevent Violent Conflict: Orientations for External Partners*, Paris: OECD Development Committee, <www.oecd.org/dac/pdf/G-con-e.pdf>.

Stewart, F. (2000) 'The root causes of humanitarian emergencies', in E. W. Nafzinger, F. Stewart and R. Väyrynen (eds), *War, Hunger and Displacement: The Origins of Humanitarian Emergencies*, Vol. I, Oxford: Oxford University Press.

UNDP (c. 2000) 'Promoting conflict prevention and conflict resolution through effective governance. A conceptual survey and literature review', New York: UNDP, Management Development and Governance Division, Bureau for Development Policy, <http://magnet.undp.org/Docs/crisis/Default.htm>.

United Nations Security Council (2001) S/PRST/2001/5, New York, 20 February 2001.

World Bank (1998) *Post-Conflict Reconstruction: The Role of the World Bank*, Washington, DC (the executive summary of this report is located on the Bank's website: <wbln0018.worldbank.org/essd/kb.nsf/PostConflictHome? OpenView>, under 'Policies').

— (1998) *The World Bank's Experience with Post-conflict Reconstruction*, Report No. 17769, 5 Volumes, Washington, DC: World Bank Operations Department.

— (2000) 'Bureaucracy hampering Balkans aid, EU will be told', *Development News*, 23 March.

TWO

An Independent Judiciary in Crisis Regions: Challenges for International Law in Cases of State Failure and Armed Conflicts

HANS-JOACHIM HEINTZE

§ An independent judiciary is an indispensable element of the modern constitutional state as well as of good governance. The development of an independent judiciary constitutes a historical breakthrough in that hitherto the judiciary was invariably linked to the will of the rulers at the time. The latter not only administered justice, but also created the rules. The legal system was a means of sustaining the balance of power. This meant that ecclesiastical and secular rulers alike selected those who were to interpret the law in cases of conflict. This link between law and power gave rise to a symbiosis between justice and politics. Up to and into the Middle Ages, this relationship between state and society was legitimized as a God-given order. It was the Enlightenment and the breakdown of a unified Christian creed (in Europe) that saw the emergence of doubts as to whether rulers in fact applied the law justly. This development gave rise to the demand for independent judges whose activity was geared to establishing the truth and justly administering the law. A further element of the rule of law is that it makes unnecessary the use of special courts, since under it everyone is entitled to appear before a magistrate. This demand was first raised in connection with the French Revolution with a view to putting an end to the arbitrary justice administered by an absolutist state authority.

Today the judiciary has the status of the third power constituting the rule of law. Like the legislative and the executive, which, in the norms they establish, provide the judiciary with the foundations of jurisdiction, the judiciary is one component of the system marked by the separation of powers. In the end, it is the judiciary that is entrusted with the task of protecting the basic rights of the individual against infringements on the part of politics or third parties. This sphere of basic rights is in need of ongoing reinterpretation (Mengel 1998: 310). It must, however, be noted that the rule of law is not in place in all parts of the world. In totalitarian states, the judiciary continues to be a tool used to secure and exercise political power. But in cases of state failure or armed conflicts an independent judiciary is, as a rule, not feasible either.

AN INDEPENDENT JUDICIARY IN CRISIS REGIONS

One feature typical of crisis structures is the lack of an independent judiciary. The absence of a functioning legal system is a typical expression of state failure, general anarchy and absence of a monopoly power firmly in the hands of government. States of this kind must be seen as being in collapse. They lack the core element of the functioning state, which Max Weber (1966: 27) saw in its monopoly of power. Police, the judiciary and other regulative systems are in such cases no longer functionable. International assistance is often needed to overcome this state of affairs. This is what the *Süddeutsche Zeitung* meant when it wrote, at the end of the twentieth century, that, in the absence of intervention on the part of the international community, many African countries were doomed to be carved up by warlords.

The modern world view based on international law goes back to what is known as the Westphalian Order, a system made up of sovereign states. Proceeding from this system, states were gradually consolidated as territorial power structures (Hobbes), subsequently developing into liberal states governed by the rule of law (Locke) and, finally, performance-oriented social states. Yet this conceptual view has coincided more or less with political reality only in certain periods – for instance, in the creation of the United Nations. More recently, unmistakable tendencies towards a breakdown of the classic nation-state in many regions of the world have cast doubts on it. The response of the international community has generally been to support – albeit with different degrees of intensity – the restitution of state functions; in the end a return to the Westphalian Order. An independent judiciary has a key role in this process. The field of politics has coined a rather vague catchphrase for this challenge: human security. In international law the term is derived from a concept familiar from its prominence in the UN

Charter: international security, which originally denoted security of states. Now that the individual has become, in terms of the protection of human rights anchored in international law, at least in part a subject of international law, we are faced with the question of the extent to which the claim to state security is at the same time also applicable to the individual. This issue is all the more important as, in situations marked by state failure, the problem of national (external) security can, in many cases, hardly be said to exist.

This situation, though, entails risks all the more drastic for individuals since in such cases the state is no longer able to comply with its duty to protect its citizens. In short, the politically coloured – and legally undefined – concept of 'human security' is seen by its proponents as meaning that individuals must be safeguarded against infringements of their basic rights as well as against threats to their security and their life (Kirn 2000: 29). It is self-evident that only an independent judiciary can ensure this.

The framework under international law Modern international law increasingly obliges states to abide by democratic and constitutionally defined rules in their dealings with their populations (Heintze 1998a: 76). This remarkable progress was achieved within a period of only two decades. When it was adopted in 1945, the UN Charter contained no such provision. The UN Charter limited UN membership to 'peace-loving states', remaining silent about their internal constitution. It was in regional organizations that the turn of international law towards democracy and the rule of law was first instituted; and the Council of Europe, founded in 1949 and defining itself as a community based on certain shared values, took the lead here. Democracy and human rights were seen as constituting its underlying values. In 1989, in its *Copenhagen Document*, the Conference on Security and Cooperation in Europe (CSCE) took up this idea, demanding that its member states abide by democratic constitutional principles. Finally, in 2000, this development reached the UN, which, in its *Millennium Declaration*, expressly stated in the name of all its member states: 'We will spare no effort to promote democracy and strengthen the rule of law' (Resolution 55/2). One other element of the *Millennium Declaration* is 'respect for the rule of law in international as in national affairs'.

The binding legal force of this last document, adopted within a global framework, is, however, rather weak. We must therefore examine whether there are other – legal – obligations that bind states to respect the independence of the judiciary. Protection of human rights is the chief issue here. This contractual right is reflected in Article 9 of the 1966 International Covenant on Civil and Political Rights (ICCPR) (16 December 1966, BGBl, 1973 II: 1553), which contains provisions on personal liberty. It states that 'No one shall be subjected to arbitrary arrest or detention. No one shall be deprived of his liberty except on such grounds and in accordance with such procedure as are established by law'; and that 'anyone arrested or detained on a criminal charge shall be brought promptly before a judge' (Nowak 1993: 158). This obligation has been repeatedly underlined, most recently, and urgently, at the 1993 Vienna World Conference on Human Rights (UN-Doc. A/CONF. 157/23, para. 27). The matter is of great importance because this conference also expressly upheld the principle of the universality of human rights. This means that all cultures are obliged to respect a certain basic number of human rights. These include, incontrovertibly, the independence of the judiciary (van Hoof 1995: 4).

SAFEGUARDING AN INDEPENDENT JUDICIARY IN CASES OF STATE FAILURE

Human rights entail an obligation under international law to establish and maintain an independent judiciary. This obligation is binding on all the signatories of the Vienna Human Rights Convention. Apart from this, however, the international community also sees in the safeguarding of an independent judiciary a universal imperative stemming from the democratically legitimized state monopoly of power. This is why numerous programmes of nearly all pertinent non-governmental organizations (NGOs) and international organizations centre on the rule of law (see Mani 1998: 2).

Creation of an independent judiciary by national means In cases of state failure, the challenge is to use national means and methods, including an independent judiciary, to restore government functions. What this means above all is a successive (re)building of the state from the bottom up through the self-constitution of a people in the framework of civil society (Cohen and Arato 1992: 10). It is in this way possible to create focal points of public awareness and the national will. By building local administrations and institutions of public and private infrastructure, it is possible to mobilize the will to make a new start. Such fragmented sub-systems can provide the impulses needed to create a public space that can, in the long run, bring about the legitimacy required for the task (Thürer 1995: 40). Elections play an important role here.

However, by itself, the holding of elections can be no more than a superficial and limited measure if the process does not succeed in creating 'bottom-up' democratic structures. It is for this reason that in Cambodia and Somalia the UN has instituted numerous information programmes geared to forming local human rights groups. In Somalia new regional councils have been created to compensate for the inability of fragmented groups to come to an agreement at national level (Hufnagel 1996: 328). Development of democratic structures by the population itself is wholly in line with the international legal norm on the right of the self-determination of peoples. This at times merely entails the obligation to create grassroots democratic structures, since otherwise the only alternative would be to call in the parties to a civil war, which are as a rule not particularly representative.

And it is only in this way that it appears possible to ensure the independence of the judiciary. For only a judiciary that is accepted by the people can be truly independent. In such cases an independent judiciary is called upon to heal the wounds inflicted in times of arbitrary rule. The example of Kosovo unambiguously illustrates the challenges involved here. When the UN assumed governmental power in Kosovo in the early summer of 1999, it was faced with the question of what legal system was to apply there. The Yugoslavian law valid in this territory prior to the abrogation of autonomy in 1989 was to be seen as applicable in this case (Büllesbach 2001: 83). The Albanian population, however, was unwilling to accept this law, which it regarded as Serbian. The judiciary therefore decided to apply the old law, but to add to it the formula 'in the KFOR version'. The consequence was growing public acceptance of this legal system.

The existence of an independent judiciary need not imply that courts alone are in a position to deal effectively with past events. Experiences gained in the recent past point to other possibilities, such as roundtables and truth commissions, which can, in specific situations, contribute to the formation of social consensus and the reconciliation of offenders and victims (Schulz 2000: 52ff). Still, measures of this kind can prove successful only against the background of an independent judiciary. If such attempts at reconciliation are not accepted by individuals, it must be possible to seek judicial redress (Bronkhorst 2000: 40).

Creation of an independent judiciary by external intervention External intervention used to restore governmental functions gives rise to a situation even more complicated than that involved in recourse to national means. The parties to the relevant human rights conventions are mutually bound to one another by a legal relationship. They have committed themselves to safeguarding an independent judiciary at home. If they fail to do so, such states are guilty of a violation of international law. Other parties can demand that the state in question comply with the law and restore the independence of the judiciary. The monitoring bodies established by the relevant individual conventions are also authorized to lodge complaints: the UN Human Rights Commission, for instance, in cases of violations of the UN Human Rights Convention. Under certain circumstances, member states can also lodge national complaints concerning non-compliance with treaty obligations, although this does not imply further-reaching competences such as a right to intervene.

Theoretically, an intervention would be unlikely to pose problems, since in cases of state failure there is no reason to assume the existence of a state. However, practical experience shows that even in such cases the international community continues to abide by the fiction of sovereignty. The most impressive example in this case is Somalia. In 1992 this 'state' was already largely deprived of its effectiveness, and yet the UN Security Council took action only when requested to by the Somali UN ambassador – even though she no longer represented a functioning government (Herbst 1999: 240). This stance of the international community appears to indicate an unwillingness to create precedents (Heintze 1998: 170).

The search for local partners International peace missions have as a rule been most successful when the parties to a civil war have assented to such a mission. In the literature there are many sources that point out that international assistance measures are bound to fail if they are not supported by local forces, which mainly means securing the support of

NGOs (Thune 2000: 207). However, any such cooperation presupposes coordination and harmonization between various national and international NGOs. Numerous overlaps have been observed precisely for rule-of-law programmes. Many initiatives are weakened by duplications and conceptual contradictions in the measures taken, as has been noted for the cases of Rwanda, Congo/Zaire and El Salvador (Mani 1998: 3ff).

Yet the assent of conflict parties can play a positive role only if the groups concerned are clearly defined and stable ones that are representative of certain segments of the population. This is most clearly the case when a group has been recognized as a conflict party or has already created a stabilized *de facto* regime (Epping 1999: 89). The situation is far more complicated when the players are a number of small splinter groups, and it is not clear whether and to what extent such groups in fact represent forces of society. Often such heterogeneous players in fact prove unable to fulfil obligations either inside or outside their own group. In situations of this kind, international assistance must be directed, via local authorities, to the population itself. In civil war situations it is important to bring the most important groups to the negotiation table to provide the legitimacy needed to rebuild the state.

Independent judiciary and international courts Solutions from the outside, geared to an independent judiciary and imposed without the assent of the local population, are highly problematic. This is demonstrated by the practice of the ICTY. This *ad hoc* criminal court – a peace-keeping measure, yet at the same time one with a coercive mandate – was created by the UN Security Council (Resolution 827, 1995) under Chapter VII of the UN Charter – in other words, without the assent of the parties to the conflict. From the very beginning, the international community has been accused of acquiescing in this measure simply in order to 'do something because something obviously had to be done' (Heintschel von Heinegg 1999: 86). The court's legality is thus entirely open to question.

This legal problem was very soon to become the grounds for an appeal in the Tadic case (Case No. IT-94-1-AR72). Pointing to the European Convention on Human Rights and the International Covenant on Civil and Political Rights, the petitioner claimed that the ICTY was not a 'law-based court'. What was needed to create such a court, the argument went, was a legislative act, in other words a democratically controlled legal norm, and not merely an executive measure.

The Appeals Chamber rejected this view, pointing to the fact that UN organs cannot be classified in terms of national categories and noting that for this reason the principle of the separation of powers was not applicable in this case. Consequently, the Chamber went on, the 'law-based' principle was applicable only within states, not under international law. It further noted that as long as the UN Security Council remained within the scope of the powers defined by the UN Charter, it was also entitled to establish courts. The decision further stated, however, that such courts were then obliged to act in conformity with the rule of law, which meant that the rights of the accused had to be ensured by means of adequate procedural and court rules. In legal terms, the Chamber's line of argument raises a number of questions, though the establishment of the Tribunal must be seen as correct in political and practical terms (Uertz-Retzlaff 1999: 89).

The example of the Yugoslavia Tribunal clearly illustrates the difficulty involved in actually complying with the stringent standards implied by the rule of law and the principle of an independent judiciary in cases of armed conflict. If even an organization like the UN, endowed as it is with considerable powers, reached the limits of the principle of the rule of law in creating the criminal court, it is easy to understand how complicated it is for small states with unconsolidated structures to respect the principles associated with the rule of law.

Another important factor is that even an international criminal court cannot function without local support. The first point here is the extradition of accused persons, as we saw in the tug of war surrounding the handing over of Slobodan Milosevic to the Hague Tribunal. The successor states of the former Yugoslavia are also expected, among other things, to provide help in securing evidence and protecting witnesses. Since the ICTY was established as a coercive measure as per Chapter VII of the UN Charter, all states are required to cooperate with it. Croatia and Serbia's behaviour for many years has shown that it is possible to refuse such cooperation, even though such refusal is unlawful. There is little doubt that the main reason for the 'soft' stance the international community has long maintained towards this resistance, as well as for the reticence it has shown in making arrests on its own, stems from fears of negative impacts on the peace process in Bosnia-Herzegovina (Böhme

2000: 118). The pictures of UN blue-helmets taken hostage have left their mark.

All this gives an inkling of the difficulties faced by the international community in dealing with crimes against international law if the process is not backed by the authority of the Security Council or if, for political reasons, the mandate the Council gives its blue-helmet forces is inadequate to the task at hand.

Taking local factors into account The example of the ICTY, as well as that provided by different kinds of national resistance to cooperation with this organ of the international community, show how sensitively states may react when they feel that inroads are being made into their sovereign rights – in this case, into their sovereign penal jurisdiction. This also explains why the Cambodian government decided to set up a national criminal tribunal to try the cases of genocide committed in the country. In this case UN international experts and expertise were allowed, even though the court was established on a national basis.

This mirrors a general problem faced by international assistance for crisis regions. The problem consists in the fact that it is very difficult to take adequate account of regional factors. Yet the political context can prove to be an impediment to the rule of law. Because they see political and economic tasks as more urgent, new rulers often accord low priority to the establishment of an independent judiciary following a crisis situation. In addition, those in power must frequently fear a loss of their power if an independent judiciary is in fact established. The literature (see Mani 1998: 6ff) cites a number of examples. The government of El Salvador, for instance, dragged its feet in implementing the binding recommendations of the Truth Commission and disbanding the country's corrupt supreme court. When Namibia became independent, the government also neglected to take the steps required to sanction infractions of the law committed by the country's liberation movement, SWAPO, during the struggle for independence.

The situation in Cambodia was for years even worse: with an eye to securing the fragile peace, the international community insisted on a continuing participation of the Khmer Rouge in the Cambodian government. Under these circumstances it was quite inconceivable to build an independent judiciary. Western legal experts, calling for the introduction of a new legal order – common law for the Americans, the Code

Napoléon for the French – were themselves running the risk of disregarding the interests of the local population and showing insufficient understanding for the country's historical and mental peculiarities (Lithgow 1994: 44ff). This missionary zeal necessarily gave rise to the – false – impression that Cambodia is a territory without any centuries-old legal traditions of its own. Any approach of this kind is likely to put off the local population, whereas the aim should be to ensure its involvement as a means of building an independent judiciary. It is therefore imperative to ensure a strong involvement of local NGOs at the earliest possible date in order to gain the participation of a given region's civil society in the process of rebuilding government structures. The case of East Timor underlines this fact (Patrick 2001: 52ff).

PRACTICAL EXPERIENCE IN THE ROLE OF LAW FOLLOWING CONFLICTS

The rule of law is a key element in rebuilding social structures after conflict and collapse. This is seen in the medium term as a precondition essential for peace and durable internal stability. It is for this reason that a large number of international players are involved in supporting efforts aimed at creating an independent judiciary. These include various UN bodies such as the Office of the High Commissioner for Human Rights.

The World Bank lists ten elements on which legal reforms in developing countries should be based (Thürer 1995: 30). These centre on:

- the creation of an independent judiciary;
- security for judges;
- the streamlining of legal procedures and improvement of legal management;
- the selection and training of judges;
- the establishment of legal institutions and an information system;
- the opening up of access to courts; and
- legal groundwork needed to create courts or bodies of arbitration and mediation commissions.

The growing importance of the fields of justice and security has also found expression in UN peace operations. Practitioners have proposed setting a new priority here (Brahimi Report 2000). The means available to promote the consolidation of peace include the use of civilian police and other law-oriented forces such as justice experts to secure both the rule of law and human rights (UN-Doc. A/55/305, para. 29ff). A central role is assigned to the reform of the judiciary and criminal justice as well as to support for the process of democratization (Cumaraswamy 1996. para. 4ff).

The implementation of an independent judiciary Compared with national law, international law is difficult to enforce. Apart from the responses of the UN Security Council to threats to or breaches of peace, there is no central international enforcement mechanism. Consequently, it is as a rule not possible to use international coercion to force countries to institute an independent judiciary. Instead, customary international law and treaties binding under international law oblige the world's states to guarantee an independent judiciary at national level. If such countries are called upon by other countries or by international bodies to do so, this can in no way be seen as constituting interference in internal affairs. However, the international community has no choice but to rely on the cooperation of the states concerned in addressing grievances.

This being a cross-cutting problem, various UN organs have been concerned, since 1980, with the independence of the judiciary as well as with related issues. As early as 1980, the UN Economic and Social Council (ECOSOC), in its Resolution 1989/124, proposed appointing a Special Rapporteur on these issues. Such a Special Rapporteur was finally appointed by the Human Rights Commission in Resolution 1995/36. His mandate consisted in assessing, on the basis of international best practices, the significance of an independent judiciary and analysing the impact of international assistance such as advisory services and technical support. The aim was to adapt relevant international assistance to the challenges posed by the task of supporting democratization processes and the protection of human rights in the post-Cold War era. The reports, analysing above all relevant existing human rights instruments, reflect the present state of international legal affairs. The second part of these documents describes the situation in various crisis-torn countries of the world. Since most of these countries have declared their willingness to cooperate with the Special Rapporteur, the reports also reflect the positions of both the countries concerned and the relevant aid organizations. Interested parties will be able to distil some general information from the reports as well as from UN practice.

GENERAL FINDINGS DERIVED FROM UN PRACTICE

In its peace missions in collapsing states in the 1990s, the UN increasingly assumed a trusteeship role (Hufnagel 1996: 320). Any such concrete activities of course require a detailed mandate for specific operations and must be geared to local conditions. Still, some main lines of development have become visible in practice. The international community is, for instance, unable to rebuild government structures in crisis regions without reference to certain values. Such activity is based on a concept of good governance that is reflected in the specific mandates adopted by the UN Security Council. If we look, for instance, at the UN missions in Namibia, Cambodia and Somalia, we find that they share a number of common characteristics. These show that efforts aimed at instituting the rule of law and setting up an independent judiciary have been embedded in a comprehensive catalogue of measures, described below.

Democratic governmental structures are aimed for in all such cases. In Namibia and Cambodia this was achieved by means of nationwide elections, while in Somalia efforts have been aimed at forming representative organs at local level. The UN's commitment here was not restricted to the expression of the population's democratic will, but also extended to the preparatory work for elections. Comprehensive awareness campaigns were used to inform people of their basic rights. This was aimed at countering any attempts to intimidate the population. These activities included information on gaining access to the media, presentation of the general right to vote, and a declaration that this right applied to all persons, including refugees.

All UN operations have also been based on the aim of improving the human rights situation on the ground. This was approached by means of information programmes geared to creating an awareness of human rights and educating people to respect human rights. In addition, the missions also had the task of investigating human rights violations on their own initiative.[1] In Cambodia the mission included a special human rights component. One important task of these UN interventions was to secure the state's monopoly of power. Since both police and military, as armed and organized groups, play a key role in internal conflicts, any solution must begin with them. It is for this reason that control over the armed organs of the state and their subordination under the political leadership has always been a priority task.

Apart from the ceasefire, peace operations have focused on disarming, barracking and demobilizing the conflict parties. In practice, however, there have been major problems here. Disarming the conflict parties proved impracticable, for instance, in Cambodia and Somalia.

The experience gained in building armed organs in the countries to be stabilized has likewise differed from case to case. In Namibia, the task was merely to monitor the process of reorganizing an existing police force. In Somalia, on the other hand, the police force had to be rebuilt from scratch.

One feature shared by these operations is the aim of creating a police force that acts not as an instrument of oppression but as a protector of human rights on the basis of the rule of law. This task is derived from the human rights of personal security and the right of freedom from fear. The monopoly of power, which at the same time implies a subordination of executive power under the democratically legitimized political leadership, is one of the core elements of any democratic order.

The goals named above cannot be achieved if care is not taken at the same time to institute the rule of law and create an independent judiciary. This is why the UN devoted so much effort in Cambodia and Somalia to creating a new system of courts designed to operate independently of the government. As far as human rights and the right to vote are concerned, international organizations or bodies have in some individual cases even assumed jurisdictional functions. Under Annex 6 of the Dayton Agreement, for instance, a Human Rights Chamber was created for Bosnia-Herzegovina. Its task is to ensure that the country maintains the highest possible standard of internationally recognized human rights. This court is made up of 14 judges, six from Bosnia-Herzegovina's constituent states, and eight international experts (Nowak 1998: 192). Furthermore, the international community is also providing support for the training of judges, lawyers and judicial staff. These missions have also been engaged in monitoring prison systems and the treatment of prisoners (Bartole 2000: 162ff). Numerous changes in the national protection of human rights as well as in electoral laws are likewise due to UN missions. And such countries have also, not least, been provided support in working out democratic constitutions.

The task of building an independent judiciary in crisis areas can prove successful only if it is accompanied by efforts aimed at reviving the economy, although this is not a task immediately associated with

UN peace operations. Still, practice shows that it is in many cases impossible to strictly separate the tasks of instituting the rule of law and (re)building an economic infrastructure. To this extent, development-assistance measures are also instrumental in creating the conditions needed for an independent judiciary. In his 1992 'Agenda for Peace' (UN-Doc. A/47/277), former UN Secretary General Boutros Boutros-Ghali expressly referred to this state of affairs and called for a new type of technical assistance. The issues involved here are support for the reshaping of inadequate national structures and capacities as well as the strengthening of new democratic institutions. The fact that the UN has had every reason to become active in this field becomes evident when we consider that social peace is just as important as strategic or political peace: 'There is an obvious connection between democratic practices – such as the rule of law and transparency in decision-making – and the achievement of true peace and security in any new and stable political order. These elements of good governance need to be promoted at all levels of international and national political communities' (Agenda for Peace, para. 59).

(Translation: Paul Knowlton)

NOTE

1. In Somalia, though, the credibility of UN commitment suffered heavily when, in 1993, at the height of the conflicts with General Aidid and other warlords, UN and US troops were themselves involved in severe human rights violations; and human rights organizations such as Amnesty International and African Rights levelled serious charges against them. What were at issue here were, first – as noted above all for the Canadian contingent – cases of torture and racist excesses perpetrated on Somalis. In the second place, hundreds of Somalis were detained for months without trial. And, finally, UNOSOM troops had used wholly unreasonable force against the civilian population, in this way violating international humanitarian law. After the charges levelled by UN representatives had been rejected on problematic or indeed flimsy grounds, a UN commission of investigation appointed by the Security Council, while clearly placing the blame on Aidid, also criticized the USA and the UN for the aggressive nature of their actions and recommended payment of compensation to the victims among the Somali civilian population. Furthermore, in September 2001 the UN human rights representative for Somalia, Ghanim Alnajar, recommended a comprehensive investigation of war crimes committed during the phase in which the UN troops were withdrawn.

REFERENCES

Bartole, S. (2000) 'The contribution of law and democracy to conflict resolution in the Republic of Albania', in European Commission for Democracy through Law (ed.), *Societies in Conflict: The Contribution of Law and Democracy to Conflict Resolution*, Strasbourg: Council of Europe Publishing, pp. 153–66.

Böhme, O. (2000) 'Von Nürnberg nach Den Haag – Erfahrungen mit internationalen Tribunalen', in Gabriele von Arnim et al. (eds), *Jahrbuch Menschenrechte 2000*, Frankfurt/Main: Suhrkamp, pp. 109–21.

Brahimi Report (2000) 'Report of the Panel on United Nations Peace Operations: Comprehensive Review of the Whole Question of Peacekeeping Operations in All Their Aspects', New York, United Nations (A/44/305 – S/2000/809, 21 August 2000) <http://www.un.org/peace/reports/peace_operations/report.htm>.

Bronkhorst, D. (2000) 'Sieben Überlegungen zu Wahrheitskommissionen', in Gabriele von Arnim et al. (eds), *Jahrbuch Menschenrechte 2000*, Frankfurt/Main: Suhrkamp, pp. 33–45.

Büllesbach, R. (2001) 'Aufgaben öffentlicher Sicherheit für KFOR-Soldaten im Kosovo', in *Humanitäres Völkerrecht – Informationsschriften*, No. 15, pp. 83–8.

Cohen, J. L. and A. Arato (1992) *Civil Society and Political Theory*, Cambridge: Cambridge University Press.

Cumaraswamy, Dato'Param (1996) 'Report of the Special Rapporteur on the independence of judges and lawyers', UN-Doc. E/CN.4/1996/37.

Epping, V. (1999) 'Völkerrechtssubjekte', in Knut Ipsen (ed.), *Völkerrecht*, 4th edn, Munich: Beck, pp. 51–91.

Heintschel von Heinegg, W. (1999) 'Die Errichtung des Jugoslawien-Strafgerichtshofes durch Resolution 827 (1993)', in Horst Fischer und Sascha Lüder (eds), *Völkerrechtliche Verbrechen vor dem Jugoslawien-Tribunal, nationalen Gerichten und dem Internationalen Strafgerichtshof*, Berlin: Berlin Verlag, pp. 63–86.

Heintze, H.-J. (1998) 'Interventionsverbot, Interventionsrecht und Interventionspflicht im Völkerrecht', in Erich Reiter (ed.), *Maßnahmen zur internationalen Friedenssicherung*, Graz: Styria, pp. 163–94.

— (1998a) 'Selbstbestimmungsrecht und Demokratisierung', in Erich Reiter (ed.), *Jahrbuch für internationale Sicherheitspolitik*, Hamburg: Mittler, pp. 52–76.

Herbst, J. (1999) *Rechtskontrolle des UN-Sicherheitsrates*, Frankfurt/Main: Lang.

Hoof, F. van (1995) 'Asian challenges to the concept of universality: afterthoughts on the Vienna Conference on Human Rights', in Jacqueline Smith (ed.), *Human Rights: Chinese and Dutch Perspectives*, The Hague: Kluwer, pp. 1–16.

Hufnagel, F.-E. (1996) *UN-Friedensoperationen der zweiten Generation*, Berlin: Duncker.

Kirn, R. (2000) 'Ensuring human security in conflict situations', in European Commission for Democracy through Law (ed.), *Societies in Conflict: The Contribution of Law and Democracy to Conflict Resolution*, Strasbourg: Council of Europe Publishing, pp. 28–32.

Lithgow, S. (1994) 'Cambodia', in Kevin Clements and Robin Ward (eds), *Building International Community*, Canberra, pp. 27–57.

Mani, R. (1998) 'Conflict resolution, justice and the law: rebuilding the rule of law in the aftermath of complex political emergencies', in *International Peacekeeping*, Vol. 5, No. 3, pp. 1–25.

Mengel, H.-J. (1998) 'Justiz und Politik', in Dieter Nohlen (ed.), *Wörterbuch Staat und Politik*, Bonn: Bundeszentrale für politische Bildung, pp. 306–10.

Nowak, M. (1993) 'CCPR Commentary', Kehl: Engel.

— (1998) 'Die Rechtsprechung der Menschenrechtskammer für Bosnien-Herzegowina', in Gabriele von Arnim et al. (eds), *Jahrbuch Menschenrechte 1999*, Frankfurt/Main: Suhrkamp, pp. 191–214.

Osinbajo, Y. (1996), 'Legality in a collapsed state: the Somali experience', *International and Comparative Law Quarterly*, Vol. 45, pp. 910–23.

Patrick, I. (2001): 'East Timor emerging from conflict: the role of local NGOs and international assistance', *Disasters*, Vol. 5, No. 1, pp. 48–66.

Schulz, C. (2000): 'Guatemala: die Schwierigkeiten der Vergangenheitsbewältigung', in Gabriele von Arnim et al. (eds), *Jahrbuch Menschenrechte 2000*, Frankfurt/Main: Suhrkamp, pp. 46–53.

Thune, G. H. (2000) 'Lessons and challenges', in European Commission for Democracy through Law (ed.), *Societies in Conflict: The Contribution of Law and Democracy to Conflict Resolution*, Strasbourg: Council of Europe Publishing, pp. 197–213.

Thürer, D. (1995): 'Der Wegfall effektiver Staatsgewalt' ['The failed state'], in *Berichte der Deutschen Gesellschaft für Völkerrecht*, Vol. 34, Heidelberg: F. C. Muller, pp. 9–47.

Uertz-Retzlaff, H. (1999): 'Über die praktische Arbeit des Jugoslawien-Gerichtshofes', in Horst Fischer und Sascha Lüder (eds), *Völkerrechtliche Verbrechen vor dem Jugoslawien-Tribunal, nationalen Gerichten und dem Internationalen Strafgerichtshof*, Berlin: Berlin-Verlag, pp. 87–100.

Weber, M. (1966) *Staatssoziologie*, Johannes Winkelmann (ed.), 2nd edn, Berlin: Duncker.

THREE

Decentralization, Division of Power and Crisis Prevention: A Theoretical Exploration with Reference to Africa

ANDREAS MEHLER

§ In Germany, the term 'decentralization' has positive associations for activists and theoreticians right across the political spectrum: from proponents of the subsidiarity principle, rooted in local patriotism, to efficiency-oriented 'engineers' of state and statehood, to the champions of intense participation at the grassroots. In countries set on a different historical trajectory, the advocates of a centralized executive may still resist the process of decentralization without, however, attacking the term itself. This is well illustrated by the discussion on autonomy for Corsica that has been raging in France since the summer of 2000. The former minister for the interior, Jean-Pierre Chevènement, maintained that a new statute for the island was promoting political-criminal interests (*interêts politico-mafieux*), and contained a 'time-bomb,' a reference to Corsican terrorism. While he has continued to stick to his position even after his resignation, the new legislation was passed by the French parliament on 22 May 2001. Opponents of the reform still worry about the 'revival of tribalism'. Its supporters, in turn, regard the adjustment of national regulations to local realities, including recognition of the Corsican language, as a long overdue response to the 'cultural imperialism' of the mainland.

In Germany, where concerns over decentralization are confined to small groups of experts, little notice has been taken of this debate. Even in the field of development cooperation the notion of decentralization is subject to little controversy. One of the reasons may lie in the belief that German actors have a comparative advantage on this issue, owing to the range of diverse communal constitutions and the large number of potential experts.

In view of the literal use of the term, there is a need for some semantic clarification:

- Decentralization refers to a process, and not the existing state of local self-government. It is therefore not certain that the term is still applicable to contemporary Germany.
- Decentralization presupposes the existence of a centralized state, hence it remains to be seen whether the term is relevant to all states recognized under international law, including those that have collapsed.

Our intention is not to concentrate on definitions, but to clarify the theoretical substance of the argument: decentralization addresses the division of power, and provides a way out of autocracy. The division of power between a central authority and territorial units along the periphery is a political necessity for large states, if their continuation is not to be based on repression. But, the persuasive logic of this theory can run into considerable resistance when applied in practice. We will discuss the character of these difficulties, in particular the link between decentralization and violent conflict (or its prevention).

A closer look at the relationship between decentralization and the intensification of conflict will be followed by a discussion of the peace-promoting aspects of decentralization. My particular interest lies in those conflicts that 'are socially disruptive and dis-integrating, the prevention of which does not involve the stabilization of existing social relations, but promotes instead the peaceful and constructive transformation of a society or a state' (Engel and Mehler 1998: 138). Numerous conflicts between central governments and decentralized units over juridicial, fiscal and administrative competence do not fall under this definition and are therefore excluded.

DECENTRALIZATION AND THE INTENSIFICATION OF CONFLICT

A major reform of state such as decentralization can serve to intensify existing conflicts and contribute to their violent escalation. Where, for example, the demographic relations between different population groups at the local level differ widely from those at the national level, local elections, possibly unprecedented, can have serious implications. Where the group forming the national majority finds itself locally in a minority position, a defeat at the ballot box can prompt 'calls for help'. These may contain requests for the despatch of military forces, or the cancellation of the election results.

In Cameroon, for example, the communal elections, held in 1996 after a five-year delay, were followed by disturbances in a number of places, including the coastal town of Limbe. Although an opposition party had clearly won the election, the leading candidate of the government party was appointed mayor by the president. The security forces put down subsequent popular protests, resulting in a death toll of five. One is tempted to infer that without elections there would have been no unrest, but that would be simply to focus on the immediate trigger for the violence.

A different variant of the argument: in some countries the central government is regarded as having a neutral position in ongoing local conflicts. Once the competence and the capacity for playing the arbiter has been lost in the process of decentralization, opposing local forces may clash with one another. This type of situation could unfold in western Cameroon, where local land disputes are being regulated and kept in check by central government officials. These, including district prefects, and provincial governors, are systematically recruited from different regions.[1] We must also take into consideration the fact that local government has a history and a dynamic which, as a rule, is neither 'democratic' nor 'representative'. One variant commonly found in colonial Africa, for example, was that of 'decentralized despotism' (Mamdani 1996). The chiefs, acting with the support of the colonial government or a colonial official, would impose their rule with little contribution from their subjects, and frequently with equally little effective control from 'above'. In Latin America, local authority figures were equally free from control by either the people or the colonial power, hence the prevalence of local despots. These developments are of major significance for the political and cultural basis of decentralization.

Most developing countries contain diverse, multi-ethnic populations, and therefore cannot resort to a uniform system of pre-colonial local government and local political culture. But it is difficult to decentralize without a system of identical institutions across a country (exceptions prove the rule). Some political units, such as regions and communes, will invariably be better able than others to exercise the new power. Is there a potential for a multi-track process, or a graded model, or will this only serve to spark off new conflicts?

Differences in the response to the opportunities presented and risks posed by decentralization are likely to exacerbate the development differential between regions and communities. Adherents of the 'public choice' school, who employ mathematical models and economic concepts to analyse decision-making processes, may regard inter-community competition as a positive, development-promoting outcome (Adamolekun 1999). In societies that are already polarized, a blatant inequality in the distribution of development benefits can be disruptive, and is likely to stir up envy between different regions. From the perspective of crisis prevention, there are significant issues surrounding the regulated structural transfer of funds between regions and communes, and the range of further regulations, including exemption rules and direct distributive interventions.

Decentralization does affect the lines of conflict: it is highly likely that a number of ongoing conflicts between citizens and the central government over such issues as taxation or the curtailing of civil rights will, in the aftermath of decentralization, take place between the citizens and the region or the commune. There is little to suggest that these conflicts will be less violent or better managed.

Every radical structural reform entails the eventual redistribution of competencies, and theoretically, or in the second phase, of finances. As this inevitably touches on existing power arrangements it will create new conflicts of interest. Where tension between government and opposition is running high, the decentralization process can itself become a direct object of conflict, thereby compromising its peace-building potential from the outset (see, for example, Tag 1996).

Representatives of the central government are among the losers in the decentralization process, but they may still be able to cause mischief at local level, depending on their real and juridical powers. For example, a prefect or equivalent who was hitherto all-powerful will retain in the first phase of decentralization considerable police powers, with a well-armed gendarmerie at his disposal. The traditional authorities also lose their position as the preferred, local interlocutors for central government, but they too can avail themselves of considerable powers. Some traditional chiefs control their own police forces and jails. Moreover, they are believed to control ritual and occult powers. The victory of an opposition party in local elections can have serious ramifications, especially in strongholds of traditional authority. Another example from Cameroon involves the Sultan of Foumban, a high-ranking member of the government party, who lost to the chairman of an opposition party during the local elections of 1996. This triggered a series of violent clashes as party political rivalry was overlaid and interwoven with the confrontation between tradition and modernity and the sectarian differences between Islamic brotherhoods.

Table 3.1 Levels of potential conflict intensification after decentralization

Level	Variant
Relationship between individual citizen and community	Falling performance from incompetence, waste, harassment • Tax strike • Individual protest Inadequate local democratic structures, lack of competence, corruption • Popular uprising against decentralized units
Relationship between local groups with conflict potential	Competition over, and changes in the balance of power in the local arena, for example native groups versus immigrants, or between clans or families, without neutral arbitrators (from central government) • Violent conflict over land, or • Religious issues
Relationship between communities and regions	New rivalries, blockages, boundaries, refusal of cooperation, for example • Communication routes • Violent conflict over land in border zone
Relationship between community/region and central government	Resurgent autonomy movements, calls for independence • Rebellion • Repression Weakening of central state • Tilt towards state collapse

Important questions surrounding decentralization processes are: how will the losers respond, and what advantages can they recognize for themselves? Central government officials are often anxious lest the transfer of fiscal competencies to incompetent political and administrative personnel lead to the bankruptcy of some communities. Without the appropriate training of all participants, and in the absence of institutional safety measures, this poses indeed one more danger for the intensification of conflict.

The political implications are even more acute, since decentralization – as a fundamental reform, by creating a new arena and a new rivalry – will impact on the competitive behaviour of groups and factions of the élite (Blundo 1996; Bierschenk and Olivier de Sardan 1999: 51ff). The relationship between autochthonous groups and immigrants may be particularly affected. One instance is the attempt by traditional local authorities to control the real estate market, including the resort to customary law. This is a hot potato, as the invention of tradition can be used to construct 'ancient rights', that put 'strangers', for which read immigrants, into a disadvantageous position, and open the possibility for the re-examination of land titles – with the ultimate aim of expropriation and displacement. Immigrants too will defend their interests. This happens first in the big cities, where the native groups are already in a minority (Abidjan, Douala, Conakry). In some remote areas similar problems are found; for example in the provincial town of Bangangte, Cameroon, the traditional ruler, from fear of foreign infiltration, issued a new *code foncier* in 1995 (Rohde 1997: 312ff). The transfer of power from the central government to local authorities is risky. Here the community council was evidently not involved in the issue, reflecting its low status in the centralized structure of Cameroon.

POLITICAL TRANSFORMATION THROUGH DECENTRALIZATION?

One should not expect miracles from decentralization: local élites are no less high-handed than élites at the centre. Municipal leaders of peripheral communities have often learned their trade in large cities, and will continue to keep their clientelistic networks active. They are likely to keep living in the capital, where they earn the bulk of their income from office jobs. They are likely to extend anti-democratic practices commonly encountered at the centre to the local level, where constructing a system of checks and balances is particularly difficult. Civil society, which is supposed to provide a counterweight to state power, is not well developed, and is plagued by poor educational levels. The meetings of community councils are frequently held behind closed doors, leaving the ideals of participation as little more than a pious prayer. It seems, however, that at least Somaliland and Puntland, two successor 'states' of the former Somalia, have developed relatively well-functioning civil society control mechanisms at local levels.

The full impact of the decentralization process on secession movements is open to debate. Opponents argue that decentralization will form the basis for the subsequent secession of entire regions, which is hardly likely to proceed along peaceful lines. The supporters argue, on the other hand, that regional autonomy and federalism offer the only lasting solution to minority problems. Once such politicized and highly emotional conflicts are regulated locally, opposition groups are less likely to reject the state in its entirety. It is the position of the author, however, that if the decentralization project is to succeed, all participants need to agree on the objectives and the extent of local autonomy, and to prepare the requisite consensus carefully.

How does decentralization relate to the problems of state collapse? Bringing the distant state closer to the citizen could prevent the collapse of the state at inception. It would open the possibility of a constructive 'reconfiguration of the political order' (Boone 1998: 138ff). Supporters of decentralization have shifted the focus by speaking of 'state building from below' and the 'reconstruction of collapsed states' (Steinich 2000; Forrest 1998), usually with reference to Africa. How does this translate into practical terms? Experiences have been gathered in Somalia (Heinrich 1997), and the Central African Republic (Africa Consulting 1998). There are even visionary suggestions of 'quasi-imperial systems of decentralized power' (Forrest 1998: 56). Where this path is to be pursued, a clear idea is needed of the functions to be performed by the rump state at the centre. The communes could indeed begin with the 'state-building from below', by setting up depersonalized institutions at local level. The most feasible candidates for the implementation of such processes are those failed states currently under quasi-protectorate administration (Kosovo, East Timor). Yet if 'state-building' is a core objective, difficulties will arise once the institutions evolving in different locales are eventually to be integrated within a federal system. The next step is therefore of critical importance: the construction of a regional level to integrate and interlock the local developments, leading eventually to state-building at national level. Highly problematic in this debate is the role of external forces engaging in political engineering, especially in regard to the sustainability of imported institutional designs.

It is likely that the recipients of such external intervention will resist even the process of 'decentralization from above'. There is some concern that the proposed decentralization in developing countries will follow on from where structural (economic) adjustment left off, in the abandonment of the state. Structural adjustment has delivered mixed results, including the drastically reduced welfare role of the state. There are therefore justified concerns that a decentralized state will further cut back on the service delivery of the centralized state, and hence merely provide an excuse for poor performance.

OPPORTUNITIES OF DECENTRALIZATION

Ultimately, it is the overall performance of a state system that bears responsibility for effective crisis prevention. Helpful here is the key term 'structural stability', referring to the stability needed to cope with the dynamics inherent in (emerging) democratic societies. In contrast to conventional notions of stability, this refers to the interplay of sustainable economic development, democracy, respect for human rights, viable political structures, and healthy social and environmental conditions. These conditions will determine the capacity for managing change without resorting to violent conflict.[2] As structural stability is a comprehensive objective, it is frequently in need of simultaneous initiatives from within and without.

The key term 'structural stability' also implies the subsidiarity principle, and hence decentralization. It is assumed that it should be easier to empower a society to regulate internal conflicts within the framework of a federal system than in a centralized one, because violent conflicts often have a local trigger, such as land use, water conflict or cattle rustling. Being familiar with the object of dispute should enable the decision-makers to analyse the core issues, suggest measures for settling the dispute and arrange for participation in the resolution of the problem.

A situation marred by bad governance at regional level could be alleviated by an adjusted community development plan designed by participative methodology, a regional land-use plan respecting existing ownership patterns, and a 'bottom-up' local economic policy. Efficiency gains can even result from the competition between different communities. While this can be achieved under overall positive conditions, it cannot be guaranteed. If scarce resources are really to be husbanded more carefully, the waste involved in the duplication of institutions in neighbouring communities has to be avoided.

One highly persuasive argument in favour of decentralization calculates the cost of doing nothing, including a number of instances of state failure where the opportunity for decentralization was missed. The 'risk of doing nothing' is also apt for the mega-cities in the developing world, where the formal structures of state, politics and economy have largely been eroded, and the informal sector and networks determine social life. In highly personalized and essentially authoritarian states all decision-making powers are often concentrated in the head of state, who in turn is frequently absent, either in his home village or on extensive visits to Europe. In these cases, the distribution of some of the responsibility may at least remove a few bottlenecks in the decision-making process.

In the end any consideration of decentralization will have to be situated within the framework of the good governance discussion. It is assumed that local decision-making will allow for greater transparency, enhance the chances of a more rational utilization of scarce resources and facilitate greater participation, all of which combine to function as crisis-prevention measures. This is based on the belief in the existence of institutional interests, and that local élites have a genuine interest in the development of their homeland.

Decentralization also allows minority groups, excluded from power at the national level, to participate in decision-making processes in their immediate environment. This should also reduce conflict potential. Where the governing party controls national institutions, while the opposition parties capture several important regional units, a structural stalemate may ensue, leading to security-enhancing coalitions between hitherto irreconcilable opponents (Fandrych 2001: 461).

Decentralization, runs a further argument, engenders the formation of local associations and grassroots organizations. Many of the existing non-governmental organizations (NGOs) are often too limited in their scope, or too dependent upon particular personalities, to be able to impact on national policy-making. At local level, however, such civil society organizations may well be in a better position to participate in and control political developments. One more argument can be cited: local government acts as a training ground for participatory, democratic culture, and has an important integrating function, as the first instance where minorities can enjoy a measure of autonomy (Steinich 2000). Such an initiative, however, has to be tied in with the political trans-

Table 3.2 Levels of potential conflict mitigation after decentralization

Level	Impact on Crisis Prevention
Relationship between individual citizen and the state	Improved performance, direct responsibility, local democracy, government close to the people • Efficiency gains • Legitimacy gains
Relationship between local/regional groups with conflict potential and the state	Local-level conflicts • Appropriate solutions through legitimate institutions • Greater acceptance of national institutions • Ethnic identification superseded by formation of sub-groups Structural power balance between national government and opposition enjoying local dominance • Impulses for coalition-building, cooperation
Relationship between communities and regions	New opportunities for cooperation • Municipal associations • Common interest groups • Coordination of development projects • Equitable allocation of finances across communes and regions
Relationship between community/region and state	Strengthening of autonomy: demands met • No rebellion, no repression

formation of the central state at an early stage of the process, otherwise there is a danger that conflicts at the centre will develop a momentum all of their own, with repercussions for communities and regions. To summarize: the democratization process at local level that has been initiated by decentralization can contribute to the transformation of authoritarian regimes if this is part of a wider development of the state.

CONCLUSION

How dangerous or useful, then, is the decentralization process in view of the arguments for and against it? In order to evaluate the risks and opportunities involved in the sense of a Conflict Impact Assessment (Lund 2000; Miall 2000), it is instructive to consider the 'political economy of local politics'. The discussion focuses on the concrete analysis of the capacity and legitimacy of existing state structures and institutions at different levels. In addition, we need to take into account the political and economic strategies of the main parties involved, at both local and national levels.

For the purposes of crisis prevention three questions seem of particular relevance:

- Does decentralization contribute significantly to reducing structural disparities between groups in conflict, especially the more equitable distribution of central goods and services? Or does it exacerbate such disparities?
- Does decentralization further or obstruct the formation of autonomous spheres of social power outside official or oppositional organizations?
- Does decentralization enhance or undermine the ability of local actors to promote crisis prevention and reconciliation?

In the final analysis, then, the process of decentralization may make a considerable contribution to 'structural stability' (through subsidiarity), to good governance (through transparency, the rational use of scarce resources, and participation), and democracy (by stimulating a local civil society and local ownership). In all probability, decentralization is the only sustainable solution to minority problems in nation-states, and hence a significant avenue to peace.

In spite of this, there is no guarantee that local actors are any more peace-loving, or that local élites are any less corrupt, than those at central level. New conflicts may break out, old ones may become intensified, and new minorities may emerge. There will be consequences for the level of competition between groups and élites. The redistribution of considerable resources and competencies has, by definition, plenty of conflict potential. The decisive factor is what becomes of the losers in the process, and how their fears, as well as those of the population at large, are to be accommodated.

The existing political culture as a basis of decentralization is often problematic, as the diverse traditions of local government complicate the systematic and uniform process of decentralization. Decentralization may also accelerate the development differentials between different communities and regions. Finally, it is often not clear what functions remain for the central government after the process has been completed.

There are, nevertheless, trenchant arguments in favour of decentralization in addition to the issue of crisis prevention. A well-planned, long-term strategy can yield benefits in terms of efficiency gains and democracy-building. Positive outcomes can also be expected, from the improved performance of the public sector and greater equity in the distribution of development benefits (Thomi 2001: 35). In order to realize these objectives, however, it is important to ascertain that the right conditions obtain, and to reserve the possibility of continuous adjustment should a crisis develop.

(Translation: Axel Klein)

NOTES

1. The official translation of the French prefect in Cameroon is 'senior divisional officer', but this might not help readers who are not familiar with the country.

2. Cf. the definition in EU 1996, 6.3: 2. 'Structural stability is to be understood as a term denoting a dynamic situation, a situation of stability able to cope with the dynamics inherent in (emerging) democratic societies. Structural stability could thus be defined as a situation involving sustainable economic development, democracy and respect for human rights, viable political structures, and healthy social and environmental conditions, with the capacity to manage change without resorting to violent conflict.'

REFERENCES

Adamolekun, L. (1999) 'Decentralization, subnational governments, and intergovernmental relations', in Ladipo Adamolekun (ed.), *Public Administration in Africa: Main Issues and Selected Country Studies*, Boulder, CO and Cologne: Westview Press, pp. 49–67.

Africa Consulting (1999) *République Centrafricaine: évaluation sociale et institutionnelle*, final report.

Bierschenk, T. and Jean-Pierre Olivier de Sardan (1999) 'Dezentralisierung und lokale Demokratie. Macht und Politik im ländlichen Bénin in den 1980er Jahren', in Jakob Rösel and Trutz von Trotha (eds), *Dezentralisierung, Demokratisierung und die lokale Repräsentation des Staates*, Cologne: Koppe, pp. 37–68.

Blundo, G. (1996) 'Gérer les conflits fonciers au Sénégal: le rôle de l'administration locale dans le sud-est du bassin arachidier', in Paul Mathieu, Pierre-Joseph Laurent and Jean-Claude Willame (eds), *Démocratie, Enjeux Fonciers et Pratiques Locales en Afrique, Cahiers Africains* 23–4, Brussels and Paris: L'Hormattan, pp. 101–19.

Boone, C. (1998) '"Empirical statehood" and reconfigurations of political order', in L. A. Villalón and P. A. Huxtable (eds), *The African State at a Critical Juncture: Between Disintegration and Reconfiguration*, London, Boulder, CO and Cologne: Lynne Rienner, pp. 129–41.

Engel, U. and A. Mehler (eds) (1998) *Gewaltsame Konflikte und ihre Prävention in Afrika. Hintergründe, Analysen und Strategien für die entwicklungspolitische Praxis*, Hamburg: Institut für Afrika-Kunde.

EU (European Union) (1996) 'Communication from the Commission to the Council: the European Union and the issue of conflicts in Africa: peace-building, conflict prevention and beyond', 6.3: 2.

Fandrych, S. (2001) *Kommunalreform und Lokalpolitik in Mosambik: Demokratisierung und Konflikttransformation jenseits des zentralistischen Staates*, Hamburg: Institut für Afrika-Kunde.

Forrest, J. B. (1998) 'State inversion and nonstate politics', in L. A. Villalón and P. A. Huxtable (eds), *The African State at a Critical Juncture. Between Disintegration and Reconfiguration*, London, Boulder CO and Cologne: Lynne Rienner, pp. 45–56.

Heinrich, W. (1997) *Building the Peace. Experiences of Collaborative Peacebuilding in Somalia, 1993–1996*, Uppsala: Life and Peace Institute.

Lund, M. S. (2000) 'Improving conflict prevention by learning from experience: issues, approaches and results', in Michael Lund and Guenola Rasamoelina (eds), *The Impact of Conflict Prevention Policy: Cases, Measures, Assessments*, Baden-Baden: CPN Yearbook 1999/2000, pp. 63–88.

Mamdani, M. (1996) *Citizen and Subject: Contemporary Africa and the Legacy of Late Colonialism*, Kampala, Cape Town and London: James Currey.

Mehler, A. (1998) 'Demokratisierung und Demokratieförderung im frankophonen Westafrika. Ein Beitrag zur Vermeidung gewaltförmiger Konflikte?', in Österreichisches Studienzentrum für Frieden und Konfliktlösung/Schweizerische Friedensstiftung (eds), *Friedensbericht 1998, Afrikanische Perspektiven*, Chur/Zürich: Rüegger Verlag, pp. 223–34.

— (2001) 'Dezentralisierung und Krisenprävention', in W. Thomi, M. Steinich and W. Polte (eds), *Dezentralisierung in Entwicklungsländern. Jüngere Ursachen, Ergebnisse und Perspektiven staatlicher Reformpolitik*, Baden-Baden: Nomos, pp. 287–99.

Mehler, A. and C. Ribaux (2000) *Crisis Prevention and Conflict Management in Technical Cooperation: An Overview of the National and International Debate*, Wiesbaden: Schriftenreihe der GTZ, No. 270.

Miall, H. (2000) 'Preventing potential conflicts: assessing the impact of "light" and "deep" conflict prevention in central and eastern Europe and the Balkans', in M. Lund and Guenola Rasamoelina (eds), *The Impact of Conflict Prevention Policy: Cases, Measures, Assessments*, Baden-Baden: CPN Yearbook 1999/2000, pp. 23–45.

Rohde, E. (1997) *Grundbesitz und Landkonflikte in Kamerun. Der Bedeutungswandel von Land in der Bamiléké-Region während der europäischen Kolonisation*, Hamburg: Lit.

Steinich, M. (2000) 'Decentralisation as an instrument for institutional conflict management', draft Eschborn (GTZ).

Tag, S. (1996) 'Mehr Demokratisierung durch Dezentralisierung? Analyse eines umstrittenen Reformvorhabens in der Zentralafrikanischen Republik', *Afrika Spectrum*, 31 (3), Hamburg, pp. 235–53.

Thomi, W. (2001) 'Hoffnungsträger Dezentralisierung?', in W. Thomi, M. Steinich and W. Polte (eds), *Dezentralisierung in Entwicklungsländern. Jüngere Ursachen, Ergebnisse und Perspektiven staatlicher Reformpolitik*, Baden-Baden: Nomos, pp. 17–42.

PART TWO

Crisis Regions between Violence and Development

FOUR

State-building and Solving Conflicts in the South Caucasus

RAINER FREITAG-WIRMINGHAUS

§ The Caucasus is one of today's most explosive arenas of ethno-territorial conflicts. The interaction of transformation-related structures, conflicts surrounding pipeline routes and geo-strategic ambitions in the power struggle resulting from the so-called great game for the prize of the oil in the Caspian Sea have turned the region into a trouble-spot that is unique in the world. With big powers and regional powers deeply involved, the situation in these countries on the European periphery is potentially more explosive than that in the Balkans, and reminiscent of the Cold War.

The US and Turkey on the one side and Russia on the other side are engaged here in a struggle for spheres of influence. In times of NATO expansion and eastward enlargement of the EU, this has a substantial impact on the security of Europe. New regional alliances involving close ties with NATO, which have emerged as a counterbalance to the hegemonic power-policy position of Russia, are creating a new potential for conflict.

CONFLICT CONSTELLATIONS FOLLOWING THE DEMISE OF THE SOVIET UNION

Following the collapse of the Soviet Union, inter-ethnic conflicts arose in the Caucasus at various levels. These included clashes between the former central power and the former republics of the Union, as well as between the new states and their autonomous republics and regions. In most cases the issue was that of secession, while others were concerned with the relevant political status. What they have in common is

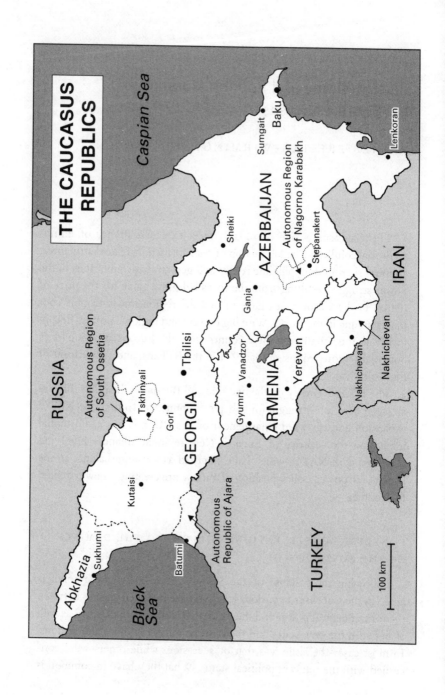

that they all harbour the potential for violent excesses. At least five conflicts have turned into wars: the conflict in Chechnya, the clashes surrounding Abkhazia and South Ossetia in Georgia, and those between Ossetia and Ingushetia in the Russian Federation. The conflict affecting Nagorno Karabakh even led to a war between two states: Armenia and Azerbaijan. This latter dispute also provides the clearest evidence of the rift between pro-Western and pro-Russian positions, which is responsible for a progressive militarization of the region, and is illustrated on the one hand by Russia's supply of arms to Armenia, including a joint air traffic control system, and on the other hand by the desire for NATO bases expressed by Baku.

The demise of the Soviet Union is associated with the loss of the central authority that had previously regulated relations between the different levels – the central power, the Union republics, the autonomous republics and the autonomous regions. This led to the formation of new states, which were guaranteed territorial integrity at international level as a symbol of their independence. The picture was different for the formerly autonomous republics or regions such as Chechnya, Nagorno Karabakh and Abkhazia, which also wanted to be recognized as independent states or, in the case of Nagorno Karabakh, had initially sought unification with a state of the same ethnic community (Armenia). They also invoked their right to self-determination. However, the titular nations of the former Soviet republics were not prepared to give up their territorial integrity or grant them any form of autonomy. The separatist regions, in turn, did not accept subordination under the new statehood. With Russia, Georgia and Azerbaijan all having defined their new political sovereignty in terms of territorial integrity, any proposals of a confederate-type political order were viewed with deep suspicion.

Although there is agreement at international level that existing borders should not be altered, the titular nations of the former Soviet republics feared, not without reason, that autonomy would lead to full secession in view of the dynamic and unpredictable developments in the region.

The conflict surrounding Nagorno Karabakh, though on ice since the 1994 ceasefire, is undoubtedly the most significant in the Caucasus. In the meantime, a *de facto* independent second Armenian state has been created in Nagorno Karabakh, which belongs to Azerbaijan. Almost a million people have been made refugees through the occupation of wide

areas of Azerbaijan territory. The conflict prevents economic cooperation among the Caucasian states, casts a shadow over the relationship
between Armenia and Turkey, and burdens Turkey's relations with
Russia. It blocks pipeline plans and economic renewal and affects the
political balance of the entire region.

In 1999 Western pressure did bring about a meeting between
Presidents Robert Kocharian (Armenia, 1998–) and Haidar Aliyev
(Azerbaijan, 1993–), while the efforts of the Organization for Security
and Cooperation in Europe (OSCE) within the Minsk Group[1] and the
talks on a regional stability pact for the South Caucasus over the past two
years all signal positive changes. There is an increasing awareness at
international level that a dead end has been reached and that new
concepts and initiatives are needed. At the same time, however, the
readiness of the adversaries to reach painful compromises has not grown
to the same extent. The reactions observed most recently in Armenia as
well as Azerbaijan in relation to the negotiations and discussions on
possible solutions for peace make this only too clear.

Although the present situation of frozen conflict can continue to exist
for years – as in the case of Cyprus, for example – it is associated with
the permanent risk and danger of new military confrontation. The
prospects of economic benefits derived in particular from the Caspian oil
and gas fields may render conference participants more amenable to
compromise and concession. It has, however, now been acknowledged
that the West is not in a position to provide the hoped-for security
guarantees of Georgia and Azerbaijan. Although the USA has been able
to strengthen the political independence of both states, it has, at the same
time, aroused expectations in those countries that it cannot and does not
intend to fulfil. A *Pax Americana* is not possible; rather a solution for
peace can succeed only with the approval of and support from Moscow,
which continues to regard the South Caucasus region as a traditional
hegemonic sphere. The EU support will bear fruit, and the economy –
not just the oil sector – will be able to develop only once a solution for
peace has been found. When the Council of Europe admitted Armenia
and Azerbaijan together in January 2001, despite severe criticism of the
procedure for elections to the Azerbaijan parliament in November 2000
and deficiencies in the area of human rights, this was done in the hope
that membership of that organization could contribute towards a solution
to the conflict as well as to democratization.

The three states in the South Caucasus region will be able to safeguard their independence only through regional integration – integration with the long-term aim of being incorporated into European structures. Future prosperity is dependent upon the degree of regional cooperation. Such insights are, however, repressed by emotions. This is made extremely evident by the newly aroused readiness for war in Azerbaijan and Armenia and the declared resistance against 'selling out one's own interests' together with the feeling of being betrayed and deceived by the international community. In much the same way as in the early 1990s, the Nagorno Karabakh conflict again plays an especially significant role in the way the not yet consolidated states see themselves and in their process of nation-building.

THE WEAKNESS OF STATE STRUCTURES AS A CAUSE OF CONFLICT

The collapse of the USSR resulted first of all in a general loss of state authority and considerable fragility of the new nation-states. Local and supra-regional economic structures also broke down. Besides ethnic conflicts, the initial post-Soviet years were characterized by a not inconsiderable number of successful and unsuccessful coups and a massive redistribution of public property in favour of a new ownership class, which predominantly comprised and still comprises the old *nomenklatura*. This economic transformation was accompanied and encouraged by the general weakness of the state structures. The Soviet system had produced a series of weak states. The so-called weak-state syndrome first means that the state is unable to collect taxes in order to finance its organizational structure. However, a weak state that fails as an institution by no means signifies that power is not distributed in a clear and definite manner. Chaos and authoritarianism are not mutually exclusive; rather, chaotic states often strengthen the tendency towards an authoritarian system.

Georgia, for example, can still not regard itself as an integrated state in the regions that belong to its territories. It does not have control over Abkhazia, South Ossetia or Adsharia, or over Javakhetia, settled by Armenians. Sub-national players have assumed power at the expense of the central authority. Abkhazia and South Ossetia are, like Nagorno Karabakh, *de facto* independent states. Cynics even claim that the

Georgian president, Edward Shevardnadze (since 1992), is simply the president of Tbilisi and its surroundings. It may also appear that 'ethnic cleansing' has temporarily brought a certain degree of stability in some regions. At the same time, those displaced internally frequently live in wretched conditions. Violence and displacement have pushed any thought of peaceful coexistence far into the distance.

State-building in the South Caucasus has long since been hindered by ethnic conflicts, even going back to the independent republics of the 1918–20 period before the seizure of power by the Bolsheviks. The subsequent administrative structure in the Soviet Union – with autonomous territories of ethnic minorities within Georgia and Azerbaijan, controlled and funded by Moscow – entailed alienation from the respective titular nation of the republic. Another problem was that the Armenians in Nagorno Karabakh, for example, had more rights than the Azerbaijanis in Armenia. They were, furthermore, better organized – an important requirement for the emergence of secession plans.

Inter-ethnic tensions leading to reciprocal pogroms before the First World War, and between 1918 and 1920, remained latent during the Soviet era. After the collapse of the Soviet Union in 1988, the resurgence of nationalist ambitions led once more to the escalation of tension. In Armenia, nationalism was not directed against control by Moscow but, rather, resulted in an attempt to restore 'historical justice'. It appeared easier to 'win back' Nagorno Karabakh than the territories in Turkey formerly settled by Armenians. When the official call for the affiliation of Nagorno Karabakh was made in February 1988, this was supported by a mass movement, which regarded itself as being national and democratic.

The Armenians in Karabakh were not repressed to a substantial extent. Their situation was undoubtedly better than that of the Azerbaijanis in Armenia, who lived in the Zangezur region in an equally concentrated manner, though without possessing any autonomy. The autonomy of Nagorno Karabakh made the Armenians all the more determined in their claim for independence. As one of the oldest Christian peoples, their identity is shaped by religious and cultural isolation. They see themselves as being surrounded by non-Christian peoples and as the victims of persecution. This results in a feeling of uniqueness, of being the chosen people and of superiority over neighbouring countries. Armenian nationalism is characterized by the collective trauma of 1915, when the Young Turks carried out forced deportations and hundreds of thousands lost their lives. The memory of this, as well as the embitterment over the loss of settled territories in eastern Anatolia and the allocation of the regions of Nakhchivan and Nagorno Karabakh to Azerbaijan, also continued throughout the Soviet era. Hardly any differences are made between Turks and Azerbaijanis, which is why the affiliation of Nagorno Karabakh to Azerbaijan was so difficult to stomach.

TAKEOVER OF POWER BY NATIONAL INDEPENDENCE MOVEMENTS

The movements that determined the conflict were, at the same time, the upholders of the struggle for independence on both sides. Just as in Armenia, the Nagorno Karabakh problem also led to the forming of a national democratic independence movement in Azerbaijan. Although the development of a national identity was closely linked with the conflict, the struggle for Nagorno Karabakh united different forces only sporadically in Azerbaijan. In contrast to Armenia, Azerbaijan has a more fragmented society and although the Karabakh conflict was able to act as a catalyst for unity, it could not surmount the social division in a sustained manner. National mobilization in Azerbaijan occurred later than in Armenia and was, in essence, a reaction to the Armenian movement. This can be attributed to the greater persecution of national forces by the strongly entrenched communist bureaucracy in Azerbaijan. The nationalist forces did not come to power until two years after this happened in Georgia and Armenia. This impacted on the ability to develop state structures and institutions capable of defending the territory and its citizens. As they are part of the 'Turkish World', the feelings of uniqueness and tendency towards isolation are alien to the Azeris.

For Azerbaijan, the reason for the war lies in the unjustified territorial claims asserted by Armenian chauvinism and irredentism. Armenia, on the other hand, regards the right to self-determination and the guarantee of human rights as being the core of the conflict. While the special situation of the ethnic minorities in Georgia and Azerbaijan has made transformation and state-building more difficult, Armenia has, through the displacement of the Azerbaijanis, established itself as a mono-ethnic, homogeneous state.

It is not so easy for Azerbaijanis to unite around an ideal of national importance. They represent the passive side of the conflict, which only reacts – and often irrationally, by virtue of being unprepared. It was Nagorno Karabakh that first kindled national consciousness. If Moscow had annexed Karabakh to Armenia in Soviet times, it can be assumed that this would have met with hardly any resistance. It was the reforms of *perestroika* that first sparked off the conflict.

On taking over power, the nationalist movements in Georgia and Azerbaijan found fragmented societies with separatist groups, broken-down economic and administrative structures, and the resistance of the old communist bureaucracy and an all-pervasive system of corruption, which they themselves were not free from. Building new state structures while at the same time fighting against the dissolution of the state by secessionist movements was to be carried out under the maxim of democratization, modernization and defending territorial integrity. The overall approach was wrapped in the cloak of nationalistic ideology. It failed because of the persistence of the old system and the inexperience of the new rulers, as well as their lack of pragmatism and the ideologization of their politics. Ebulfez Elçibey (1992–93) in Azerbaijan and Zwiad Gamsachurdia (1990–91) in Georgia were the first freely elected presidents to be popular leaders of the nationalistic dissident groups. However, the popularity they enjoyed by virtue of their idealistic convictions did not last much longer after they had seized power.

The new nationalistic and not strictly democratic élites considered the old state to be an obstacle to the establishment of a new social order. Their rise and their temporary take-over of power in Georgia and Azerbaijan were associated with excluding the old party oligarchy from the top positions of power, thus depriving the state of its infrastructure based on party discipline and clientelistic loyalty. Although the system of the old élites – characterized by experience and personal contacts – lost authority, it did hold on to its influence, which found expression in new, partly mafia-like structures.

RETURN OF THE OLD ÉLITES

The new élites could not match the experienced power politicians of the old regime, who – once detached from their ideological ballast – were able to return quickly to their positions and thus just about prevent a total collapse of the state. Without personalities such as Shevardnadze and Aliyev, who rose to high office in the Soviet Union, Georgia and Azerbaijan would possibly not have survived as sovereign states. Both countries had reached an abyss, where it was more important to maintain some semblance of order under chaotic conditions than steer a course of transformation to democracy.

Following the collapse of the nationalist, anti-communist people's front government in Azerbaijan, only the charismatic Aliyev, relying on old contacts and his popularity stemming from the 1970s, was able to give the country a certain degree of stability despite the wretched economic situation and losing the war. Elçibey, on the other hand, had not succeeded in carrying out parliamentary or local elections during the one-year period for which the Popular Front held power. He appointed incompetent Popular Front members to the administration without coming to any arrangement with the old bureaucracy. When the coup – supported by Russian forces – was mounted against him in 1993, he was, typically enough, not able to mobilize any public support for himself.

This failure contributed to the Popular Front – from which the most prominent part of today's opposition emerged – being associated for a number of years with the anarchic conditions of the early post-Soviet period and a unilaterally anti-Russian foreign policy direction. In contrast, the strong leader Haidar Aliyev was – like Shevardnadze in Georgia – associated with order and security, and with the good aspects and times of the old regime. The result was a system of populist authoritarianism. The representatives of the old élite, hardened in their careers through the political institutions of the old system and experienced in all angles of Soviet policy, demonstrated a great understanding of political realism. Despite extreme pressure from the Russian side with regard to foreign policy, they were successful in pursuing a foreign policy direction clearly oriented towards the West while at the same time carrying out a balanced policy that did not provoke Russia to any great extent. In a system of personal networks, patronage and corruption, the practices of the Soviet system are useful in dealing with both internal and external rivals. The fact that Shevardnadze and Aliyev survived several attempted coups further strengthened their positions of power. The Soviet system had produced leaders that were capable of dealing with power struggles and intrigues as well as eliminating their opponents – especially in the military domain – through establishing dependencies and alliances and conducting purges. This secured them legitimacy among the public at large, which tended to be confirmed by the elections – whether manipulated or not.

In the area of foreign policy, the former Soviet cadres have been able to achieve a balance by skilfully exploiting rivalries and differences.

Whereas the dissidents had formed their foreign policy according to ideological criteria – the Turkist Elçibey backing Turkey unilaterally, thereby angering Russia and Iran – the former communists (turned into nationalists) geared themselves towards economic interests. Aliyev and Shevardnadze both based their orientation towards the West on oil, the former relying on the large deposits in his country and the latter focusing on Georgia's function as a transit country. They both combined their opportunism and power instincts with visions, namely the integration of their nations into Western and European structures. This strategy regards regional cooperation, together with the consideration of Russian interests, as prerequisites for success. The model of greater independence oriented towards Europe brings together the government and opposition in Azerbaijan. Indeed, foreign policy is the area on which the two sides extensively agree.

The political approach of the old cadre is, of course, faced with a major problem in that although the skills acquired during the Soviet era were sufficient to ride out the internal turmoil, they have not been up to the task of implementing far-reaching reforms and establishing modern state structures.

Although there are undoubtedly some successes in the area of foreign policy, it is precisely the integration into Western structures that generates external demands for the abolition of the personality cult, patronage and corruption on which the power structures are based. As a result, the will to integrate with the West clashes with the refusal to accept the associated consequences.

PRESIDENTIAL RULE AND AN ALL-POWERFUL EXECUTIVE

The combination of patrimonial structures and the communist control machinery has made the old system particularly resistant to fundamental changes – a fact aided by the absence of democratic traditions in the region. Apart from the legacy of the Soviet era, the security situation in the states of the South Caucasus has also ensured that the presidential form of state rule with strong executive powers and far-reaching control of parliament and the judiciary has become the model for the still young states. The social conditions for this were a weak opposition and a civil society that had hardly developed. The centralization of the regime consolidated the state's power, with its structures remaining inadequate at the same time.

Democratization and liberalization were considered to be inconsistent with consolidation of power and control over the national territory. It was argued that democratization would hinder economic reforms, while a middle class and civil society as the prerequisites for a functioning democracy could emerge only through an economic upturn. In other words, the population was not yet ready for democracy. Aliyev's supporters carried this argument to the extreme with the paradoxical thesis that the prerequisites for democracy could themselves be created only through authoritarian measures. Aliyev's understanding of the state is correspondingly patriarchal insofar as he likes to compare the state with a family in which everything goes wrong if the man does not have authority as head of the household. This harbours the far from unjustified fear that breaking down the traditional structures endangers the continued existence of society.

Free and fair elections are generally deemed to be the symbol for democratization of a society. No poll in the Caucasus has yet deserved to be classified under the heading of *free and fair* as applied by the OSCE in its observation of elections. It is not parties or ideals that establish political identification here but, rather, regional loyalties. The Soviet system was built on networks of bureaucratic interests along traditional family and regional lines. These form the basis for political rule and obstruct the establishment of independent civil and political institutions. The main problem in post-communist societies is the gulf between the public at large and the decision-makers such as the élites extensively educated during the Soviet era, and a lack of intermediary structures or institutions.

The call for democratization from outside is problematic in this context. The new states are, in contrast to the Middle East states, for example, members of the OSCE and therefore committed to democratization. Georgia and Azerbaijan chose the West as the guarantor of their independence *vis-à-vis* Russia. Georgia was the first country in the

Caucasus to become a member of the Council of Europe, with Azerbaijan and Armenia following at the beginning of 2001. Apart from formal deficiencies (election and party legislation), the constitutions ostensibly meet the requirements of a democratic state according to the Western definition, in that they establish republicanism and the division of powers, and uphold the fundamental liberties of freedom of speech, assembly and religion.

The presidential system dominates in the new states, and the presidents would have clearly won all the elections even without any manipulation. Nevertheless, they prefer to convey a picture of power beyond challenge, in the old Soviet tradition. To accomplish this, an overwhelming majority is needed, which means approval ratings of over 90 per cent as in the old Stalinist days. Although it is often not even needed, manipulation is considered to be almost legitimate. It is expressed in the same distinctive ways every time: not permitting opposition parties to put up candidates, excluding observers and manipulating votes. Since elections of the – in any case powerless – Azerbaijani parliament were rigged, the elected representatives fail to reflect the existing balance of power. The small number of seats held in parliament by the opposition does not correspond to its real political influence. This puts into question the hypothesis that a patrimonial dictatorship is a suitable model for state-building in the Muslim parts of the post-Soviet world, as the potential for a functioning parliamentarianism must be assessed as being far higher here than in the Central Asian states, for example.

An all-powerful executive can also be justified by the threat or actuality of external powers exerting pressure to undermine the state – in Azerbaijan's case, this is purported to be Russia in unison with Armenia. The authoritarian regime undoubtedly permits more options for action. If the territory cannot be regained, the president can strive for a diplomatic solution in a relatively independent manner. In practice, this means that only he is in a position to choose options other than war. This hypothesis is supported by the behaviour of different presidents in the negotiations on Nagorno Karabakh.

The example of the first Armenian president, Levon Ter-Petrosian (1991–98), who emerged as a dissident from the Karabakh movement, shows how even a democratically minded president fell or could not help falling into the authoritarian style in order to establish legitimized authority during the state-building process. Although he had recognized that neither the unification of Karabakh nor complete independence could be achieved, the Armenian public could not understand this step. Ter-Petrosian failed internally because of his willingness to compromise with Azerbaijan and had to resign in 1998. He was succeeded by the tougher and more nationalistic Kocharian, a war veteran and former president of Karabakh, who had the support of the military. Ter-Petrosian linked Armenia's future stability to the resolution of the Nagorno Karabakh conflict and strove to normalize relations with Turkey as a precondition of economic growth and ending the country's isolation. Kocharian, by contrast, made the genocide issue one of the central elements of his foreign policy with the support of the Armenian diaspora. In this regard he also relied on the hardened nationalists, who see themselves as the guardians of the Armenian nation. At the same time, sections of this group benefited from the failure to settle the conflict, since retaining the status quo provided them with economic advantages. Domestic policy clashes have become fiercer since Aliyev and Kocharian commenced direct negotiations under international pressure.

Compared with Azerbaijan, the parliament in Armenia is undoubtedly of greater significance. In October 1999, the vulnerability of these young democratic institutions was borne out by the assassination of Prime Minister Vasgen Sarkisian and Speaker of the Parliament Karen Demirchian – both opponents of Kocharian and advocates of an even tougher stance.

The political skills and the background of an individual leader all go towards shaping the politics of conciliation and conflict resolution. When political power is centralized, foreign policy is insulated from the influence of factions and particular interest groups. There is, however, the risk that this very exclusion from the decision-making process is brought to a head by the secret negotiations, and provides a rallying point as in Azerbaijan. Here the opposition has united to call for the re-conquest of Nagorno Karabakh and the territories occupied by Armenia. The evident distrust between the President and the opposition can therefore become an obstacle to an acceptable peace agreement.

EXTERNAL INFLUENCES AND NEW ALLIANCES

In Azerbaijan, one of the legacies of the Soviet era is the widely held sense of victimization by foreign powers. It is believed to a large degree that the key to resolving the Nagorno Karabakh conflict lies solely with Moscow, thus diverting attention away from one's own responsibility to find a solution. The apportioning of blame does, of course, have its justification, given Russia's policy over the past ten years. The deep distrust of Russia does not exactly make Moscow the ideal mediator. Even though the 1994 ceasefire was achieved through Russian mediation and despite Moscow stressing its impartiality, its intentions are still regarded as hostile in Azerbaijan. Russian conflict management is perceived as a pretext for strengthening Moscow's influence. Doubts about Russia's commitment to solving the conflict are indeed justified, given that Moscow contributed to freezing the conflicts in Georgia and Armenia once its military presence was assured. Russia's non-constructive role caused Azerbaijan and Georgia to lean towards the West, resulting in a consolidation of the present security policy structures – in other words, Georgia and Azerbaijan see Russia as a threat, while Armenia regards it as a guarantee for security. However fragmented Russian foreign policy was, the strategic importance of the region for Russia has put Georgia and Azerbaijan under constant pressure because neither country can exclude Russia from any possible peace accord.

Over the past few years, so-called strategic alliances have been formed in the region. Although these are not without contradiction in themselves, they do not exclude the possibility of military alliances. On the one side are states that have joined together in the organization GUUAM (Georgia, Ukraine, Uzbekistan, Azerbaijan, Moldova), a loose and not very effective alliance held together by the common desire to avert Russia's hegemonic claims. On the other side, we find the remainder of the CIS (Community of Independent States), led by Russia itself.

As a response to this development and the growing influence of the USA, since taking office Vladimir Putin has encouraged and supported the strengthening of military cooperation within the CIS. The actions of radical Islamic terrorists in the North Caucasus provides him with ample justification, and has allowed him to turn the 1992 CIS Collective Security Treaty into a serious instrument. This means that the central Asian states – with the exception of Uzbekistan and neutral Turkmenistan – have joined together with Belarus and Armenia to form a permanent CIS core under Russian leadership.[2] Armenia, beneficiary of substantial Russian arms shipments over recent years, is playing a central role in the Caucasus. The military alliance, which places Russia under a binding obligation to provide support should Armenia be threatened, is seen in Azerbaijan as a threat. Baku's hasty offer to provide military facilities to NATO should be seen in this light.

THE KARABAKH CONFLICT: A KEY ROLE FOR THE SOUTH CAUCASUS

The tentative attitude of Western powers towards the Caucasus in the 1990s, when attention was focused on Russia, has been replaced by a flurry of diplomatic activity in an attempt to find a peaceful resolution to the Nagorno Karabakh problem. Both the USA and the EU, in partnership with Russia, are making strenuous efforts to find a peaceful resolution. Azerbaijan is in no position to implement the required structural reforms as long as it remains bogged down in the Karabakh conflict, to the chagrin of US oil interests and pipeline plans. The EU, in turn, is disturbed by the presence of a conflict-prone Caucasus region on its doorstep. As US policy-makers are seeking to come to terms with the unpredictability of Russian policy, they have to contend with enormous contradictions. With Section 907 of the 1992 US Freedom Support Act, for example, the US Congress adopted sanctions against Azerbaijan to the extent that direct economic or military aid is forbidden as long as Baku maintains the blockade against Armenia, even though this was imposed because of the Armenian occupation of Azerbaijan territory. The activities of the Armenian lobby in the USA, which were instrumental in the fall of President Elçibey, continue to fan popular mistrust of US intentions in Azerbaijan despite the predominant general approval for the government's Western-oriented course.

The disappointment was exacerbated after the Kosovo conflict, when the NATO intervention expected in Azerbaijan and Georgia failed to materialize. There are also deep-seated suspicions of the OSCE, which intensified when the OSCE increased its pressure for a peace agreement. The parties concerned simply do not feel that they are taken seriously by the organization. Azerbaijan does not feel adequately represented by any of the three countries presently chairing the Minsk Group.[3] This is linked with tendencies towards a new, anti-West stance and the feeling of being the victim 'once again'. The defiant stance arising from this situation is giving rise to a call for the people at last to reflect and rely on its own strength. In the final consequence, this will result in a readiness for war that misjudges the existing balance of power and disregards the devastating effects of a further armed conflict.

Gains were made in the peace progress after the presidents succumbed to US pressure, and held a meeting in 1999. In October the process was stalled, however, by the assassination of two leading Armenian politicians, throwing Armenia into turmoil. In view of the heated internal political climate, a compromise solution is also a risky undertaking in Armenia as no settlement is likely to be satisfactory to all groups. In consequence, the Nagorno Karabakh army sees no reason in altering the status quo and withdrawing from the occupied territories in Azerbaijan as long as it enjoys military superiority.

PEACE PROPOSALS MADE BY THE MINSK GROUP AND THE COMMON-STATE MODEL

Since the beginning of 1997, the Minsk Group has submitted three peace proposals to the OSCE.[4] The latest of these, presented in November 1998, provides for the concept of a common state between Azerbaijan and Nagorno Karabakh. While this proposal does accommodate Armenian demands, it is far less advantageous for Azerbaijan than the first two proposals. Essentially, Baku sees the common state principle as an attempt to legalize in a diplomatic manner what has been achieved by force. In its view, an agreement that accepts the existing realities – the occupation of Azerbaijani territories – cannot constitute the core of a peace agreement. The plan for a common state solution is attributed by Baku to the Russian influence within the Minsk Group, and is believed to have been authored by Yevgeni Primakov, Russian foreign minister at the time, and his Armenian counterpart, Vartan Oskanian.

Within the context of intensified efforts to find a peace solution, there has been increased discussion on the possibility of a stability pact for the South Caucasus. At the OSCE summit held in Istanbul in 1999, both Armenia and Azerbaijan proposed a stability pact as a forum for multilateral cooperation in the Caucasus. The Turkish president at the time, Süleyman Demirel, also took up this idea. However, none of the proposals was set out in any great detail. The stagnation of the peace process following the events in Armenia also showed that a peace agreement in Nagorno Karabakh as a prerequisite for a stability pact is unlikely as long as the internal political situation in the respective states remains tense. This raises the fundamental question of whether the internal instability in both countries permits a peace accord at all, or whether the many particular interests do not make a settlement an Utopian ideal from the outset. Although at international level the existing delimitation of state borders is held to be inviolable, Armenia's military victory remains a *fait accompli*, which Azerbaijan is widely expected to accept at some stage.

The way out of the dead end is seen to be via a confederation that safeguards the principle of territorial integrity while at the same time introducing non-hierarchic relations between the federal entities. The weak point of all the proposals concerning a common state solution is, however, that this can lead to complete secession. In other words, the biggest difficulty lies in translating the details into the reality of the South Caucasus. Up to now, all proposals for a stability pact have been at the theoretical level.

The only proposal regarding a stability pact for the South Caucasus that has actually been elaborated so far was made by the independent Centre for European Policy Studies in Brussels in spring 2000. This also includes the common state as a basic concept, whereby territorial-ethnic conflicts would be solved not through uncompromising subordination or independence but, rather, through a complex system of horizontal and asymmetric relations between different entities. This would also embrace horizontal relations between different levels of governmental forms, including the possible self-administration of political entities, which could establish independent relations with other states.

This concept would open up the possibility for Nagorno Karabakh to cooperate with Armenia in a large number of areas without threatening the territorial integrity of Azerbaijan. For Karabakh and Abkhazia, this would entail a high degree of self-administration, with the devolution of powers in many areas, their own constitutions, horizontal relations with state and regional authorities, as well as shared competencies in economic, foreign policy and security matters.

The view in Azerbaijan, however, is that the offer of vertical autonomy for Karabakh within Azerbaijan already constitutes a far-reaching concession. A solution that merely promises some sort of autonomy, on the other hand, is not acceptable to Armenia. Furthermore, there is a third position in this conflict, namely that of Nagorno Karabakh. And the leadership in Karabakh opposes any form of a common state with Azerbaijan and insists on full independence.

A confederate solution as in the model of the common state, balancing the principles of territorial integrity and the right to self-determination, is seen by Azerbaijan as abandoning territorial integrity, whereas for Armenia it represents the logical consequence of the military reality. It would be the ratification of the already existing *de facto* independence of Karabakh. From the Azerbaijani viewpoint, this solution would merely represent a concealed transition to full independence or a veiled affiliation of Karabakh with Armenia.

The question of status is thus the key issue of the conflict. A vertical model of the autonomy of Nagorno Karabakh within Azerbaijan would theoretically offer Azerbaijani refugees the possibility of returning to their homeland. The principle of territorial integrity would be protected, as desired by the international community, and the Armenian conquests would not be 'rewarded'. From the Karabakh point of view, however, such a constellation would clearly not solve the conflict either.

In the light of the above, and the lack of any tangible successes over the years, Azerbaijan's displeasure with the OSCE's mediation attempts is therefore understandable. The fact that the contents of the 1998 common state proposal were not made public until February 2001 succeeded in outraging broad sections of the Azerbaijani population, and the subsequent threats of war from leading politicians and high-ranking army officers illustrate the difficult situation of the leadership under Aliyev. There is a deep rift between the need for a peaceful resolution and the realization that Azerbaijan has to make the most concessions – an insight that asks a lot of politicians and the public at large. The only alternative to the subjectively painful compromise solution would be renewed war.[5]

KEY WEST AND THE BOUNDARIES OF AUTHORITARIAN PRESIDENTIAL RULE

The negotiations conducted in Key West, USA at the beginning of April 2001 under the auspices of US Secretary of State Colin Powell have further inflamed public opinion on both sides. Mediators conveyed the impression of substantial progress being made, and a compromise solution being within reach, while keeping details of the proceedings in total secrecy. In both countries, the respective oppositions are taking advantage of the current negotiations to arouse agitation against the leadership. Seen in superficial terms, a front line is being drawn in Azerbaijan between an opposition that sees itself as democratic and is calling for war on the one hand, and an authoritarian president who has recognized the necessity for a compromise solution but whose scope for action is very limited on the other.

Although both presidents softened their stance during the talks, they struck a far more hawkish pose when back in their respective countries. There could be tactical reasons for this, inasmuch as intransigence can buy time at the negotiating table. However, they also have to be afraid of agreeing on something that they will not be able to 'sell' to their people. Indignation could release a tide of rebellion that would wash them away.

The authoritarian system has reached its limits: it cannot ignore the mood of the public at large without running the risk of a protest movement emerging. This illustrates the correlation between the resolution of the conflict and the process of democratization most clearly. An opposition that is partly excluded from the political process, as is the case in Azerbaijan, is more likely to turn against a compromise solution. Arbitrary presidential decision-making in a democracy established only in formal terms makes the peace process very blurred for the public at large. Even in Azerbaijan itself, it is not possible for anyone to judge what drives the sick 77-year-old president more: the desire for peace or the endeavour to smooth the way for his son, Ilham Aliyev, as his successor.

External demands for the simultaneous democratization of the political system and a greater willingness for compromises in the inter-state negotiations are met with incomprehension and resistance. The idea of restricted and shared sovereignty has evidently not yet found any resonance in the states of the South Caucasus, although this is hardly surprising, given the region's experiences with outside interference. Furthermore, the region has only just started the long process of nation-building, based on experiences of suffering and warlike conflicts with heavy losses, which, in turn, caused a large part of the population to strengthen its national identity through the ideal of territorial integrity. Moderating this in favour of ideals that have not yet really matured in the Caucasus and that also took a long time to develop in Europe is something that is difficult to imagine and even more difficult to put into practice in the region.

(*Translation: Barry Stone*)

NOTES

1. The so-called Minsk Group is responsible within the OSCE for solving the Karabakh conflict. It comprises representatives of the conflicting parties and the following countries: the USA, Russia, France, Germany, the Czech Republic, Sweden, Italy, Belarus and Turkey. The USA, Russia and France currently hold the co-chairmanship of the Group.

2. On 11 October 2000, the presidents of Russia, Belarus, Armenia, Kazakhstan, Kyrgyzstan and Tajikistan laid the foundations in Bishkek for forming a military-polity bloc under Russian leadership. The agreement on Creating Forces and Installations of the Collective Security System permits the setting up of joint troops. Cf. Monitor – A daily briefing on the post-Soviet states, 16 October 2000, Vol. VI, Issue 192 (CIS collective security system fleshed out at Bishkek summit).

3. In the USA and France, the Armenian lobby is the decisive factor, and Russia is an ally of Armenia. In Baku, the view is often heard that Germany should take the chair in place of France.

4. The first proposal made in July 1997 (All-Around Agreement on Adjustment of Karabakh) contained an overall package of solutions, including the question of the status of Karabakh. It was accepted by Azerbaijan with reservations and rejected by Armenia. The second proposal submitted in September 1997 was accepted by Azerbaijan, while Armenia accepted it with reservations.

5. It is still impossible for the Azerbaijani leadership to accept the OSCE proposal, as it would amount to virtually full independence for Nagorno Karabakh. The resignation of Aliyev's closest advisers has to be understood in this context. Under this model, Karabakh would have its own constitution and its own legislature, executive and judiciary, as well as the right to determine its own foreign and economic policy within a loose confederation with Azerbaijan. A buffer zone would be created as a security guarantee, which would be controlled by an OSCE multi-national peace-keeping force. Karabakh would have its own national guard, with the Azerbaijani army denied access to Karabakh, which raises the issue for Baku of the protection of Azerbaijanis returning to Karabakh. Furthermore, Karabakh would have its own currency and its own flag. The state language would be Armenian, with Azeri as the second language. Its citizens would have Azerbaijani passports issued by the authorities in Karabakh. Cf. BBC Monitoring Service – United Kingdom 2001.

REFERENCES

Alieva, L. (2000) 'Reshaping Eurasia: foreign policy strategies and leadership assets in post-Soviet South Caucasus', University of California, Berkeley, Berkeley Program in Soviet and Post-Soviet Studies, Working Paper Series.

Auch, E.-M. (1999) 'Aserbaidschan: Regierungsinstitutionen – politisches System. Zur Entwicklung der politischen Machtverhältnisse in den neunziger Jahren', in Gerhard Mangott (ed), *Brennpunkt Südkaukasus, Aufbruch trotʒ Krieg, Vertreibung und Willkürherrschaft?* Vienna: Braumüller, pp. 61–104.

BBC Monitoring Service – United Kingdom (2001) 23 February 2001 (OSCE's 'common state' proposal for Karabakh, as published in Azeri paper. *Source*: *Bakinskiy Rabochiy*, Baku, in Russian, 21 February 2001, p. 3).

Centre for European Policy Studies (2000) 'A stability pact for the Caucasus. A new deal for the whole region, incorporating: a South Caucasus community, Russian/EU/US Southern dimension cooperation, enhanced Black Sea–Caucasus–Caspian cooperation. A consultative document of the CEPS Task Force for the Caucasus', Brussels, Working Document No. 145, May.

Dehdashti, R. (2000) *Internationale Organisationen als Vermittler in innerstaatlichen Konflikten. Die OSZE und der Karabakh-Konflikt*, Frankfurt/Main: Campus Verlag.

Freitag-Wirminghaus, R. (1999a) 'Politische Konstellationen im Südkaukasus', in *Aus Politik und Zeitgeschichte, Beilage ʒur Wochenʒeitung Das Parlament*, B 42/ 99 (15 October), pp. 21–31.

— (1999b) 'Südkaukasien und die Erdöl-Problematik am Kaspischen Meer', in Gerhard Mangott (ed.), *Brennpunkt Südkaukasus*, Vienna: Braumüller, pp. 247– 82.

Herzig, E. (1999) *The New Caucasus: Armenia, Aʒerbaijan and Georgia*, London: Pinter.

Malek, M. (2000) *Determinanten der Sicherheitspolitik Armeniens*, Bundesinstitut für Cologne, Internationale und Ostwissenschaftliche Studien (BIOST).

Mangott, G. (ed) (1999) 'Brennpunkt Südkaukasus, Aufbruch trotz Krieg, Vertrei-bung und Willkürherrschaft?', *Laxenburgher internationale Studien* 14, Vienna: Braumüller.

Manutscharjan, A. (1999) 'Das Regierungs- und Parteiensystem Armeniens', in Gerhard Mangott (ed.), *Brennpunkt Südkaukasus*, Vienna: Braumüller, pp. 19–60.

Monitor – A daily briefing on the post-Soviet states, <http://www.jamestown. org>

Nodia, G. (1999) 'Trying to build (democratic) state institutions in independent Georgia', in Gerhard Mangott (ed.), *Brennpunkt Südkaukasus*, Vienna: Brau-müller, pp. 105–138.

Perspective – edited by the Institute for the Study of Conflict, Ideology and Policy, <http://www.bu.edu/iscip/>

Suny, R. G. (1999) 'Armenia and Azerbaijan: thinking a way out of Karabakh', in *Middle East Policy*, Washington, DC, 6 (3) (7 October), pp. 145–76.

Tchilingirian, H. (1999) 'Nagorno Karabakh: transition and the élite', in *Central Asian Survey*, Abingdon, 18 (4) (December): 435–61.

Trenin, D. (1999) 'Conflicts in the South Caucasus', in Gerhard Mangott (ed.), *Brennpunkt Südkaukasus*, Vienna: Braumüller, pp. 283–306.

FIVE

Human Security, Liberal Democracy and the Power of Nationalism: The State Crisis in Georgia and Possible Solutions

DAVID DARCHIASHVILI

§ The debate surrounding national and state security in Georgia reveals a range of clearly definable problems. The list is long:

- an insufficient legal system; deficiencies in security policy and crisis management;
- a lack of experienced personnel and necessary funding as well as inefficient use of available resources;
- the absence of a culture of civil and democratic control of the institutions responsible for enforcing the law;
- low level of awareness of individual rights and 'human security' on the part of state institutions;
- political and economic vulnerability of the state;
- internal conflicts with minorities demanding territorial autonomy or even independence; and
- threats presented by external risks and challenges.

Furthermore, the widespread corruption prevailing in the state institutions is an expression and consequence of the points referred to above. Security experts regard corruption, which can hardly be differentiated from organized crime, as a serious national threat. 'Corruption is a security threat in its own right, as well as contributory factor to the governmental failings ... Indeed, it is the single most serious threat to the viability of several countries of the former Soviet Union and a severe problem everywhere' (Donnelly 2000–01: 33). This corresponds very precisely to the reality in Georgia, where 'corruption has become a way of life in certain areas. Corruptive thinking so broadly embraced public perception, that we have to be extremely cautious while drawing a line between the roots of national originality and corruptive customary practices causing national catastrophe' (Republic of Georgia 2000: 9). If the view of the Georgian experts who drew up *The Main Directions of the National Anti-Corruption Program of Georgia* in 2000 is shared, it then becomes evident that traditional reform instruments in the security domain, such as passing democratic laws, training public servants and enhancing the transparency of Georgian politics, will not be sufficient in themselves. The success of reforms in the security sector depends – to a great extent – more on a political culture, which requires public consensus on particular ideological questions. Public consensus plus common ideals and goals are the prerequisites for creating a civil society and a state governed by the rule of law. A viable national security system that can overcome the many diverse challenges confronting Georgia, be they external threats, internal conflicts or the ubiquitous corruption, cannot otherwise be expected.

This chapter attempts to uncover the systemic reasons for the evident crisis concerning national security and statehood in Georgia. This crisis finds expression in the insecurity of large numbers of citizens in the face of state despotism and the lack of protection against crime in everyday life. However, it is also reflected to a very substantial degree in the warlike conflicts that have rocked Georgia since the collapse of Soviet territorial dominance. The first of these was the civil war fought in 1992–93 between the supporters of Zwiad Gamsachurdia, who was elected president and then subsequently removed from office (1990–91), and an alliance surrounding his successor, the current President Edward Shevardnadze (since 1992) – a conflict that continued to smoulder even after Gamsachurdia's death on 31 December 1993. Furthermore, the conflicts affecting South Ossetia and Abkhazia, which led to open warlike clashes in 1991–92 and 1992–94, are still virulent in nature. Besides protecting its cultural identity, the autonomous region of South Ossetia has at times wanted to break away from Georgia and join together with the Autonomous Republic of North Ossetia (Russian Federation). The political leadership in Abkhazia is still striving to attain independence. The status of both regions has still not been clarified. Georgia does not have territorial control there, nor is the power of the Georgian state consolidated in Ajaria (see Chapter 4).

My endeavour is to develop a conceptual approach against the background of these conflicts that could serve as an orientation for overcoming the crisis in the state of Georgia and guaranteeing extensive security for its citizens. I will first outline the conditions for creating state security, emphasizing the crucial importance of a liberal, constitutional democracy. Second, I will address the reciprocal relationship of conditions for national and human security, paying particular attention to the significance of parliamentary, judicial and public control of the security sector (police, military). Third, I will look at the argument that Georgia's greatest threat comes from external powers – from Russia, in particular. In this context, I would plead for the undeniably negative consequences of external interference not to be over-emphasized and, rather, for a greater awareness of the significant political leeway also open to a small country such as Georgia. The key to a workable security policy, both inward and outward, lies more in the loyalty of the citizens to their state than in external factors. Georgian politics is characterized by severe failings in this regard, resulting in the unclear distribution of constitutional competencies in the security sector as well as considerable inconsistencies in the area of foreign policy. I am in favour of these failings being remedied. At the same time, I would urge that the power and significance of nationalism for state and democratic consolidation should not be underestimated in this regard. In my opinion, there cannot be a case for fighting against the legacy of the nationalistic ideology of the nineteenth century; rather, it must be endeavoured to civilize and pacify nationalism.

CONDITIONS FOR CREATING STATE SECURITY

The creation of effective public institutions that afford protection for the individual, thereby gaining the trust and loyalty of the country's citizens, is an essential responsibility of every society. This derives from the nature of political activity and, in particular, from the forming of the state by virtue of the fact that the state and politics essentially revolve around the protection of life and property as well as the establishment of rules for relations between the members of a society.

According to the traditional liberal approach, which calls for the maximum possible realm of liberty for the individual, security is the true function of the state (Buzan et al. 1998: 37). According to this logic, the state is nothing more than a security system in a given society.

Whether or not one agrees with the state and security being equated in this way, one thing is clear: security is one of the most important foundations for political power. However, it is also true that individual rights and the security of the state and/or society pervade each other. If one area or the other becomes predominant, they will both be harmed, thus calling the stability of society and the security of its members into question.

What form a state's security system takes depends on this balance, that is, the relationship between the citizens' rights and obligations, as well as on the extent and depth to which security policy has matured in terms of whether it is considered satisfactory by the members of a given society, and the system is thus legitimized by them. Originally conceived as a means of combating armed external opponents or internal unrest, security policy now includes economic, social and ecological dimensions. In general terms, it is concerned with promoting the collective will, which is translated into so-called vital national interests as articulated by governments.

A more recent development worthy of mention in the security domain, at both the practical-political and the conceptual levels, is that of 'human security'. This concept goes beyond the traditional core issues of statism and national security, which are sometimes focused on 'political high grounds', sacrificing individual liberties and interests for collective prosperity. Without ignoring the existence of state interests in an anarchic international system, as postulated by the 'realist school', the human security approach argues that 'national security is insufficient to guarantee people's security' (CDFAIT 1999: 2).

The supporters of this concept stress the need to protect citizens from fear and anxiety, wherever this may stem from (see Chapter 1). In emphasizing that the state is not an end in itself and that the most important objective of security concerns the people and not the government (CDFAIT 1999: 3–4) the concept calls for the state's citizens to be protected against abuse and crime in their everyday lives. It also advocates humanization of the security system through giving preference to respect for human rights over the short-term efficiency of the security institutions.

Human security and national security can and should be compatible with each other, since they are not inconsistent with each other: 'Improving the human security of its people strengthens the legitimacy, stability and security of a state' (CDFAIT 1999: 6). The key to bringing different security aspects together in this way and providing an equal measure of security for both the state and society lies in democracy and the rule of law. These criteria justify and legitimize the institutions established for the protection of society. Legitimation is nothing other than recognition and loyalty *vis-à-vis* the state and its servants on the part of the citizens of the state. No regime can be regarded as stable and secure without such legitimacy – and this cannot be had for nothing, rather it requires constant and continuous endeavour.

Fair elections are obviously the best way of determining who or what is to be legitimate in a given society. However, elections are not the be-all and end-all of the matter. Rules and regulations are also needed that cannot be disregarded by any elected holder of public office. The constitutional precedence of statutes requires a division of powers with strong emphasis on an independent administration of justice with the authority to interpret the statutes as well as political intentions:

- in order to avoid partiality by state servants resulting from the assumption of human inadequacy;
- in order to protect individuals against the majority, who often blindly follow populism and emotions and entrust enormous power to irresponsible persons; and
- in order to protect the views and needs of minorities in a given society, who must have the opportunity to express themselves and possibly even convince the majority.

HUMAN AND NATIONAL SECURITY IN GEORGIA

The modern state of Georgia has been in existence for ten years now. It has been a decade filled with tragic events, and the echo of these developments can still be heard. The young state is suffering from unsolved political and socio-economic problems, with both subjective and objective reasons contributing to the cruel failure. The latter include, first of all, the complex geopolitical location, with numerous regional and external political interests clashing in the Caucasus. Second, the demise of the Soviet Union gave rise to economic chaos and ethnic conflicts. Georgia was very seriously affected in this regard by virtue of being ethnically heterogeneous and having been entirely integrated into the Soviet economic area because of its scarcity of natural resources. Added to this is the fact that the Georgian population did not have the experience that is required for taking autonomous political action. The last political entity on Georgian territory was abolished in the second half of the nineteenth century, after which the country was able to enjoy only a brief spell of independence between 1918 and 1921. Any independent social activity was then suppressed by communist totalitarianism.

The leaders of the national movement who cleaned up in Georgia after *perestroika* in the late 1980s and the political élite that followed them also bear considerable co-responsibility for the Georgian state crisis, such as a constant budget deficits and an impoverished population, a rising crime rate, lost territories or unprotected national borders, and a capricious foreign policy. Improper behaviour by a number of public officials and abuse of their position has made this reality even worse, as has the merciless confrontation between economic and social groupings in their struggle to gain influence.

Nevertheless, the state of Georgia is making advances despite its fragility and there have been a number of successes over the past ten years. Of these, the two most important are the ending of the military confrontation in numerous internal conflicts (Abkhazia, South Ossetia, Ajaria, supporters of former President Gamsachurdia), and the adoption of a new constitution (1995), as well as presidential and parliamentary elections plus initial steps towards uniting the military.

From the point of view of democratic reforms, the most significant achievement in the area of legislative enforcement and national security is the establishment of parliamentary control. In addition to relevant committees, a so-called 'Fiduciary Group' has been set up to monitor programmes that touch on state and military secrets. Transparency in these central areas is provided for by an administrative code that entered into force in 2000. Among other things, this code contains provisions for removing the secrecy label from military decisions where violations of individual constitutional rights and liberties occur (General Administrative Code, Tbilisi 2000, § 4). Furthermore, the effectiveness of the authority – the Chamber of Control – responsible for monitoring Ministry of Defence expenditure increased over the 1999/2000 period.

Legal stability has also been enhanced through the adoption of new criminal laws and criminal court procedures. Police and other members of the security forces can now be prosecuted if they violate human rights or intern citizens without any legal basis. The reform of the administration of justice carried out in the late 1990s has led to the substantial restructuring of and new appointments in its institutions, ending a long struggle between the disreputable Ministry of the Interior and the Ministry of Justice over the supervision of the penal institutions, which have now been placed under the authority of the latter.

On being recognized as an independent country by the international community and becoming a member of the UN, Georgia quickly endeavoured to become more closely integrated into the economic, political and security policy architecture of Europe and the North Atlantic alliance. Georgia was admitted to the Council of Europe on 27 April 1999, signifying both encouragement and support for the country on its path to democratization. Its determination to reform the defence sector and abide by a cooperative security policy was underscored by the signing of an agreement on Conventional Armed Forces in Europe (the CFE Treaty) within the framework of the OSCE and participation in NATOs 'Partnership for Peace' programme. Initiatives for a 'Peaceful Caucasus' and the creation of GUUAM (Georgia, Ukraine, Uzbekistan, Azerbaijan, Moldova) followed this line.

In 2000, the Georgian Ministry of Foreign Affairs together with Western experts drew up an official document entitled *Georgia and the World: Vision for the Future*. The document provided proof of an increasingly pro-Western trend in Georgian foreign policy. As a result of this, strengthening the partnership with the European Union is a top priority for Georgia, with the partnership with NATO being seen as a necessary precondition for subsequent NATO membership. The document points out that it would be desirable for all Russian military to withdraw and is critical of the Commonwealth of Independent States (CIS).

After being forcibly integrated into the CIS and consenting to the presence of Russian military bases on its territory in the early 1990s, Georgia made efforts in the late 1990s to escape from the 'protective custody' of the former mother country. International security institutions and Western states played a huge role in this process. Above all else, the agreement on the partial withdrawal of Russian troops negotiated with Russia in Istanbul during the OSCE summit in November 1999 signified a major step towards genuine independence.

Despite these accomplishments, Georgia is still faced with numerous problems today. Not only is the political system far removed from a consolidated democracy, but some of its democratic institutions are merely a sham. Laws are not adequately enforced, and human rights violations by state bodies rarely punished. Furthermore, the political climate in Tbilisi, where pluralism and a free independent press are more than mere rhetoric, does not spread as far as the periphery.

Even independent media, which many Georgians are proud of, are repeatedly restricted with regard to the freedom of their reporting. The OSCE representative on freedom of the media, Freimut Duve, identified the following three central obstacles for the press in his report:

- The public authorities are prepared to develop freedom and diversity to only a limited extent – a problem that is particularly relevant in the regions.
- Protection through an independent administration of justice is inadequate.
- The economic conditions for an independent press are only in their initial stages (OSCE 2001: 3).

Furthermore, the electronic media need clear regulations with regard to what constitutes libel or slander, the manner in which frequencies are distributed and how licences can be obtained. The strongest pressure is evidently exerted on state media – which have the largest share of the market – by biased state officials (OSCE 2001: 5ff).

This results in a picture of a still barely consolidated democracy with a fragile rule of law. If we then also add kidnapping, rampant corruption, a rise in crime in trouble-spots plus the fact that the institutions responsible for enforcing the law exist only on paper in some parts of the country with the central government unable to assert its power, the crisis of human security becomes all too vivid. High unemployment and poverty levels together with a lack of energy resources make the environmental situation even more bleak and exacerbate the feeling of total insecurity. As a consequence, between 300,000 and 700,000 persons (between 6 per cent and 13 per cent of the total population) have left the country over the past decade.[1]

THE INTERNATIONAL STAGE AND THE ROLE OF RUSSIA

The argument can often be heard that the critical risk factors for Georgia lie outside rather than inside the country, as do the resources for overcoming such risks. Georgia is indeed situated in a region where external powers are struggling to gain influence and where there are serious internal rivalries (see Chapter 4). Internal conflicts have been worsened by intervention from outside sources, leading to the loss of state control over a substantial part of Georgian territory, namely Abkhazia and South Ossetia.

Russia's stance towards Georgia's independence and territorial integrity is sometimes considered to be crucial where it concerns making predictions about the future of Georgian statism or the overcoming of ethnic conflicts (Darchiashvili 1997, 2000). This logic follows the widely held view of an all-pervading power on the part of the metropolis as well as the traditional standpoint that small states are essentially subjected to an alien will, an idea whose roots can be found in the realism school of international relations. Although this assumption is justified to a certain extent, it should be remembered that there is currently more scope in the international arena for independent and democratic developments in small countries such as Georgia than in more recent history.

Communities that are not significant in numerical terms possess a remarkable ability to make strong and bigger players bend to their will. Just as minorities within a state are frequently able to bring about changes in the strategies decided on by the majority, smaller states also have considerable influence in the international arena from time to time. The emergence of states that have just attained independence is proof of this.

Relations with Russia do indeed represent the most difficult problem for Georgian foreign policy. Russian troops are still stationed in the country, and the population is still dependent on Russian goods, Russian energy and the Russian labour market. In view of the perception that 'the hidden agenda of Russian leaders ... is their wish to restore the country's hegemonic position, at least on a regional basis, and regain control of territories and other natural and man-made resources that they lost' (Sheffer 1997: 30), Russia remains a risk factor for the independence of Georgia. These circumstances reinforce the way of thinking of local observers – as outlined above – that the key to solving

Georgia's problems still lies in Moscow and that Georgia cannot do anything under its own steam. However, this view is not only misleading but is also extremely problematic, since even if Russia does behave in an imperial manner towards Georgia, such a situation is certainly not irreversible. The current state of international relations favours the independence of smaller states as never before. Support is emerging through universally applicable political paradigms, the prevailing logic of which must also be heeded by Russia. For this reason, any sudden threat to Georgian independence from the north remains rather unlikely. There is, of course, always leeway for covert actions aimed at undermining the sovereignty of the Georgian state.

However, if Georgian society can reach a fundamental consensus on socio-political structures as well as relations within the country and if the government tackles the issues of *good governance*, development and cooperative security in the correct manner, conspiracies will then be uncovered automatically. They will then turn into open intervention or – much more likely – come to nothing.

However weak it may be, Georgia does have legitimation in the international arena. Georgia's legitimacy as an independent state and its significance in the eyes of the members of the Euro-Atlantic security system are reinforced by the prospect of its becoming a bridge between Asia and Europe. The independence and stable future of Georgia are also important for Western democracy for other reasons. The fact that Georgia professes democratic values and that a new democracy is emerging on the periphery of Europe are in both the West's ideological and security interests, while also enabling the West to unite its interest in keeping Russia's remaining imperial ambitions in check. This will not succeed, however, if Russia is able to assert itself in just one instance. Any further weakening of Georgian independence would be the litmus test for Russian ambitions, which harbour dangers for the entire world. Globalization and the so-called CNN effect represent a further guarantor for Georgia's independence if the small country's problems are well communicated and understood by the international community.

INTERNAL FAILINGS

Despite the difficulties presently confronting Georgia, the large number of foreign missions in its capital confirms the impression that

Georgian independence is no longer just a mere idea, but is, rather, gradually becoming reality and – even more importantly – normality. If there is some power or other that can cast doubt on Georgian statism, this can, at most, be its citizens, its society or a part of that society and the political élite.

There are still a number of constitutional regulations outstanding in relation to important security issues. The constitution makes no mention of the territorial arrangement within Georgia or of the status of autonomous entities, for example. Moreover, the responsibilities of the president and the parliament clash to a certain extent in that the president does not have the right to dissolve parliament or the authority to use military force without the approval of parliament, while the parliament's right to impeach the president exists only in formal terms. The result of this is, first of all, that the present structures for territorial division are lacking in constitutionality and, second, that there are no clear crisis management guidelines. When crises occur, such as the uprising at one of the military bases in October 1998, these are resolved informally and according to the will of a single person without any legal basis.

The president's personal power frequently hinders parliament in the exercising of its control functions. The latter acts selectively in almost all cases and is dependent upon the will of the president. As a powerful patron, the president counts on patronage relationships and clientelism from Soviet times (Losaberidze and Kikabidze 2000). There is also an element of clan loyalty in the parliament, where resignations or hearings in relation to corruption accusations levelled at public servants are demanded only in very rare cases. In some instances, the division of powers is fictitious, being replaced, in truth, by a complex balance between different clans.

The meagre budget expenditure in no way reflects any particular priority. Organizations often continue to receive funding even though they ceased operating in an orderly manner some years previously. The pitiful financial situation is, however, sufficient to give the semblance of functioning and conceal the real level of unemployment. The numerous institutions responsible for security and defence are widely scattered and provided with unbelievably scarce resources. Military entities are placed under the control of four independent institutions. Furthermore, in two of these, the Ministry of the Interior and the Ministry of Defence, the national guard and domestic troops even enjoy their own autonomy.

All of this makes it impossible even to dream of any real efficiency on the part of the navy, air force or other armed forces.

Despite the foreign policy successes already referred to, the national security policy is marked by inconsistencies. While strategic documents stress the need for integration into the Euro-Atlantic security architecture, indicating that Georgia would like to become a member of the EU and, indeed, NATO, the official rhetoric has, from time to time, also veered towards the idea of a neutral state. The fate of the Russian military bases is still unclear. Although Georgian members of parliament emphasize that the official position has not changed on this issue and that the Russians should withdraw as quickly as possible, the president remains vague on this point, explaining that this and other matters will be regulated within the framework of a major convention between Russia and Georgia.

The talk of possible neutrality and cautious utterances on the subject of Russian military bases are probably motivated by the wish not to annoy Russia. Not long ago, during the years 1993–94, Georgian foreign policy *vis-à-vis* Russia reflected anything but allegiance. However, there may also be other explanations as to why the bureaucracy has become so cautious with regard to determining a strategy on this matter, for example the ideological breakdown of the political élite. It must be remembered that the political and the intellectual élite have the following very different social origins:

- young democrats with a Western education, who have relatively little idea of or thought for the ethno-national peculiarities of the Georgian public at large;
- clans and corrupt personalities lacking any conviction and who consider corruption to be a national sport;
- radical ethno-nationalists who regard ethnic myths as being the truth, stressing the importance of the purity of blood and culture;
- and, finally, those who possess elements of all these traits.

There are also reasonable and honest people, of course, but unfortunately either they do not offer any clear strategy or are not sufficiently influential. They often seek support from clans and corrupt groups, thus forfeiting their integrity.

The ruling party and the parliamentary majority are also heterogeneous in nature. If there is something that brings them together, it is

Edward Shevardnaze's charismatic personality. However, the president himself frequently adopts inconsistent positions. It is clear that a group made up in this manner and its leader cannot come to any agreement on a set of fundamental values.

HOW CAN THE VICIOUS CIRCLE OF NATIONALISM FOUNDED ON ETHNICITY BE BROKEN?

When assessing universal principles, people – especially those in countries that import the Western ideas of liberal democracy – tend to see things in the light of their own culture, comparing its general principles with the perceived standards and contents of their own identity. The power associated with these variables is obvious. It is, indeed, a positive aspect that there is now hardly any culture that has an entirely negative attitude towards the ideals of democracy. It is also positive that culture and identity are historical constructs, which therefore adapt and change gradually. Negative or onerous for liberal democrats, however, is the fact that, in far too many cases, cultures and – based on this – collective identities perceive others in terms of 'us' and 'them' or as adversaries.

Conflicts that have their origin in cultural rivalries assume an ethnic nature in most instances. Up to now, ethnicity has been an especially strong expression of collective culture and a genuine search for identity. The ethnic community – or 'ethnie' as Anthony D. Smith calls it – is an identity founded on the myth of common forefathers, on a collectively shared memory and culture, as well as on ethnic solidarity and references to a historical territory on which the turning point in the life of a respected community took place (Smith 1993: 1ff). There are two opposing standpoints for explaining ethnicity: that of the primordialists, which argues for the thousand years of existence of modern nations and their eternity, and that of the modernists, which sometimes presents nationalistic feelings as an entirely new, artificial phenomenon not justified by history. The happy medium is the so-called synthetic-ethnicist approach, which traces ethnic solidarity in parts of the world back over centuries, emphasizing that this was not typical of all representatives of indigenous populations but was, rather, mostly confined to nobles and clerical circles (Smith 1993: 3; Sheffer 1997: 17ff).

The modern ideology of nationalism obviously differs from traditional ethnic solidarity in that it strives for the sovereignty of peoples and equality of all representatives of an 'ethnie', as well as the bringing together of 'high' and 'low' culture. Finally, the state's frontiers are intended to correspond to the cultural and linguistic frontiers. In contrast, the ideals of ethnic solidarity had more to do with the division of classes within the ethnic community and were not necessarily directed against outside rulers.

Some experts distinguish between ethnic and civil nationalism, arguing that the civil variety is more rational and compatible with democracy whereas the ethnic variant is characterized by a dangerous insistence on common national forefathers and the struggle for racial and cultural purity, which causes it to produce conflicts. In reality, most of the civilly defined nations also have a number of ethnic foundations, that is to say that in determining what constitutes the nation, a number, if not all (blood or common ancestor) ethnic components (language, religion, common heritage and other aspects of culture) are cited. According to Anthony D. Smith (1993: 9), the 'ethnic element was always present' in the first Western European forms of nationalism, which were of a civil nature, 'if only through identification of the nation with the ideal of popular sovereignty'.

A new wave of national awareness associated with the collapse of the Communist Bloc has a clearly ethnic characteristic. Ethnic memories alone form the grounds for various Eastern European nationalists to demand independence for their respective communities. Fortunately, not all the leaders of the new ethnically defined states emphasize the necessity of racial and cultural purity for their nations.[2] Whether a policy of 'ethnic cleansing', which is part of the logic of many ethnic nationalists, is pursued in a consistent manner depends on a range of factors (Smith 1993: 8). A large number of ethnic nations attempt, for example, to incorporate methods of civil nationalism and enrich their cultural and ethnic characteristics with distinctive features of minorities living within their borders. Globalization factors are also absorbed from time to time. However, what really impedes peaceful relations between ethnic nations striving for independence is that a) in many cases there is more than one ethnic group that can link its past to a particular stretch of land and b) ethnic groups awake at different times and draw inspiration from examples of their own, belated modernization. Previously passive minorities then suddenly start fighting for their share of a world of independent nation-states. Such demands by ethnic minorities awaking late in the day lead to radical ethnic resentments among the representatives of the ethnic majority of a given state, thus undermining the prospects of liberal-democratic development – sometimes in an entire region, as happened in the case of the former Yugoslavia.

Civilizing ethnic nationalism   What is the way out of the vicious circle that so often results from ethnically founded nationalism? Is there any possibility of planting a liberal democracy on the soil of ethno-national convictions, which is the only basis for long-lasting internal and external peace? The answer is in principle 'yes', because there is no alternative: the world will essentially remain a multi-ethnic jigsaw puzzle for the foreseeable future. Consequently one general recipe is a 'shift in political culture' and 'legal and institutional innovations to foster accommodation and mutual security among different national and ethnic groups' (Diamond 1996: 11). It is almost impossible to give a more precise and, at the same time, universal recommendation because of the unique nature of each of the ethnic histories.

One thing is evident, however: where a state needs legitimacy, there is no sense in politicians fighting ethnic nationalism, as that signals the moment where nationalism becomes invincible. The complete transformation of ethnic nationalism into civic nationalism, that is to say reconciling the instinctive inclination towards an ethnic heritage and one's own language, appears to be impossible. It is better to modify the rhetoric and politics of liberal-democratic forces favouring civil nationalism in transitional democracies and to direct these towards 'civilizing and pacifying' ethnic nationalism. Although there are various techniques available for satisfying ethnic groups engaged in dispute, it is extremely risky to generalize these. In some cases, it may be possible to integrate ethnic minorities into the dominant ethnic culture of a given state easily and peacefully. International activities in the sense of an 'early warning system' can be artificial and counterproductive in this instance by virtue of their unleashing emotions. If not only politicians but also political analysts and anthropologists reach the view that a particular ethnic minority is developing into an ethnic community with its own claims to an ethnic nation, the *unionist state* should be transformed into a *common state*.

Should this fail and should the possible loss of stability and democracy be greater than the pursuit of unity, the difficult process of division should be commenced. One point, in particular, must be heeded in such cases: the ethnic majority generally links its own memories and ideals to the area of land predominantly populated by the minority. The majority will therefore regard it not only as legitimate but, for reasons of moral and material satisfaction, also as necessary to regain at least a certain piece of territory in that part of the country. It is important to find solutions that are specific and unique to the case in question. In this way, a formerly dominant ethnic community can be granted sovereignty over its 'sacred sites'. 'Graded election systems' are also conceivable, as used in Switzerland, for example, when the Jura region separated from the canton of Berne.

Although it is made responsible for a multitude of sins, it is hardly possible, in general terms, to separate nationalism from democracy if we understand democracy not as a series of institutions but, rather, as an ideology of its own that invokes the sovereignty of the individual as well as of a people. Although the search for democracy may have preceded the emergence of modern nations, 'it is as if we have been dealing with twin concepts that would not be dissociated: the territorial nation and sovereignty of people' (Daniel 2000: 82). If nationalism is officially ignored, it will still find its way into the population, but could fall into 'dirty' hands.

It remains the eternal task of all politicians and other leaders to hold the 'twin brothers' of democracy and nationalism together: protecting democrats against disregard by collective entities while, at the same time, stopping populist nationalists from pursuing ethnic purity and xenophobia. In this context, the cultural characteristics and identity traits of a community must be gradually adapted to the impetus of globalization and a modern understanding of human rights. At the same time liberal-democratic ideals must also be brought closer to local views and perceptions. Instead of insistently declaring ethnic prejudices, myths and the iniquity of ethnic solidarity to be outdated and irrational, greater attention should be paid to finding proof and examples of respect for universal values and multi-ethnicity in the local culture. The nation is halfway between the individual and the universal and as such only can enable the universal to take root (Daniel 2000: 87).

As Larry Diamond puts it: the consolidation [of democracy] is the process of achieving broad and deep legitimation (Diamond 1996: 11).

The legitimacy of a state – and, in specific terms, democratic statehood – derives from a wide variety of sources. Security, prosperity, effectiveness and fair treatment of its citizens contribute towards this manifestation. Last but not least, cautiously keeping the dialectically linked forces of democracy and nationalism in step with each other is also part of the legitimation of a concrete national project.

Nationalism and conflicts between minorities By virtue of its freeing the ground for anti-Western sentiments and protecting corrupt public officials and/or criminals, the ethnic nationalism in Georgia is presently one of the reasons for the brutal conflict with Abkhazian and Ossetian minorities, which respond in the same manner. However, if nationalism has so far been a weapon of the enemies of democracy and human rights, who have been able to hide behind ethnically mobilized masses, democrats should now defeat their opponents with their own weapons. Democrats should change their tactics *vis-à-vis* ethnic nationalism and attempt to civilize it. Summed up briefly, they should find a formula to turn the ethno-cultural emotions rooted so deeply in the Georgian soul into a constructive element of democracy instead of making them a weapon against it. First, all possible efforts should be directed towards seeing ethnic identity as a cultural entity, recognizing the tradition of coexistence and not helping to confuse identity with racial purity.

The Georgian model of the convergence of ethnic emotions and liberal-democratic ideology can take root if historical facts are sought; for example an ethnic culture and ethic that support and propagate the ideal of individual liberty and tolerance and create or revive appropriate ethnic myths. Democratic politicians should not allow themselves to be taken in by the still widespread modernistic approach of nationalism, which contends that ethno-national solidarity is an entirely modern phenomenon.

The nineteenth-century art inspired by Georgian nationalism contains, for example, truly great works in which the individual fights for his 'foreign' friend and against the strict rules as well as the exclusiveness of the community. Also remarkable is the fact that the Georgian nobility, one of the sources of the ethnic genesis, very rarely paid any heed to the purity of ethnic blood.

Instead of fighting against the legacy of the nationalist ideology of the nineteenth century and accusing it of being outdated, it should be stressed that even the founder of the modern Georgian nation, Ilia Chavchavadze, had a good share of 'Armenian' blood in his veins. He spoke out in favour of the homeland, language and faith, regarding them as the nation's supports – he did not insist on the question of blood. At the same time, Chavchavadze, like many other Georgian nationalists of the nineteenth century, considered Muslim Georgians to be part of the nation, thus even abandoning the ideal of the 'purity of faith' in favour of nation-building.

Georgia's ethnic democracy should develop the following stance towards other well-developed ethnic communities on Georgian territory: no fear of modern techniques of territorially or culturally based division of power, and acceptance of a concordance democracy and/or federalism in the Swiss or Dutch sense, whereby the role of central government is to ensure protection using all suitable means. Otherwise, 69 per cent of Georgia's population could be pushed in the direction of undemocratic ethno-nationalism or be left to political nihilism, which is no less dangerous. Should the advantage of the state's territorial integrity substantially outweigh the cost of security, stability, development and even independence in a particular part of the country, and should the benefit of territorial integrity also cause prolonged military conflicts with virtually the entire minority with no prospect of reconciliation (as in the case of the Israelis and Arabs), a division of the disputed territory could then be considered. The justification in this context may be that the disputed land is 'sacred' in the perception of both identities and both ethnic communities can lay claim to a physical part of it. Only under such conditions can ethnic groups waging war with each other save face. However, the traditional argument of the indivisibility of internationally recognized borders should, of course, retain its importance insofar and for as long as it represents an effective framework for security and the settlement of conflicts.

(*Translation: Barry Stone*)

NOTES

1. Statement by the Minister of Health and Social Affairs to the Georgian parliament on 24 May 2001. More precise data are not available as the last census carried out in Georgia was in 1989.

2. In fact, all newly founded states are regarded as ethnic by Gabriel Sheffer (1997).

REFERENCES

Buzan, B., Ole Woever and J. de Wilde (1998) *A New Framework for Analysis*, London: Lynne Rienner.

CDFAIT (Canadian Department of Foreign Affairs and International Trade) (1999) 'Human security. Safety for people in a changing world', *Reading Materials of the Executive Course*, 01–1, Garmisch Partenkirchen: George Marshall Center.

Daniel, J. (2000) 'Democracy and nation', in M. F. Plattner and J. C. Espada (eds), *The Democratic Intervention*, Baltimore, MD: Johns Hopkins University Press.

Darchiashvili, D. (1997) 'Georgia – the search for state security', *Caucasus Working Papers*, Center for International Security and Arms Control, Stanford University.

— (2000) 'Trends of strategic thinking in Georgia: achievements, problems and prospects', in G. K. Cassady Craft, S. A. Jones and M. Beck (eds), *Crossroads and Conflict: Security and Foreign Policy in the Caucasus and Central Asia*, London and New York: Routledge, pp. 66–74.

Diamond, L. (1996) 'Is the third wave over?', *Journal of Democracy*, 7 (3) (July).

Donnelly, C. (2000–01) 'Rethinking security', *NATO Review*, 48 (Winter): 32–4.

Losaberidze, D. and K. Kikabidze (2000) 'Institutionalism and clientelism in Georgia', *UNDP Discussion Papers*, 3, Tbilisi, Georgia.

OSCE (2001) *Current Media Situation in Georgia*, Report of the OSCE Representative on Freedom of the Media, Vienna, 16 March.

Republic of Georgia (2000) *The Main Directions of the National Anti-Corruption Program of Georgia*, pamphlet, Tbilisi, 31 October.

Sheffer, G. (1997) 'The security of small ethnic states: a counter neo-realist argument', in Efraim Inbar and G. Sheffer (eds), *The National Security of Small States in a Changing World*, London and Portland, OH: Frank Cass.

Smith, A. D. (1993) 'The ethnic sources of nationalism', in *Survival*, 35 (1) (Spring): 48–62.

SIX

The Central American Conflict System: External Players and Changing Violence

SABINE KURTENBACH

§ In the 1980s Central America was one of the world's trouble-spots in which long-standing conflicts were linked with the confrontation between the USA and the Soviet Union. Following over a decade of violence and devastation, the three wars on the isthmus – in Nicaragua, El Salvador and Guatemala – were brought to a negotiated end with the support of a number of internal and external players, with the guerrilla combatants turning in their weapons and the armed forces sharply reducing the size of their forces.

The development of Central America is often cited as a success story because it is marked, at least at first glance, by peace and democratization. Despite indisputable progress, however, numerous problems remain unsolved, and these give reason for doubt as to the sustainability and stability of peace and democracy in the region.

Peace – and this goes for the entire sub-region (including Belize, Costa Rica and Honduras) – means above all the termination and absence of armed political conflict. Yet violence has not declined in Central America – on the contrary, since the mid-1990s the region overall has been experiencing a dramatic increase in violent crime. In the second half of the 1990s, for instance, more people died by violent means in El Salvador than during the war there. Viewed in terms of murders per 100,000 of its population, El Salvador has at times ranked ahead even of Colombia as the world's most violent country.[1] In other words, what we see in Central America is not so much pacification and a winding down of social conflict than a transformation of the form of violence encountered there. While in the 1970s and 1980s violence was politically motivated, the only collective use of violence today is by

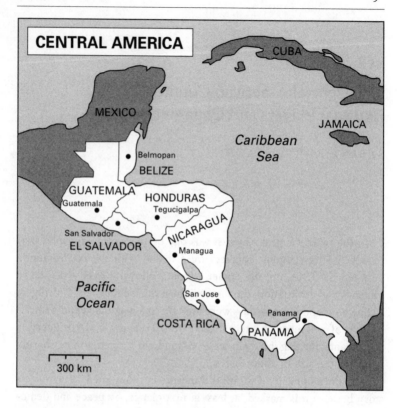

organized criminal groups. Most violence today, however, is individualized. The main causes, though, have, at least materially, largely remained the same: the poverty and the marginalization of large segments of the population are the breeding grounds of both old and new forms of violence. Moreover, continuing violence is also laying bare some basic deficiencies of the peace processes in the region.

THE CENTRAL AMERICAN CONFLICT SYSTEM

Even though the civil wars of the 1980s were internal armed conflicts that had little to do with one another, the unfolding of these conflicts was marked by a number of common features, and their internal and external dynamics showed a large measure of reciprocal influence. This is mirrored in the traditionally close interrelationship between developments in the region, which, during the period of Spanish colonial rule, was known as the Captaincy General of Guatemala.[2] Furthermore, key external players have viewed Central America as an entity.

The common features of these armed conflicts must be sought at the structural level, and their causes may be summed up under the headings of: extreme social inequality, the lack of political participation, and governmental repression. The dynamics that led to an escalation of the political violence and to war in Nicaragua, Guatemala and El Salvador was at that time, however, strongly influenced by concrete developments and experiences at the national level.[3] It is by no means a chance fact of history that Nicaragua was the first of these countries to experience the formation of a broad-based opposition movement far wider in scope than the armed groups active in the 1960s. In 1979, the movement toppled the corrupt Somoza regime within weeks and without the use of excessive violence. From 1981 onwards, however, a heterogeneous alliance, massively backed by the USA and ranging from former Somozistas to disgruntled Sandinistas, waged war on the revolutionary project launched by the Sandinistas, and the 1980s were again marked by armed conflict.

In El Salvador, on the other hand, the organization of armed resistance to the authoritarian government coalition, consisting of the military and the country's oligarchy, was a comparatively lengthy process, one inextricably bound up with the 1932 massacre in which over ten thousand people lost their lives. At that juncture, the government used massive repression to stave off an attempted coup staged by a small, poorly organized group associated with the Communist Party; this repression was mainly felt by the country's small Indio farmers. This traumatic experience prevented any further attempts to organize the marginalized population politically, especially in rural areas. It was only in the 1980s that El Salvador, the region's smallest country, saw the rise of Latin America's undoubtedly best-organized and strongest guerrilla movement. It took massive intervention by the USA on behalf of the government to prevent a guerrilla military victory.

Beginning in 1960, Guatemala experienced the region's longest and bloodiest armed conflict, in which considerable sections of the Indio majority of the population participated in the 1970s. The key factor behind this war, which in part escalated to the point of genocide, was the issue of ethnic diversity and / or equal rights for the entire population.

The peace negotiations and the agreements reached on 29 December 1996, which have to a large extent yet to be implemented, were also largely defined by this issue.

Developments in Nicaragua were a decisive factor in the regionalization and internationalization of these various conflicts in the 1980s. On the one hand, following the overthrow of the Somoza regime, these developments constituted the point of reference for the opposition movements in El Salvador and Guatemala. The opposition movements in these countries hoped for swift progress following Nicaragua's example. On the other hand, the events in Nicaragua decisively influenced the policies of the governments in power both in these countries and the USA – even before Ronald Reagan had been elected.

In view of the clash between the superpowers in the 1980s, which saw the policy of détente supplanted by a new 'Cold War', counterinsurgency assumed paramount priority for the governments concerned. Another exacerbating factor was that the Castro regime in Cuba proved to be tenacious and was able to assert itself in the region as a countermodel to the élites backed by the USA. This interlinking of developments in Nicaragua, El Salvador, and – to a lesser extent – Guatemala also drew Honduras and Costa Rica into the conflict. The US government made Honduras its central military base for operations in the region, and Costa Rica, which had abolished its own army in 1948, was unable to evade this pull towards militarization.[4]

In 1983, the tense situation in the region nearly led to an outright war between Honduras and Nicaragua. It took a resolute intervention by their neighbouring countries, Mexico, Panama, Colombia and Venezuela – which had, in January 1983, joined forces to form the Contadora Group – to prevent any further escalation of the conflict. In the following years, the group strove to bring about a regional peace agreement. Even though, in the end, this initiative proved unsuccessful, the three years of effort that went into it were undoubtedly instrumental in laying the groundwork for the so-called Guatemala Agreement signed in August 1987. The regional peace treaty made it possible to reduce the armed conflicts to the national level, thus preparing the ground for attempts to settle them. One of the central mechanisms provided for was a ban on support for insurgent groups fighting against the governments of neighbouring countries. The signatory governments furthermore committed themselves to engaging in talks, at least with the unarmed opposition, and to work towards a ceasefire at the earliest opportunity with the armed groups involved. The Agreement was the first step in a peace process that led, between 1990 and 1996, to the termination of all three armed conflicts at the negotiating table.

THE PACIFICATION OF CENTRAL AMERICA

Even though the national dimension of the conflicts moved into the foreground after 1987, the peace agreements would not have been possible without the strong commitment of numerous external players.

While in the early stages various National Reconciliation Commissions played the main role in the initial talks held between national governments and armed and unarmed opposition groups, these efforts were later, after some attempts to block them, succeeded in El Salvador and Guatemala by UN mediation efforts.[5] The individual peace agreements were to a large extent conditioned by specific internal political constellations as well as by the relative strengths and weaknesses of the warring parties. But at the same time – and in a way resembling the situation pertaining during the escalation of the conflicts – reciprocal regional effects and, in some cases, 'learning effects' were also in play here. Once again, Nicaragua was in the vanguard of regional developments.

As early as January 1988, President Daniel Ortega unexpectedly announced his willingness to negotiate directly with the Contra forces. Apart from persistent international pressure, one crucial factor was the absence of any major military threat from the Contras since the Honduran government had discontinued its logistical support in accordance with the Guatemala Agreement. Following some initial snags – a meeting held at the end of January in Costa Rica producing no results – in March 1988 the parties to the conflict consented, in the Sapoa Agreement, to a 60-day armistice. This ceasefire, which was, despite some major problems, on the whole respected, made progress possible in other areas too. While the Contra groups continued to refuse to lay down their arms, the civilian opposition reached agreement with the Sandinista government to hold early elections in February 1990. This split between the civilian and military opposition further weakened the Contras. The loss of the elections by the Sandinistas and the accession to office of a new president, Violeta Chamorro, then led to a final delegitimization of the armed conflict in Nicaragua, even though pacification of the country was still to be some time in coming.

The end of the war in Nicaragua differs in some important respects from later developments in El Salvador and Guatemala, and these differences must essentially be sought in the structure of the conflict in Nicaragua:

- Due to the change in government, the post-Sapoa process was no longer rooted in an agreement between the original conflict parties and now entailed negotiations between the Contra groups and their former civilian allies.
- The fragmentation of the Contras prevented the emergence of a centralized peace agreement. Instead, there were a total of 40 agreements with different Contra factions. Unlike the guerrilla groups in El Salvador and Guatemala, the Contras, owing to their highly heterogeneous make-up, were unable to hammer out a uniform (party-linked) political agenda.
- The talks did not include any political agreements on the country's future development. The agreements focused on demobilization involving material concessions aimed at ending the armed struggle.
- In this case, the international community played no mediating role, but a mission of observers from the Organization of American States (OAS) was dispatched to monitor the agreements.

In spite of their evident limitations, the dynamics of the developments in Nicaragua placed both the governments and opposition groups in El Salvador and Guatemala under pressure to succeed. In both of these countries there had been, in the 1980s, some initial national mediation initiatives, although they had failed to bring about an end to the armed conflicts. In El Salvador, national peace efforts spearheaded by the Catholic Church collapsed when, in November 1989, killer commandos linked to the country's armed forces brutally murdered six Jesuits from the Central American University, as well as their housekeeper and her daughter.

At the same time, guerrilla forces launched a major new offensive, bringing the affluent neighbourhoods of the capital, San Salvador, under their control for a number of days. It was this military escalation that brought home to all the parties involved that they were faced with a military stalemate that no party could break in its own favour, so in

December 1989 they called upon the United Nations to mediate in the conflict. The following two years saw the emergence of a number of partial agreements which came into effect following the official signing of the Peace Agreement in January 1992. The only agreement to take effect immediately was the Agreement on Human Rights signed in 1991.

In Guatemala, the situation was different for various reasons. The relative strengths of the conflict parties were very different from those of the parties involved in El Salvador. There was no stalemate, although in political and military terms the Guatemalan guerrillas were not as isolated as the Nicaraguan Contras, which enabled them to assert substantive political demands. Following some initial national peace efforts, which, as in El Salvador, took place under the auspices of the Catholic Church, the international community here too became increasingly involved in the search for peace, starting in 1989/90. But it was only after six years of tough negotiations, repeatedly marked by setbacks, that, in December 1996, Central America's most protracted armed struggle came to an end with the signing of a peace agreement.

The peace process in Central America, nearly ten years in the making, is seen internationally as one of the few successes in pacifying a world region. This is essentially due to the interplay between various national, regional and international factors: at the national level it became evident at the end of the 1980s that none of the armed players was in a position to achieve their aims by military means. This led to a strategic stalemate between the conflict parties that, according to the theorem of the 'ripe moment' (William Zartmann), must be seen as the most important precondition for success in mediation efforts. At the regional level, a minimum consensus was reached in 1987 with the signing of the Guatemala Agreement. Its central elements included mutual recognition of the governments in power and renunciation of any support for attempts to overthrow governments in neighbouring countries. Internationally, various steps were undertaken that had positive effects on the pacification of Central America. These included the rapprochement between the USA and the Soviet Union in the second half of the 1980s and the end of the Cold War, dramatically expressed in the fall of the Berlin Wall in 1989. This spelled the end of a momentous dynamic that had long hung over and masked national developments. In addition, the domestic problems besetting the second Reagan administration – one need only think here of Iran-Contragate[6] – also entailed positive effects to the extent that they undermined the options available to the USA to exert pressure on its Central American allies and increased the latter's political leeway.

In all three countries, agreements were signed on two issues: first, on the processes of the demobilization and reintegration of the armed opposition, as well as the monitoring of the parties by international organizations; second, on the opening of these countries' political systems and the redefinition of national civilian–military relations. This led to the start of a series of legal and constitutional reforms that provided for civilian control over the armed forces and a sharper delineation of military and police powers, numerous changes to electoral law, and the emergence of a strengthened independent judiciary, a development that has gone some way towards re-establishing the rule of law. In the case of Nicaragua, though, these issues were not the object of negotiations between the Sandinista government and the Contra leadership, but were dealt with in a so-called 'transition protocol' between the Sandinista government and the government of Violeta Chamorro, who was elected president in February 1990.

The central issue of demobilization and reintegration was the confinement of armed factions to clearly defined zones, where they had to hand in their weapons in the presence of international observers. In return, these groups were to be provided with material support and access to the reintegration measures agreed upon, whether in the form of training programmes or in the transfer of land titles. At the same time, the governments involved undertook to cut back the force levels of the government security apparatus.

In El Salvador and Guatemala, other issues and problems also came in for discussion. Respect for human rights, in particular, and the approach to be adopted in dealing with human rights violations committed during the war assumed an important role in this context. The fact that the Agreements on Human Rights were signed and put into effect had, in both cases, the effect of a confidence-building measure, one that served in both countries as a basis for the presence there of the United Nations, which monitored compliance with the Agreements[7] with the aid of its ONUSAL (Observación de Naciones Unidas en El Salvador) and MINUGUA (Misión de Naciones Unidas para Guatemala) missions.

TRANSFORMATION OF VIOLENCE

Despite the undisputed successes the parties have achieved in de-mobilizing ex-combatants and demilitarizing Central American societies, as well as in opening up the political systems under consideration here, the major underlying causes of conflict persist in the region as a whole. This is one of the reasons why violence, rather than declining, has assumed new forms. The entire region has experienced a wave of violence and crime that goes far beyond what was observed during the immediate post-conflict period; this now threatens to blight these societies for an unforeseeable period of time (Chinchilla 1997; Call 2000; IIDH 2000).

Violence has been exacerbated by the large quantities of arms remaining in circulation. They are in the hands not only of ex-combatants, but of the civilian population. Despite international monitoring, insufficient progress has been made in collecting, scrapping or legalizing these weapons. For Nicaragua, the OAS Verification Commission assumes that every Contra member was in possession of three to four weapons. Yet 22,500 registered Contras handed over only 17,000 weapons, and these were for the most part old, rusty and in very poor working order. According to military information, 130,000 weapons were handed over in connection with subsequent buy-back and collection programmes. But there are still huge numbers of weapons in the hands of the ordinary members of the civilian population, sporadic groups and gangs, a state of affairs that requires a constant renewal of effort and fresh initiatives. For El Salvador, it is estimated that some 300,000 weapons are in circulation; according to the Guatemalan defence ministry, the figure is 500,000, of which 300,000 have been duly registered. Numerous buy-back programmes in recent years have proved unable to do much to address the problem.

Easy access to weapons is fuelling organized and unorganized crime in the region. A second factor must be seen in the lack of prospects for many ex-combatants – both former guerrillas and soldiers – as well as for large segments of the population at large to earn a livelihood without recourse to violence. Pacification and democratization have done little to address the basic social problems facing the region as a whole; indeed, the neoliberal reforms undertaken in recent years have even exacerbated them. In the 1990s, most countries in the region achieved impressive macro-economic growth rates ranging from 7 per cent (Nicaragua, 1999) to a peak of 8.3 per cent (Costa Rica, 2000), although – with the exception of Costa Rica – this development has been accompanied by persistently large and growing inequalities in the distribution of wealth and opportunities (Minkner-Bünjer 2000).

Some enclaves of prosperity in large towns are more than counterbalanced by widespread and extreme poverty in outlying metropolitan areas, as well as in the countryside. The only exception is Costa Rica. Here 'only' 17 per cent of households live below the poverty line, while the figures for neighbouring countries are: El Salvador 50 per cent, Honduras 65 per cent, Nicaragua 74 per cent, and Guatemala a staggering 86 per cent.[8] In the region as a whole, the downsizing of government machinery and the privatization of state-owned companies have led to job cuts of 15 per cent in the public sector (Sojo 2000: 43ff). Unemployment has risen further after the demobilization of some 150,000 former combatants from among the insurgents and the armed forces.

Against this background, Central America became an increasingly important player in international drug-trafficking in the 1990s, and has become an important transit region for drug shipments from the Andean countries to the USA and Europe. According to the US government, 54 per cent of the cocaine reaching the USA is routed via Mexico and Central America.[9] Drug consumption has also risen in the Central American countries themselves, resulting in increasing drug-related crime.

Apart from these material factors, the persistent violence in Central America also has a psychological aspect. Since – despite the efforts of various investigative commissions – past atrocities have so far been dealt with only in a rudimentary fashion, impunity is widespread, the judiciary continues to be weak, and the threshold of violence is low in day-to-day conflicts.

The growth in crime levels thus graphically illustrates the interaction between different problem complexes in post-conflict societies. Without any real prospects for people to earn an honest living, and in a culture prone to settle conflicts by violence, the use of weapons has developed a logic of its own. If the government takes a lenient approach, other groups will be rational in adopting this pattern of behaviour. If, on the other hand, the government responds with repressive measures, this will tend to strengthen the influence of the security forces, endangering any redefinition of civilian–military relations and the aim of subordinating the military to civilian authorities. What is called for is both a comprehensive reform of the entire security sector and the establishment of mechanisms and instruments sanctioned by the rule of law. Finally, extreme inequality, the breeding ground of violence, must be redressed. In other words: only if the old causes of conflict are dealt with constructively will the pacification of Central America prove durable and extend beyond the mere absence of war.

EXTERNAL PLAYERS

Regional and international players have had a key influence on the negotiations and peace processes in Central America. In both El Salvador and Guatemala, the various activities of internal and external mediators were remarkably well coordinated. Both the UN and other external players (such as the 'Group of Friends of the Peace Process', and also the US government) exerted substantial pressure on the parties to the conflicts in the final phase of each of the peace processes with a view to preventing a failure or breakdown of negotiations. To prevent this they threatened to impose sanctions – for instance, an end to economic and military aid – or, to encourage a cooperative stance, they promised aid for reconstruction and development cooperation.

In monitoring compliance with the agreements as well as in financing reconstruction, the international community has likewise played an important, though not altogether unproblematic, role. In Nicaragua, for instance, the mandate of the OAS monitoring mission was explicitly designed to protect the demobilized Contra groups, and so it cannot be seen as a neutral authority (Spalding 2000). While the formulation of the ONUSAL and MINUGUA mandates was more balanced, in both cases criticism was voiced of an allegedly one-sided pro-government stance. The governments involved were in any case in a better position when the conflicts ended: instead of being integrated into new security forces, the guerrillas were for the most part disarmed and demobilized.[10] For them, this meant giving up their most important means of exerting political pressure, and here they were largely forced to rely on the goodwill of their governments and the international monitoring missions. At the same time, the multilateral missions, unable to impose concrete sanctions, were reduced to exerting whatever pressure they could or appealing to world public opinion. Moreover, the principle of national sovereignty, and other legal and political considerations, have made intervention by the international community contingent on a ceasefire and an end of open hostilities. This amounts to a tendentious reduction of the concept of peace to the absence of war – an approach that is problematic for a comprehensive peace-building process, as it is averse to the objective of employing civilian means for addressing the causes of conflict.

Developments in Central America are also a good example of the counterproductive results generated by the diverse objectives pursued by different international players: while the UN and its development programme were mainly focused on consolidation of the peace, other players – above all international financial institutions such as the International Monetary Fund or the World Bank – calling for economic structural adjustment and setting their priorities accordingly, have on the whole tended *de facto* more to obstruct than to facilitate the process of peace consolidation.

In the case of El Salvador, this is obvious: the policy of macro-economic structural adjustment led to a situation in which government largely withdrew from social policy, delegating it to international partners in development cooperation. A UNDP (1995) study explicitly noted that after 1992 the Salvadorian government accorded priority to structural adjustment rather than to reconstruction. Here, the donors involved in development cooperation could have demanded more of their partners. Since 1992, individual attempts to establish conditionalities have foundered in view of large inflows of development cooperation funds. This has enabled the Salvadorian government to choose its donors according to the most suitable, or minimal, set of conditions attached. In fact, numerous donors – including the EU – were not interested in attaching any conditionalities at all. During the 1990s most donors involved in development cooperation reverted to their traditional lines of cooperation, with peace consolidation receding further and further into the background. As long as the donors fail to reach agreement on common priorities favouring comprehensive peace-building, the recipient governments will be able to push through their own agendas, which are for the most part keyed to day-to-day political interests.

THE CENTRAL AMERICAN STATE AS A PEACE-BUILDING PLAYER

Despite the great number and diversity of international influences at work here, the individual state in fact still remained the central player in the peace-building process. This meant that progress depended on two factors: first, the will and ability of individual governments to reach out beyond their own clientele, and crafting a policy of domestic social integration; second, the ability of the political opposition as well as of other social groups to organize their interests and represent them *vis-à-vis* state and government. There is no doubt that in recent years Central America has made progress in both areas in connection with the democratization process. At the same time, however, little progress has been made in the arena of politics, which has continued to be dominated by personalism and clientelism: the old ruling élites, for instance the military, still have a kind of veto power that enables them to block any comprehensive social reforms. Similar developments in Nicaragua and Guatemala in recent years must be seen as particularly critical. In Nicaragua, the leader of the Sandinistas, Daniel Ortega (revolutionary leader and the country's president in the 1980s) and the leader of the anti-Sandinistas, Arnoldo Alemán (president since 1996), fight bitterly in public, while working hand in hand at other levels to block the emergence of any independent political forces. Since President Alfonso Portillo came to power in January 2000, Guatemala has been experiencing an ongoing – partly open, partly latent – power struggle within the ruling party, between the president and Efraín Ríos Montt, the former dictator and current president of the parliament. How this struggle will end, and where it will take the country, is at present an open question. The activities of death squads, once again on the increase, give little reason for optimism.

Neither in the individual countries in question nor at regional level has any noteworthy headway been made in defining and working out a common 'national project'. This would require the various social players to reach agreement on the future development of a given country or the region as a whole. The peace agreements can be no more than a starting point here. It is of the utmost importance to implement and further develop the ideas and ideals set out in them. In Guatemala, for instance, equal rights for the Maya peoples as well as a definition of the country as a multicultural society represent a fundamental break with the past. So far, however, little tangible progress has been made here, and this is leading to frustration and disappointment.

In recent years, at least, a few steps have been taken towards the renewal and reform of governmental institutions in Central America. In both political and economic terms, the municipal level has been upgraded politically throughout the region as a whole. While, up to the 1980s, nearly all decisions – including the hiring of teachers – were taken at the national level, in the later 1980s and 1990s democratization processes contributed to the transfer of greater responsibility, and in some cases more resources, to the region's municipalities. This has given the organization of the state a new dimension that may be termed 'territorial'. Carlos Sojo (2000: 24ff) refers to this as the socio-territorial dimension of state reform. It is precisely in the process of economic globalization that players at local level could play a central role in economic development. Furthermore, thanks to the lower degree of complexity of politics and administration here, the municipal level is far more transparent since citizens and government officials are more accountable here than they are at national level.

The municipal level is for many reasons of crucial importance to the development of efficient, transparent and democratic governance, and has a decisive role to play in the concrete process of peace-building: villages, communities and towns are the places in which the population

- looks for the satisfaction of its basic needs (housing, food, jobs);
- experiences social problems and their consequences; such as escalating social violence and crime; and
- exercises the rights to participation it has gained in the framework of democratization.

A positive assessment of the potential at local level should, however, not be allowed to give rise to a new 'small-is-beautiful' dogma that pins all of the population's hopes and expectations on municipalities. Grassroots nation-building will have a chance of success only if the appropriate accompanying measures are implemented at national level. Municipalities are in need of sufficient funds if they are to tackle problems at the local level (such as transportation infrastructure, housing, wastewater disposal). Here, in the framework of development cooperation, the international community could provide an important contribution, one that could contribute to generating a positive impact on democracy, participation and transparency. It is precisely at the local level that the years to come will show how far-reaching the process of change has been in the countries of Central America.

(*Translation: Paul Knowlton*)

NOTES

1. For 1995, the Pan-American Health Organization indicated the number of murders as 156 per 100,000 of the population, while the corresponding figure for Colombia was 'only' 75, *El Tiempo*, 10 August 1997. As a rule, figures above 14 are regarded as high.

2. Besides Guatemala, Honduras, El Salvador, Nicaragua and Costa Rica, these include today's Mexican state of Chiapas – which joined Mexico when the latter became independent – and Belize, which, as British Honduras, was split off from the Spanish possessions in the nineteenth century, a fact reflecting Britain's growing influence in the Caribbean in the nineteenth century.

3. These factors may also be demonstrated for Honduras, although the conflicts did not escalate there. The main reason for this was a more flexible government distributional policy and the opposition's lower level of organization. Since the 1950s, developments in Costa Rica have been a special case within the Central American context (Kurtenbach 2000).

4. A development typical of this situation was the sharp rise in military spending in the region between 1980 and 1983, as well as the increase in US military aid for its allies in El Salvador and Honduras (data in Kurtenbach 1996). Even Costa Rica militarized the police forces to some extent.

5. On the peace process in general, see, among others, Child 1992, Dunkerley (1993); on El Salvador, see Montgomery 1995; on Guatemala, see Jonas 2000; and on the role of civil society, see Kurtenbach 2000a.

6. The Iran-Contragate scandal saw White House officials around Oliver North using drug shipments to fund arms deliveries from Iran to the Nicaraguan Contras. This was a highly sensitive matter, not only because of the drugs involved, but also on account of the then extremely poor relations between the Reagan administration and the Islamic regime in power in Iran.

7. In El Salvador these were the San José Agreement (26 July 1990) and the Mexico Agreement (27 April 1991); in Guatemala the Comprehensive Agreement on Human Rights in Guatemala (29 March 1994). On the work of the various international monitoring missions, see Lincoln and Sereseres (2000); Holiday and Stanley (2000) and Jonas (2000a).

8. Figures from FUSADES (Fundación Salvadoreña para el Desarrollo), cited from Minkner-Bünjer (1999: 28). The data cover the period 1991–94. More recent figures for the region are unavailable, though some national data indicate that the basic problem remains serious.

9. Cf. the UN World Drug Report 2001, <www.undcp.org/adhoc/report_2001_06 26_1/report_200_06-26_1.pdf>.

10. The police forces of all three countries underwent restructuring processes, integrating opposition groups at different levels.

REFERENCES

Arnson, C. (ed.) (2000) *Comparative Peace Processes in Latin America*, Washington, DC and Stanford, CA: Woodrow Wilson Center Press.

Call, C. T. (2000) 'Sustainable development in Central America: the challenges of violence, injustice and insecurity', Centroamérica 2020, Working Paper No. 8, Hamburg, Institut für Iberoamerika-Kunde.

Child, J. (1992) *The Central American Peace Process 1983–1991: Sheathing Swords, Building Confidence*, Boulder, CO and Cologne: Lynne Rienner.

Chinchilla, L. (1997) *Taller Regional Sobre Seguridad Ciudadana y Capacitación Policial*, San José.

Dunkerley, J. (1993) *The Pacification of Central America*, London: Institute of Latin American Studies.

Holiday, D. and W. Stanley (2000) 'Under the best of circumstances: ONUSAL and the challenge of verification and institution building in El Salvador', in Tommie Sue Montgomery (ed.), *Peacemaking and Democratization in the Western Hemisphere*, Miami: North South Center Press, pp. 37–65.

IIDH (Instituto Interamericano de Derechos Humanos) (2000) *Seguridad Ciudadana en Centroamérica: Diagnóstico Sobre la Situación*, San José.

Jonas, S. (2000a) *Of Centaurs and Doves: Guatemala's Peace Process*, Boulder, CO: Westview Press.

— (2000b) 'Between two worlds: the United Nations in Guatemala', in Tommie Sue Montgomery (ed.), *Peacemaking and Democratization in the Western Hemisphere*, Coral Gables, FL: North-South Press, pp. 91–106.

Kurtenbach, S. (1996) *Zentralamerikas Militär zwischen Krieg und Frieden: Demilitarisierung und Neuordnung der zivil-militärischen Beziehungen*, Hamburg: Institut für Iberoamerika-Kunde (Arbeitsunterlagen und Diskussionsbeiträge, No. 31).

— (2000a) 'Costa Rica – intelligentes Konfliktmanagement als Basis friedlicher Entwicklung', *Die Friedens-Warte*, 75 (3–4): 371–87.

— (2000b) 'Zivilgesellschaft und zivile Konfliktregelung. Der Beitrag der Zivilgesellschaft zur Beendigung bewaffneter Konflikte', in Peter Hengstenberg, Karl Kohut and Günther Maihold (eds), *Zivilgesellschaft in Lateinamerika. Interessenvertretung und Regierbarkeit*, Frankfurt/Main: Vervuert, pp. 221–34.

Lincoln, J. K. and C. Sereseres (2000) 'Resetting the contras: the OAS Verification Commission in Nicaragua', in T. S. Montgomery (ed.), *Peacemaking and Democratization in the Western Hemisphere*, Miami: North South Center Press, pp. 17–35.

Maihold, G. and R. Córdova Macías (2000) *Democracia y ciudadanía en Centro-américa. Perspectivas hacia el 2020*, Hamburg: Institut für Iberoamerika-Kunde (Centroamérica 2020, Working Paper No. 9).

Minkner-Bünjer, Mechthild (1999) *Zentralamerika nach Hurrikan Mitch (II)*, Brennpunkt, No. 04–99, Hamburg: Institut für Iberoamerika-Kunde.

— (2000) 'Zentralamerikas wirtschaftliche Entwicklung: Bilanz und Herausforderungen angesichts der Globalisierung', in *Lateinamerika. Analysen-Daten-Dokumentation*, 44, Hamburg: Institut für Iberoamerika-Kunde.

Montgomery, T. S. (1995) *Revolution in El Salvador. From Civil Strife to Civil Peace*, 2nd enlarged edn, Boulder, CO and Cologne: Westview.

— (ed.) (2000) *Peacemaking and Democratization in the Western Hemisphere*, Miami: North South Center Press.

Sieder, R. (ed.) (1996) *Central America: Fragile Transition*, Basingstoke: Houndmills.

Sojo, C. (2000) *El Traje Nuevo del Emperador: La modernización del Estado en Centro-américa*, Hamburg: Institut für Iberoamerika-Kunde (Centroamérica 2020, Working Paper No. 6).

Spalding, R. J. (2000) 'From low-intensity war to low-intensity peace: the Nicaraguan peace process', in Cynthia Arnson (ed.), *Comparative Peace Processes in Latin America*, Washington, DC and Stanford, CA: Stanford University Press, pp. 31–64.

UNDP (United Nations Development Programme) (1995) *Ajuste hacia la Paz: La Política Económica y la Reconstrucción de Posguerra en El Salvador* (coord. James K. Boyce), San Salvador: UNDP.

A comprehensive bibliography on development in Central America can be found in *Lateinamerika. Analysen-Daten-Dokumentation*, 44. Hamburg: Institut für Iberoamerika-Kunde 2000.

SEVEN

Stagnant Transformation: Democratic Transition and Military Conversion in Guatemala

BERNARDO ARÉVALO DE LEÓN

§ In Guatemala the current relationship between society, the state and the military forces can be understood only in the light of the transition process that began in 1985, and in the texture of the power relations that developed during this process. Undoubtedly the opening (*apertura*) through which a society held in thrall by a military regime starts to move towards democratization is a decisive moment in terms of the institutional set-up of these relationships. Nevertheless, the determining factor of their final shape lies in the details of the specific resolution of each and every phase of the transition. This applies especially in a situation in which, as in Guatemala, this transformation implies a dual process: from authoritarianism to democracy, and from armed conflict to peace.

The democratic opening came in 1985 with the formation of a constitutional assembly responsible for the formulation of a constitution fit for a state that would be both democratic and uphold the rule of law. In contrast to other countries in the region, these developments had not been prompted by the authoritarian regime's failure to contain the demands for democratization emerging from civil society and political movements. Instead it was a deliberate decision by the military, which, no longer able simultaneously to fulfil the duties implicit in its direct handling of government and in waging the counter-insurgency campaign, decided to concentrate on the latter.[1]

The army's intention, though, amounted to a de-militarization of government without de-militarizing the actual exercise of political power (Varas 1991). As a matter of fact, the first civilian president of the transition period, the Christian Democrat Vinico Cerezo (1986–90), has indicated that, *vis-à-vis* the Armed Forces, he could exercise only 30 per cent of political power. The civilian–military relationship established at this point responded to the model of 'asymmetric adaptation', in which the army retains power of veto over crucial aspects of national policy (Varas 1988).

The coexistence of a democratization process with a counter-insurgency campaign under absolute control of the military implied the development of contradicting dynamics within the political system that were evident between 1986 and 1996. On the one hand, the army proclaimed a 'Thesis of National Stability' which, just like the preceding doctrine of National Security, referred to the 'enemy within': the guerrilla groups. This, in turn, served to justify the integration of all national institutions in the counter-insurgency effort, and the predominant role of the military in the state.

On the other hand, however, new opportunities for political expression appeared, and civil society revived around a political agenda over which the military no longer had control (Arévalo de León 1998a). With the reopening of the political systems, the political élite and civil society secured some room for democratic manoeuvre, successfully negotiating a gradual transfer of power from the military to the political office-holders. The end of the Cold War, with its significant ideological consequences (the obsolescence of National Security Doctrine) as well as new geostrategic considerations (the transformation of the hegemonic interests in Central America and the appearance of new international actors in the region) invigorated the role of civilian actors *vis-à-vis* the military and fostered better conditions for the democratization process (Huntington 1994; Torres Rivas 1994).

THE RETURN OF CIVILIAN POLITICS

This combination of factors gradually eroded the army's veto powers, enabling civilian politicians to overcome military resistance to any kind of political contact with the insurgency, and thus to initiate peace negotiations. At the same time, as reform-oriented, modernizing military officers held sway over hard-liners, the armed forces began to accept the legitimacy of civilian authority regarding the solution to the armed conflict (Gramajo 1995; Rosada 1999; Schirmer 1999).

In the end the military decided not only to accommodate to the inevitability of a negotiated solution to the conflict between the government and the insurgency, but also to accept the reduction of institutional prerogatives and privileges implicit in the redefinition of their role within a democratic state. Its ability to pace the rhythm of the negotiations from its position of influence within government, though, enabled it to manage this transformation. It was thus prepared in advance for a range of inevitable institutional reforms arising from the negotiations.[2] In consequence, the nature and scope of this redefinition of functions were not imposed by the political leadership and civil society, but were the result of a parallel, informal negotiation that took place within the context of the peace talks (Aguilera Peralta 1994; Arévalo de León 1998a; Rosada 1999). The existence of parallel processes of democratization, peace negotiations and military conversion within the context of a general transformation of the social and political structures of the country generated political dynamics beyond the control of any single actor. In consequence, transition developed gradually and incrementally, accelerated at critical junctures by a series of qualitative leaps. One such instance was the 1993 attempt by President Serrano Elias to monopolize power: his intention to dissolve parliament and the courts and acquire dictatorial powers mobilized various social and political forces (including the modernizing faction within the armed forces) behind the democratization process. They asserted themselves in collective political action, forcing Serrano Elias into exile and Congress to elect a new president (McCleary 1999).

This pattern, though, has resulted in a troubled and uncertain democracy. After decades of state terror, during which only a formal, hollow exercise of citizenship was possible, civil society emerged polarized and fragmented, with great difficulties in organizing itself effectively for political action and in articulating positions with the political élite.

The political élite, for their part, were unable to develop the quality of leadership that could provide a clear sense of direction to the political process. Many of the political parties and politicians that became key actors in the new, democratic electoral system had their roots in the hollow ritualistic practices of façade democracy (Solórzano 1987). Thus, from the first moments of transition, political parties continued to practise the type of clientelist, opportunist politics that inhibited the emergence of strong parties with sound ideological foundations. Both conditions – a fragmented civil society and weak, ephemeral political parties – have prevented the effective mediation of interests between society and the state.

PRECARIOUS DEMOCRACY IN A WEAK STATE

Guatemala already meets the minimal formal criteria for a democracy with regard to free and fair elections (Dahl 1971). But insofar as the democratization of a society implies not only the establishment of an electoral democracy but the actual transformation of power relationships in society, the process is far from completed. The weakness of democratic actors, the ineffectiveness of political parties and the continued adherence to a code of authoritarian values and practices have in effect caused a stagnation of the democratization process and a loss of direction. The institutional and legal framework of the country follows basic democratic criteria, but the political culture that social and political actors bring with them to the system remains largely influenced by authoritarian values and outlook. The result is dysfunctionality, ambiguity and recurrent political crisis. In other words, we have the hardware of democracy, but operate it with the software of authoritarianism.

The result is a precarious democracy within a weak state characterized by a chronic state of crisis. Development, security and integration remain unobtainable due to the state's inability to mobilize material and human resources. Lack of credibility undermines any attempt by state institutions to assume the role of government. Such a structurally weak state provides fertile ground for the power games of different social groups vying for hegemony; and in the presence of an authoritarian political culture, the resort to violence is a viable option.

Within this context, the military, by its very presence, remains a key player in the political arena. It can always intervene upon the invitation of civilian factions willing to activate the latent power in order to realize factional interests, or on its own initiative. A new definition of the relations between state, society and the armed forces must therefore secure not only the effective exclusion of the military from everyday political process, but the creation of conditions that make the resort to military force unviable even in situations of impaired governability.

The 1996 agreement defining the role of civilian authority and the function of the military (AFPC – Acuerdo de Fortalecimiento del Poder

Civil y Funciòn del Ejército en una Democracia) established basic parameters for this new relationship, basing it upon two pillars: first, the conversion of the structures, profile, orientation and values of the armed forces in accordance with the needs of a democratic state; second, the appropriation of requisite powers by civilian institutions responsible for the control, supervision and leadership of the armed forces.

However, the implementation of the principles of this and other agreements that are part of the Peace Accords has been slow and hesitant (MINUGUA 2000). In the five-year period since the signing of the 'Accord of Firm and Permanent Peace', the Guatemalan state has made little headway in securing the irreversible subordination of the military to the constitutional order. The civilian authorities have failed to develop a clear political strategy to promote military conversion and the development of mechanisms for effective democratic control. The problem was exacerbated by the failure in 1999 of the Referendum on constitutional reform, which included important changes to the Constitution on the issue of the role of the armed forces, derived from the AFPC (Arévalo de León 1999). In the absence of clear policy objectives and guidelines, the political decisions in response to specific questions threaten to undo the achievements of transition. There are several indications of this already: during the government of Alvaro Arzú (1996–2000) the military presidential security outfit (Estado Mayor Presidencial), which was the main operative centre of the counter-insurgency campaign during the armed confrontation and which the AFPC agreed should be dissolved, was brought back into action in the context of the government efforts to fight crime (Arévalo de León 1999). This same unit became, under the current administration of Alfonso Portillo, the operative centre and a cadre of retired army officers, highly influential in civilian and military matters and widely suspected of having strong links to organized crime.

THE CONTINUING 'RELATIVE AUTONOMY' OF THE MILITARY

While the authority of the president over the military has been robustly asserted on several occasions, systematic mechanisms for the supervision and control of the military are still not operational. Exercised more under the logic of 'Ceasarism' than following the principles of rule of law, presidential authority serves the interests of personalized power more than those of democratic institutional consolidation. Military subordination to civilian authority thus remains fragile: the military no longer exercise political control over the state, but civilian authorities do not exercise full, democratic, institutional control over the armed forces either. The lack of capacity of the civilian institutions remains a cause for concern: parliament has neither passed the requisite laws for military reform, nor undertaken its supervisory functions. Short of mainly vague and occasionally contradictory declarations by the political authorities, so far there has been no conceptualization of the reform process. This situation threatens to institutionalize a pattern of relative military autonomy within the state, with the armed forces affirming their active or passive role as a political actor in the country.

It should be noted that this is not the outcome of a successful campaign by the armed forces aimed at sabotaging the civilian authorities. Active resistance has so far been limited to a stated refusal to cooperate with the 'Commission for Historical Enlightenment', and sporadic protests by retired officers against the new, constitutional role of the armed forces. But the absence of a clear policy on the part of civilian authorities has left the nature and scope of military conversion in the hands of the armed forces themselves. Therein lies the origin of the problem. Although the military leadership recognized the need for institutional reform – including new military missions – as part of the Peace Accords, it could not envisage the complete subordination of the armed forces to government, parliament and the rule of law, to the extent that democracy requires.

This situation of military autonomy within the context of a weak state and a non-democratic political culture poses a potential threat to the sustainability of the democratization process itself. In the event of a possible crisis of governability, some factions within the government or within the opposition are liable to send out calls for a military intervention, and ask for the use of force to restore public order.

This possibility is not remote. Venezuela, Ecuador and Peru present recent instances, each one with its own characteristics, in which political crisis within fragile democracies led to the intervention of the military in politics, in alliance with civilian political actors. And not always, as political experience in Latin America shows, do the armed forces easily agree to return to barracks.

CONCLUSION

Three conclusions can be drawn from the above discussion. First, neither causes nor solutions for the intervention of the military in politics can be found solely in the organizational or sociological character of the armed forces, or in the political dynamics of specific moments in time. They are rather to be found in the structural nature of political institutions and culture of a country, and in the web of historically developed relationships between the military, the political institutions and society at large. For Guatemala, this implies that the risk of military intervention will not disappear until the need for coercive power as a resort to governability is uprooted. Deep, structural transformations in the political, economic, social and cultural structures of the country will be required for this, and the twin tracks of military conversion and civilian democratic control of the military are strategic roads necessary to inhibit any authoritarian temptations.

Second, in this endeavour the main responsibility falls upon the shoulders of the political élite. Civilian politicians must acquire the political and institutional capacity for designing and implementing adequate security, defence and military policies. The stagnation of the process of military conversion that followed the signature of the Peace Accords has been the result of their limitations in this respect.

This seems paradoxical, as the termination of the armed confrontation created favourable conditions for the uncurtailed exercise of power by the civilian authorities, best exemplified by the Partido de Avanzada Nacional (PAN), in power from 1996 to 2000. Political authorities of that period enjoyed conditions unparalleled before: full support of the powerful business community – the allies of the military during the counterinsurgency years – parliamentarian majority in Congress, explicit financial and political support of the international community, and the benefit of a military leadership committed to the peace process. This position of strength, however, was not used to promote the kind of transformations in the military structure that were implied in the Peace Accords that those same authorities signed. At the end of the presidential period, the process of military conversion had not only stagnated, but even showed signs of regression. Against this background only the incompetence of the civilians can account for the failure to subordinate the armed forces to the constitutional order (Arévalo de León 1998a, 1998b).

And the only explanation for this was the lack of political will and the absence of a clear understanding of the issues at stake, on the side of the civilian authorities.

Third, it becomes evident that in this context of structural weakness of the state and limitations in the quality of political leadership, the involvement of civil society in overcoming stagnation and promoting adequate policies becomes crucial (Diamint 1999). The press and the NGO sector play a central role in the formation of a critical public. Scientific centres, universities and NGOs possess the technical and analytic capacity to articulate policy proposals effectively. As these can inform the political decision-making process, and enrich the agendas of party programmes, a constructive partnership with responsible state institutions is desirable. Furthermore, groups of experts should be formed from representatives of civil society (educational institutions, the press, NGOs), the political parties and the state (ministers, parliamentarians). These expert groups should develop the technical know-how, and constitute networks of communication, that are needed for the resolution and implementation of political decisions.

It is evident that neither the nature of the issue nor the social and political context of the country will allow for a short-term solution to the problem of civil–military relations in Guatemala. At the same time, it is undeniable that, even if slowly and ambiguously, there have been substantial advances since 1986. Whether these advances will amount to the effective subordination of the military to civilian authority that democracy requires, however, will depend on our ability as a society to live up to the challenge and accelerate the pace of transformations.

NOTES

1. The prestige of the military leadership was in sharp decline, especially among junior officers disgusted by the close relationship between several generals, the business community and political representatives (Gramajo 1995; Arévalo de León 1998a).

2. For example, the demobilization of the Committee of Volunteers for Civil Defence, and the implementation of compulsory recruitment.

3. In January 2000, President Alfonso Portillo retired 19 generals and admirals, and appointed a middle-ranking officer to the office of defence secretary. The reaction of the military leadership was muted.

REFERENCES

Aguilera Peralta, G. (1994) 'La Reconversión militar y procesos de negociación: el caso de Guatemala', in Gabriel Aguilera Peralta (ed.), *La Reconversión militar en América Latina*, Guatemala: FLACSO.

Arévalo de León, B. (1998a) *Sobre arenas movedizas: sociedad, estado y ejército en Guatemala*, Guatemala: FLACSO.

— (1998b) 'Apuntes sobre una tarea inconclusa. La reconversión militar en Guatemala', *Diálogo* 2 (October), Guatemala: FLACSO.

— (1999) 'Demilitarization and democracy: implications of the popular referendum for the agreement on the strengthening of civilian power and the role of the army in a democracy', in *The Popular Referendum (Consulta Popular) and the Future of the Peace Process in Guatemala*, Latin American Program, Woodrow Wilson International Center for Scholars, Washington, DC, November, Working Paper No. 241, pp. 43–50.

Dahl, R. (1971) *Poliarchy*, New Haven, CT: Yale University Press.

Diamint, R. (ed.) (1999) *Control civil y fuerzas armadas en las nuevas democracias latinoamericanas*, Buenos Aires, Universidad Torcuato di Tella: Nuevo Hacer.

Garretón, Manuel A. (1988) 'Problems of democracy in Latin America: on the process of transition and consolidation', *International Journal*, XLIII, Verano.

Gramajo, H. (1995) *De la guerra ... a la guerra*, Fondo de Cultura Editorial, S.A., Guatemala.

Huntington, S. (1994) *La tercera ola*, Buenos Aires: Paidós.

Jonas, S. (2000) *De centauros y palomas: el proceso de paz Guatemalteco*, Guatemala: FLACSO.

McCleary, R. (1999) *Imponiendo la democracia: las élites Guatemaltecas y el fin del conflicto armado*, Guatemala: Artemis Edinter.

MINUGUA (Misión de verificación de las Naciones Unidas en Guatemala) (2000) Informe del Secretario General de Naciones Unidas Sobre la Verificación de los Acuerdos de Paz de Guatemala, 1 November 1999–30 June 2000, Guatemala, September.

Rosada, H. (1999) 'Soldados en el poder: proyecto militar en Guatemala (1944–1990)', San José: FUNPADEM/The Netherlands: Universidad de Utrecht.

Schirmer, J. (1999) *Intimidades del proyecto político de los militares en Guatemala*, Guatemala: FLACSO.

Solórzano, M. (1987) *Guatemala: autoritarismo y democracia*, San José: EDUCA-FLACSO.

Stepan, A. (1983) *Rethinking Military Politics, Brazil and the Southern Cone*, Princeton, NJ: University of Princeton Press.

Torres-Rivas, E., (1994) 'Introducción a la Década', in *Historia general de Centroamérica*, Vol. VI, San José: FLACSO.

Varas, A. (1988) 'Autonomización Castrense y democracia en América Latina', in Varas Augusto (ed.), *La autonomía militar en América Latina*, Caracas: Nueva Sociedad.

— (1991) 'Las relaciones civil–militares en la democracia', in D. Kruijt and E. Torres-Rivas (eds), *América Latina: militares y sociedad*, San José: FLACSO.

Zagorsky, P. (1992) *Democracy vs National Security: Civil–Military Relations in Latin America*, Boulder, CO: Lynne Rienner.

EIGHT

The Horn of Turbulence: Political Regimes in Transition

AXEL KLEIN

§ The Horn of Africa once referred to the area occupied by Ethiopia, including Eritrea and Somalia, including Djibouti and Somaliland. It has now become standard practice to extend the definition to the member states of the regional organization IGAD (Inter Governmental Organization on Development), that is, Eritrea, Ethiopia, Djibouti, Somalia, Kenya, Uganda and Sudan (Kiplagat 2000). This institution recognizes that the fate of each country is bound up with that of its neighbours, and that the long-term interests of all are best served if resources, such as the Nile waters, are shared and managed in partnership. Equally, the close relationship between neighbouring populations, with ethnic groups and religious faiths distributed across multiple national borders, implicates neighbours in one another's internal affairs. Policies affecting Somali groups in Kenya or Ethiopia, for example, are of concern to Somalia, while the propagation of an expansionary, fundamentalist Islam by the National Islamic Front in Sudan, or the al-Ittahad al-Islami in Somalia, is a direct provocation to the majority of Orthodox Christians in Ethiopia and Eritrea.

The borders dividing the countries of the Horn are weakly defined, contested and porous, but for all that essential for the self-preservation of the state (Issa-Salwe 2000). Continuously transgressed by people, animals, political movements and ideas, they are wide open corridors of communication leading neighbouring states into a web of mutual dependence, wherein nobody can escape the travails of a close neighbour. It also allows conflict to spread readily, with warriors and weapons moving from flashpoint to flashpoint unimpeded.

Home to one of the world's largest populations of nomadic peoples, the countries of the Horn inherited a political challenge from the colonial authorities who first fixed and fetishized the delimitation of each state. For many groups such as the Afar (Ethiopia, Djibouti, Eritrea), the Ben Amer (Eritrea, Ethiopia, Sudan), and the Somali clans spanning Somalia, Ethiopia and Kenya, the claims of states are an interference with time-honoured migration patterns. But agricultural peoples are also dispersed, and the rapid rate of urbanization has spread ethnic groups across regions within each state, and across the different countries of the region. These

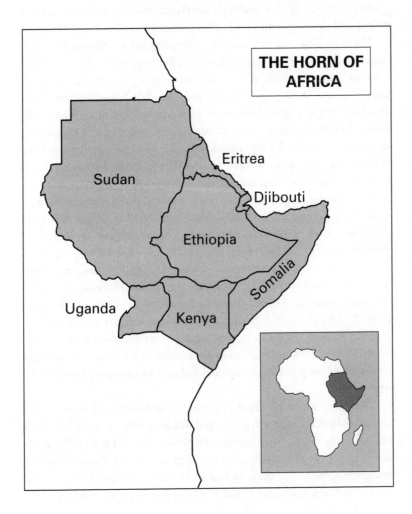

processes have made ethnic homogeneity and cultural uniformity take on the features of a mythologized past. One of the consequences of this population mobility has been the feedback loop, whereby the experiences of migrant communities in distant cities impact on their kinsmen at home. As people travel and disperse, they involve their corporate groups in new sets of relationships. It may therefore be helpful to distinguish between borders demarcating states, and frontiers, which describe the contact zone of the people of a state (Mwagiru 2000). These points of contact form a complex web well beyond immediate proximity. With the qualified exception of Somalia all the Horn countries are characterized by cultural diversity and shared ethnic, religious and cultural elements.

There is, however, a downside. The potential for violence is most apparent in the irredentism advocated by supporters of a Greater Somalia, comprising the clans in Djibouti, Ethiopia's Ogaden, Kenya's former North West province, and the renegade Somalilanders – the Puntlanders have upheld the ideal of a unified Somalia – under one political umbrella based in Mogadishu. More contrived and destructive still is the cross-border destabilization, which Horn governments have come to engage in as a matter of course. The Sudanese People's Liberation Army launches regular attacks into Sudanese territory from its bases in Uganda's Gulu region, often crossing paths with the fighters from the Ugandan Lord's Resistance Army based in Upper Nile province in Sudan. Both sides receive the overt support of their host governments. Over the years, the SPLA has enjoyed backing from Asmara and Addis Ababa, while during the 1990s Khartoum played host to both the Eritrean and Tigrayan oppositions. In the recent border war with Ethiopia, Eritrea channelled arms to the Oromo Liberation Front (OLF) through Somalia, and extended support to the warlord Hussein Aideed. Ethiopia in turn supports the Rahanwein Resistance Army (RRA). This internationalization of internal conflicts allows them to smoulder on while each expelled militant faction goes on to find a new patron.

The momentum of these processes is becoming apparent in the Congo imbroglio, where Uganda and Sudan, partly prompted by their mutual antagonism, have become deeply involved in the civil war. In the latter's case particularly, the war aims are clearly framed within a domestic agenda. The bases in Congo make a useful platform to strike against the SPLA enclave in the southern provinces of Equatoria. We thus have the conflict systems of the Horn (Djibouti, Ethiopia, Eritrea, Kenya, Somalia, Sudan, Uganda) interlock with the Congo/Great Lakes system (Congo, Rwanda, Burundi, Angola, Zimbabwe) adding a new level of complexity to the quest for peace and reconstruction.

New approaches towards conflict resolution and management are therefore urgently called for. There are some indications that changes in the political landscape, following the Eritrean–Ethiopian peace agreement and the election of a new Somali government at Arte (Djibouti), provide at least the potential for a comprehensive regional settlement. For this transition to succeed, policy-makers need to develop their understanding of two dynamics: the interrelationship of causal factors of conflict, and the scope of the diverse instruments for conflict resolution.

Significant differences still obtain between the countries. First, only Ethiopia has been involved in two large-scale inter-state conflicts (Somalia 1977–78, Eritrea 1998–2000), both of which it concluded successfully, underlining its position as a regional power. Nevertheless, the integrity of the Ethiopian state has been subject to sustained challenges from within, most significantly by the Eritrean war of independence, which began in the early 1960s and culminated in Eritrean independence in 1991. Several other groups such as the Oromo Liberation Front, the Afar Liberation Front, the Gurage People's Democratic Front and the Western Somali Liberation Front are continuing the struggle to break away from the Ethiopian state. The state, however, continues to enjoy extensive foreign backing. In the late 1940s the USA emerged as the major backer of the imperial regime. It was replaced by the Soviet Union during the rule of the Derg (1974–91), and has since returned as the major overseas donor. Ethiopian skill in the art of diplomacy has contributed to Addis becoming the focus of external engagement within the region. Foreign investments and development assistance, such as the $400 million approved by the World Bank in December 2000 for post-war reconstruction, are likely to continue providing great stability to the Ethiopian ship of state.

Eritrea, by contrast, endeavoured to continue through independence as it had started out in the guerrilla war. As a self-sufficient, disciplined and united movement forged in a 30-year struggle for independence, it emerged into statehood as the first African country to have revised colonial borders and to be entirely free from external debt. The assertive foreign policy that the fledgling state embarked upon, playing brink-manship with Sudan, Djibouti, Yemen and Ethiopia in succession, ended in shattered dreams and the evaporation of the national myth of in-vincibility. Although the country has gambled away much international goodwill, and wasted its foreign exchange reserves, it is still in a position to formulate its own economic policies. The main danger is that the leadership, forged in bush war, cannot adjust to the demands of peaceful nation-building, and will stultify any form of indigenous development. However, it is hoped that the recent border war has instilled a new realism, which will break the mould of the People's Front for Democracy and Justice (PFDJ) and make way for a more open, consultative and accountable government.

Somalia, though no longer a complete fiction, is still being invented. While it represents one of few African countries that can boast a high degree of ethnic homogeneity (although this must be qualified by the significant Bantu minority), the Somalis have historically excelled at devising polities with a minimum of institutionalization. The Somali *Kulturnation* therefore emerged into independence in 1960 as a pseudo-state (Prunier 2001). The military regime of Siad Barre held on to power mainly by an aggressive foreign policy that resulted in a bitter defeat at the hands of the Ethiopian army in 1976, followed by a civil war that lead to the collapse of the state and a devastating famine. A series of peace conferences resulted in the election of a new government at Arte in 2001. It is facing an uphill task; with neither a revenue base nor armed forces it remains highly vulnerable to the major warlords. Meanwhile, the local administrative arrangements that have returned parts of the country, including Somaliland, Puntland and Jubbaland, to peace and stability have vehemently condemned the new regime.

In Sudan, by contrast, the state appears strong and effective, at least in the north of the country. Its structures are in place, and the military struggle revolves around control and configuration of the state, rather than its existence. Few countries, however, are marked by such deep ethnic and political cleavages. The opposition between Arabized, Islamic northerners and African, Christian/pagan southerners first broke into open conflict with the rebellion of southern officers at Torit. The en-suing civil war lasted from 1955 to 1972, and erupted again in 1983. While the struggle between successive regimes in Khartoum and the SPLA has remained undecided, large tracts of lands in the southern war zones have been devastated. In recent years, eastern and western provinces have also been the scenes of intense fighting, while economic decline and the fallout of the war, including large numbers of refugees, have affected the capital and other northern towns. Recognizing the stalemate, el Turabi, the leader of the National Islamic Front, did begin making concessions to the opposition, acknowledging that the conflict could be settled only by talks and cooperation. Before these tentative steps could deliver results, president el Beshir declared a state of emergency, dismissed el Turabi and consolidated his own position. With the Bentiu oilfields now pumping out black gold to the tune of £1 million dollars a day, observers have explained these events as in-fighting among the élite for the spoils of war. Short of a massive escalation of such rifts into open strife between factions of the Khartoum political class, this war looks set to go on and on. On the other hand, it may not take much for the floodgates of discontent to open and sweep the government aside.

If the conflict over the past 20 years has centred on these four countries, this has not always been so. Uganda had its share of troubles throughout the 1960s, 1970s and 1980s. Kenya too has been shaken by violence, which is usually couched in political or ethnic terms. But neither country has seen a level of conflict comparable to that witnessed in Eritrea, Ethiopia, Somalia and Sudan. Not even Djibouti, unsettled by civil war between 1991 and 1998, has undergone similar suffering. Most of our attention is therefore focused on the theatres of conflict, and the ways in which transformation has been or is being achieved.

ROOT CAUSES OF CONFLICT: RESOURCE CONFLICTS, ENVIRONMENTAL DEGRADATION AND THE ROLE OF THE STATE

It is a precept of academic engagement with conflict/peace studies that a good understanding of the causes of a conflict is a prerequisite for its resolution. As violence became entrenched in the Horn, analysts put forward diverse explanations over the years. From the outset, external observers have sought recourse to cultural explanation. Conflicts have often been explained as tribal, as if the difference of identity were a sufficient reason for conflict itself. Later, more refined approaches have identified ethnicity as a powerful cause around which forces can be mobilized (Fukui and Turton 1979; Fukui and Markakis 1994; Markakis 1987; 1998; Suliman and Klein 1998). This usually happens, however, only after conflict has already broken out. Only in few cases does ethnic difference actually function as a direct trigger.

With the escalation of violence upon the importation of modern armaments, attention focused upon the role of outsiders. Superpower competition became an important factor during the 1970s, and allowed for the presentation of the Somalia–Ethiopia conflict as a proxy war fought on behalf of the USA and the USSR. Since the end of the Cold War in the early 1990s led to the collapse of the Soviet-supported Derg regime in Addis, but not the end of warfare, new explanations were needed.

One of the most persuasive models in the post-Cold War period has been described as Greenwars – conflict as a result of environmental degradation or ecological scarcity. Accordingly, the growing demands of a growing population are depleting the natural resource base to the point where yields are declining, or even collapsing. The intensification of production leads to overgrazing and excessive planting, which results in desertification and soil erosion that render the losses irreversible. At critical points in the unfolding of crises, interest groups will form over the demand for or the denial of access to a resource base. Historical patterns of land use in the Horn and violence in disputes over access to watering holes or pastures add plausibility to this theory.

A further level of complexity has been added by government-sponsored interventions in agriculture. Such schemes, exemplified by the mechanization of cotton-growing in Darfur and Kordorfan in Sudan (Suliman 1992, 1994, 1996) or irrigation schemes in the Awash valley in Ethiopia (Ali 1995; Nicols et al. 2000), have taken large tracts of land from traditional users without paying compensation. The traditional occupants were simply evicted and displaced on to neighbouring land, where conflict has often ensued between newcomers and established groups. Moreover, the government schemes rarely succeed in absorbing the labour of the dispossessed, or in providing tangible development benefits. Instead, the production methods employed run the risk of exhausting the soil within a short period of intensive exploitation.

The involvement of external agencies, in this case central governments or commercial companies (some of which may be from overseas), raises the question of causality. Whereas local conflicts may erupt over resource distribution, the description of environmental degradation as a root cause remains unsatisfactory in its present form. What renders the depletion of natural resources into scarcity is the lack of alternative economic opportunities and the failure of economic differentiation in the absence of a manufacturing or service industry. In the Horn agriculture remains the backbone of the economy, and even exports consist principally of cash crops and livestock.

An appropriate model to explain the crisis in the Horn would therefore incorporate multiple factors: depletion of renewable natural resources; stagnant development; divergent ethnicity and weak states. Such complex, multiple effects prepare the conditions for violent conflict, which can then be triggered by natural events such as drought, or political processes such as elections (Baechler 1999). So environmental management and the distribution of renewable resources need to be included in the policy agenda, in the interest of conflict resolution and conflict prevention.

DIVERSE MECHANISMS OF CONFLICT RESOLUTIONS: IS THERE A MODERN/TRADITIONAL DICHOTOMY?

In pursuit of resolution, one of the principal developments of the last decade has been the evolution of diverse diplomatic instruments. Conventional diplomacy scored a success in settling, albeit after the loss of tens of thousands of lives, the Eritrean–Ethiopian border war. It was brokered by the Organization of African Unity (Cessation of Hostilities in June, comprehensive peace in December 2000, both signed at Algiers), and is now being implemented by a 3,000-strong UN peace-keeping force stationed in the Temporary Security Zone (TSZ) along the border. In the aftermath politics has returned and with it the structural dilemma of how to deal with opposition.

In Ethiopia the most vociferous opposition has come from hardliners in the government, led by Defence Minister Siye Abraha, who took issue with Prime Minister Meles Zenawi for being too soft on Eritrea. This is the thin wedge of dissent in the ruling Ethiopian People's Revolutionary Democratic Front (EPRDF). Grown out of the Tigrayan People's Liberation Front (TPLF), which seized power from the Mengistu regime in 1991, it now rules Ethiopia as a quasi-one-party state, controlling 533 out of 548 seats in the Council of Representatives after the May 2000 elections. Following widespread arrests and the sustained harassment of opposition politicians, activists and journalists, the elections were boycotted by the major opposition parties, which described the proceedings as a sham.

With the main opposition either banned outright or interfered with, groups such as the Oromo Liberation Front (OLF), the Western Somali Liberation Front (WSLF) or the Sidamo Liberation Front (SLF) were unable to participate in the polls. The electoral process, then, serves as a ritual to bestow minimal legitimacy at home, and meet the conditions of external donors. Equally the constitution, drafted by the transitional government to include provisions for the self-determination of any of the country's different nations, as well as civil and political rights, is all but ignored.

These processes have been paralleled in Eritrea, where the Eritrean People's Liberation Movement (EPLF) transformed itself into the People's Front for Democracy and Justice (PFDJ) led by President Issayas Afewerki, who has been holding on to power ever since. With Asmara captured and power taken in 1991, independence was officially declared after the 1993 referendum. Mounting demands for the implementation of the constitution and democratic processes were met first with the arrest of over three thousand political opponents, followed by the scheduling of elections for 1998. These were duly cancelled when Eritrean troops marched into Zalembessa in June.

With the closure of conventional routes to political power and change, the main political fora in Eritrea and Ethiopia are within the ruling parties. Some observers have therefore been anticipating a split in both parties in the coming months. Responding to popular pressure for change, factions will consolidate and turn against the leadership. In a sense this process has already occurred in the Sudan, where Hassan el Turabi, the founder of the ruling National Islamic Front, has defected to found the Popular National Congress Party. The corollary has been the declaration of a state of emergency by President el Beshir, the suspension of the National Assembly and the arrest of el Turabi and followers.

This rough sketch suggests that the structures of formal politics along imported Western models can facilitate the resolution of inter-state wars, but have failed to establish systems that allow for the presentation and redress of grievances within existing structures. Instead, political demands are first ignored, then repressed, until they become manifest in violence that results in military conflict. In this system, power is gained by force, with all benefits accruing to the winner. Yet there are alternative instruments which have come to prominence of late.

In the midst of the turmoil engulfing the Somali republic in the late 1980s and early 1990s, traditional elders of the northern Isaqu clan organized themselves into the Somali National Movement (SNM), and established a truce in the northern part of the country, which until 1960 was known as British Somaliland. A meeting of clan elders assembled at the town of Borama to hammer out a new constitution, the Peace Charter, and to select a government, and an assembly known as *guurti*. The armed militias were successfully demobilized, and government institutions set up from scratch. In 1993 power was transferred to President Mohamed Ibrahim Egal, who was re-elected in 1997. Since then, the self-declared yet still unrecognized Republic of Somaliland has enjoyed internal stability and a moderate prosperity.

The process found imitators among the elders of the neighbouring Majerteen clan, who set up their own administration in Gorawe. Though adhering to the principle of a united Somalia, the new entity has been named Puntland, and acts like a sovereign nation. More significant, perhaps, has been the Somali peace process sponsored by the Djibouti President Ismail Omar Guelleh.

From May to August 2000 delegates from most of the major Somali clans conferred at the Djibouti town of Arte on the constitution of a new government. They elected a 250-member transitional assembly and the provisional head of state, Abdiquassim Salad, who has since received pledges of support from the Eritrean, Ethiopian, Sudanese and Kenyan leaderships, and has been celebrated at the UN and the OAU. However, the euphoria of a war-fatigued population over the new government was soon dissipated with the resistance of major warlords, including Hussein Aideed and Mohamed Quaranyeh Afrarh.

It may be that the ambit of the Arte accord has simply been too ambitious. Success in Somaliland and Puntland was predicated on the close relationship between sub-clan groups in regions dominated by a single clan. At the national level inter-clan cooperation is far more precarious. Furthermore, the inclusion of figures from the Siad Barre era, and the stated intentions of the pretenders, have given rise to the fear that they simply seek to re-run Somalia. In view of the likely failure of the Salad regime to establish itself, we should beware of co-classifying initiatives that resemble traditional mechanisms but pursue different sets of objectives.

Yet the efficacy of traditional mechanisms, based principally on extensive consultation and dialogue over long periods of time, is already being appreciated by Somalia's neighbours. In Ethiopia and Sudan, for example, outbreaks of violence between different ethnic groups are systematically settled by such committees. In the Awash valley, the scene of frequent clashes between Afar and Issa herders, tribal elders regularly hold *xeraas*, meetings where grievances are voiced and settled. They have the power to levy fines on their kin- and clansmen, and will represent their interest in the council. The most pressing issues are inter-ethnic killings, cattle thefts and resource allocation. Through the *diya*, the blood money paid by the murderers' family to the victims' relatives, restitution is made and vengeance buried. Stolen cattle are returned, and the use of the local resource base divided.

Interestingly, these conferences have become institutionalized recently under the auspices of a government body, known as Peace and Reconciliation Committees (PRC). These emerged initially under the Derg, when, with the realization of the central government's limited penetration of rural areas, traditional mechanisms were utilized for administration and law enforcement. The effectiveness of these became apparent in 1991–92. With the demise of the regime law and order broke down in many rural areas, resulting in widespread inter-ethnic violence (Gebre-Selassie 2001).

As the PRCs are now gaining a permanent presence it remains to be seen whether the impact of government-supported development schemes on the local resource base will enter the equation. So far, government officials involved in the peace conferences have sidestepped this issue. Yet the appropriation of vast tracts of land is often one of the key factors in upsetting local balances, and turning the inter-group relationship from one of cooperation to antagonism. Land distribution and misguided development policy are not the only adverse interventions by government agencies. In the peace conferences officials can not only contribute to the outbreak of violence, but also jeopardize the arrangement of a truce. Research into groups conflict in Western Sudan (el Battahani 2001), shows that the grievances listed by warring groups (in this case Reizegat, Zaghawa and Masalit) in explanation of the conflict refer to such natural issues as: demarcation of state boundaries, the role domination of the market by traders from a particular group, appointment to government positions. The stuff of which ethnic conflict is made is pork-barrel politics, not the management of nature.

Government officers attending the 1995 *joudiyya* (peace conference) between the Masalit and Reizegat in Western Darfur only exacerbated the situation by heavily supporting the Rezeigat cause. On land use, for instance, where the Masalit appealed to customary practice, the verdict was that under national law all Sudanese were entitled to public goods. And land, which since 1975 officially belonged to the state, was not for local notables to withhold. The biased distribution of government positions to Reizegat officials was also defended and left unaltered. The Reizegat aggressors emerged with impunity from the proceedings, and violence was sparked anew within days of the so-called settlement.

Reports from other parts of the Horn have described the impact of sectarian government officials on local and ethnic politics (Keen 1994; Hutchinson 1996). In Darfur, ironically, the very devolution of power to the region has encouraged this kind of abuse, as local officials are already implicated. Moreover, weak states challenged by rural opposition movements conventionally resort to 'divide and rule' tactics. In the Sudan, the NIF has long employed militias recruited from nomadic tribes such as the Reizegat, who then act with a licence, and modern arms, against other groups, particularly if these are in any form associated with the rebels.

CONCLUSION FOR EXTERNAL ACTORS

The involvement of government officials in traditional conflict-resolution processes is therefore ambiguous. The material from Ethiopia suggests that state and traditional institutions can exponentially enhance each other. On the other hand, where officials are biased towards one of the groups involved in a conflict, or where the development policy itself is aggressive and expansionist, cooperation will be regarded as collusion and will only serve to undermine traditional structures further. Losing such a valuable opportunity would be all the more regrettable in that the state is lacking the capacity to take over the functions of traditional institutions.

While the PRCs have managed to contain inter-group violence, they are frequently criticized for their failure to prevent it. This is an interesting issue with reference to the question of root causes. Traditional mechanisms have evolved in response to traditional conflict situations, which usually revolved around access to and ownership of natural resources. Their inability to settle these permanently has implications for conflict analyses. It suggests that the identification of natural resource degradation as a root cause of conflict is not necessarily helpful. Furthermore, such an interpretation is liable to lead to a call for additional technocratic interventions, and to distract from the adverse impact of so-called development projects. We can also deduce from the fragility of local accords that traditional institutions no longer hold sway over significant sections of the population – until, that is, a situation has been reached as in Somalia, where the only remaining institutions are those rooted in culture.

Meanwhile it is becoming apparent that there are no hard and fast rules as to the efficacy of different instruments for conflict resolution, and that the 'root causes' remain elusive. Perhaps war, like most complex social phenomena, simply cannot be reduced to a single denominator. As long as agricultural activities dominate the economies of the Horn, however, resource management remains at the heart of the peace process. Here valuable lessons can be learned from traditional mechanisms, which specialize in allocation, restitution and the preservation of balance. Also the modalities are valuable, as they use local idioms and work through notables from the region, with little concern for time and outside agendas.

There is also a need for donors to ensure that the impact of the interventions they are supporting is properly assessed. Unintended consequences, as in the Awash valley or Darfur, can have perverse effects on overall development. At the same time, development aspirations must be acknowledged as a fluid process, which is manifest in continuing urbanization.

As people continue to flock into the cities and into the informal economy the hold of traditional authorities based on rural production models is slipping away. New intermediary level institutions therefore have to be identified, through which 'transitionals' can voice their demands and grievances. Until measures are taken to allow for the representation of all groups, the process of marginalization will continue, and eventually degenerate into violence. Widening the political constituency by working with and developing the scope of traditional institutions should assist the passage of the Horn countries from turbulence to stable prosperity.

REFERENCES

Abbink, J. (2001) 'Anthropology and evolutionary-psychological reflections on inter-group conflict in Southern Ethiopia', in B. Schmidt and I. Schröder (eds), *Anthropology of Violence and Conflict*, London: Routledge, pp. 123–42.

Ali, S. (1995) *Survival Strategies in the Ethiopian Drylands*, Stockholm: OSSREA.

Anderson, D. and V. Broch-Due (1999) *The Poor Are Not Us: Poverty and Pastoralism*, Oxford: James Currey.

Baechler, G. (1999) 'Environmental degradation and violent conflict: hypotheses, research agendas and theory-building', in Mohamed Suliman (ed.), *Ecology, Politics and Violent Conflict*, London: Zed Books, pp. 76–112.

Battahani, A. el (2001) *Sudan: Ecology, Civil Strife and Displacement*, London: Institute for African Alternatives.

Bowman, G. (2001) 'The violence in identity', in B. Schmidt and I. Schröder (eds), *Anthropology of Violence and Conflict*, London: Routledge, pp. 25–46.

Donham, D. (1999) *Marxist Modern. Ethnographic History of the Ethiopian Revolution*, Oxford: James Currey.

Drysdale, J. (1994) *Whatever Happened to Somalia? A Tale of Tragic Blunders*, London: Haan.

Fukui, K. and J. Markakis (eds) (1994) *Ethnicity and Conflict in the Horn of Africa*, London: James Currey.

Fukui, K. and D. Turton (eds) (1979) *Warfare among East African Herders*, Osaka: Senre, National Museum of Ethnology, Ethnological Centre, No. 3.

Gebre-Selassie, S. (2001) *Resource Scarcity and Conflict Management in North Shoa*, London: Institute for African Alternatives.

Hutchinson, S. (1996) *Nuer Dilemmas: Coping with Money, War and the State*, Berkley and London: University of California Press.

Issa-Salwe, A. (2000) *Cold War Fallout. Boundary Politics and Conflict in the Horn of Africa*, London: Haan.

Keen, D. (1994) *The Benefits of Famine*, Cambridge: Cambridge University Press.

Kiplagat, B. (2000) 'Conflict Interlinkages in the Horn: Spill-over Effects of War and Peace', paper given at conference 'The Horn of Africa: Between Post-war Reconstruction and Fragmentation', <http://sef-bonn.org/events/2000/horn/paper-kiplagat-e.pdf>.

MacMichael, H. [1922] (2001) *A History of the Arabs in the Sudan*, Cambridge: Cambridge University Press

Markakis, J. (1987) *National and Class Conflict in the Horn of Africa*, Cambridge: Cambridge University Press.

Markakis, J. (1998) *Resource Conflict in the Horn of Africa*, Oslo: International Peace Research Institute.

Mwagiru, M. (2000) 'Borders, Frontiers and Conflict in the Horn of Africa: Some Preliminary Hypotheses', paper given at the Conference in Bad Honnef (2000), 'The Horn of Africa: between post-war reconstruction and fragmentation', <http://sef-bonn.org/events/2000/horn/paper-mwagiru-e.pdf.

Nicols, A., Y. Arsano and J. Raisin (2000) *Prevention of Violent Conflict and the Coherence of EU Policies Towards the Horn of Africa*, London: Saferworld.

Prunier, G. (2001) 'Wird das Friedensprojekt den Krieg neu entfachen? Die neue Regierung Somalias dürfte sich als besonders gefährliche Fraktion im Bürgerkrieg erweisen', in *der überblick – Zeitschrift für ökumenische Begegnung und internationale Zusammenarbeit*, 37 (1): 71–5.

Said, A. (1994) *Pastoralism and State Policies in the Middle Awash Valley. The Case of the Afar, Ethiopia*, Uppsala: Scandinavian Institute for African Studies.

Saqu, A. (2000) *Islamic Political Ideation in Eastern Sudan*, Khartoum: University of Khartoum.

Schmidt, B. and I. Schröder (eds) (2001) *Anthropology of Violence and Conflict. A History of the Arabs in the Sudan*, London: Routledge.

Sheik-Abdi, A. (1992) *Divine Madness: Mohammed Abdulle Hassan (1856/1920)*, London: Haan Books.

Suliman, M. (ed.) (1999) *Ecology, Politics and Violent Conflict*, London: Zed Books.

— (1992) *Civil War in the Sudan: The Impact of Environmental Degradation*, Bern: Swiss Peace Foundation, ENCOP Occasional Paper, No. 4.

— (1994) *War in Darfur*, London: Institute for African Alternatives.

— (1996) 'War in Darfur', in G. Baechler and K. Spillmann (eds), *Environmental Degradation as a Cause of War*, Bern: Ruegger Verlag.

Suliman, M. and A. Klein (1998) *Die Inversion der Ethnizität: von Wahrnehmung zur Konfliktursache*, Friedensbericht Chur/Zürich: Ruegger Verlag, pp. 257–76

NINE

Ethiopia: Crisis of State, Good Governance and the Reform of the Security Sector

SIEGFRIED PAUSEWANG

§ Ten years after the overthrow of the 'Derg'[1] - the military dictatorship (1974–91) that, following the overthrow of Emperor Haile Selassie, was led from 1977 onwards by Colonel Mengistu Haile Mariam – Ethiopia is once again in deep crisis. The government has drawn political benefits from and claims credit for the victory over Eritrea, but a split in the Tigray People's Liberation Front (TPLF), the leading party in the ruling coalition, has drawn all other members of the Ethiopian People's Revolutionary Democratic Front (EPRDF), into the confrontation.

The origins of the EPRDF go back to the conquest of Tigray by the TPLF during the war against the Derg. Since the security of an independent state of Tigray remained unviable as long as Mengistu remained in power in Addis Ababa, the TPLF had to build a coalition and extend its conquest to the entire country. Mengistu's armies were weak and demoralized, his fall only a matter of time. In order to justify the occupation of Addis Ababa, the TPLF needed allies among the other ethnic resistance groups, such as the Oromo Liberation Front (OLF). The TPLF used this alliance increasingly for its own purposes, thereby creating growing conflicts, particularly with the OLF.

At present (October 2001), Prime Minister Meles Zenawi appears firmly in charge. Dissidents within the TPLF have been suspended, arrested and accused of corruption. The affiliated parties have held purges at the request of Meles, and subjected internal critics to sanctions through the process of *gemgena* – the process of public self-criticism and justification. This process was first institutionalized during the period of the resistance struggle in Tigray, with the principal aim of securing the support of the rural population. As a mechanism for demonstrating the responsibility of the military leadership to the people, it was highly successful. Following the takeover of power, *gemgena* was introduced into all institutions, and has become a means of exerting party control.[2]

But the crisis of the state goes way beyond the internal conflict among the parties of the government coalition, and the confrontation with the OLF. Repression of the opposition can at best be an interim measure. The contradictions between constitutional rights and liberties and the reality, between decentralized democracy and the arrogation of power at the centre, between the guarantee of human rights and the daily repression and control, are becoming increasingly evident. My analysis of the historical roots of the crisis of state and the experiment with democracy in Ethiopia is set against this background. Particular emphasis will fall on the security forces, recently reinforced by rearmament, and the precarious position of the justice sector, dependent, particularly in the rural areas, on the machinery of state and party.

HISTORICAL REVIEW

On coming to power in 1991, the present government declared its commitment to preserving peace and democracy, to safeguard the ethnic and cultural diversity of the country, and to provide for the social security of the large majority of the rural poor. These were great promises, following a poor record of government with an authoritarian tradition – Ethiopia did not become colonized, but participated actively in the 'Scramble for Africa' (Gann and Duignan 1969: 15ff, 420ff). Towards the middle of the nineteenth century, King Menilek, who subsequently became emperor, extended systematically his territory southwards of the principality of Shoa in the southern reaches of the empire. Fertile lands were conquered, and the native population subjugated to form an economic and military power base for his claim to the throne (Marcus 1969; Rubenson 1976).

Accidents of history came to his aid: trading routes were relocating southwards, and therefore through his territory. This gave Menilek access to mass-produced firearms, which, in the wake of the modernization of the armed forces in Europe, were finding their way to African markets (Cooper et al. 1975). With his power rooted in the wealth of the south, Menilek could secure the throne for himself. From 1889 onwards he continued his southward expansion as emperor, and unified the Ethiopian empire. Victory over the Italian forces at Adowa (in the former heartland of the empire) in 1896 accorded him the power to safeguard Ethiopia's independence during the colonial division of Africa (Rubenson 1976; Bahru 1991).

Under his successor, Haile Selassie I, regent from 1916 and emperor from 1930, the process of modernization and centralization of the administration continued. Particular emphasis fell on the development of the economy and communications, as well as on the education system and the health sector. By building up his power base upon the landed aristocracy, which was rewarded with offices and privileges, he was in no position to alleviate the economic and personal dependence of the peasantry, many of whom had to transfer up to 75 per cent of their harvest to the landlord. These conditions explain the explosive power of the slogan *meret le arrashu* (land to the tiller), popular among internal opposition, especially the students. The politics of linguistic and cultural imperialism sparked off further opposition among the diverse peoples of the south (Rubenson 1976; Bahru 1991; Balsvik 1985).

The end of the imperial road was reached in 1973, when official silence over the famine that held large parts of the country in its grip sparked off demonstrations and strikes. A committee of junior officers, known as the Derg, took power in 1974, promising a series of socialist reforms. This was followed in 1975 by a land reform, the most radical part of the Derg programme. But within the next two years Colonel Mengistu Haile Mariam rose to the pinnacle of power and established his personal rule by outmanoeuvring his rivals, who were executed or murdered. The regime was socialist in name, and enjoyed ample Soviet support until the late 1980s, while pursuing a rigorously centralistic and nationalist policy. An intensive war against the Eritrean independence movements was financed by continuously rising taxes on the peasantry. The self-governing Peasant Associations, which had been formed in 1975 as the local unit of administration for the land reform programme, were brought under the control first of the state and from 1985 of the Ethiopian Workers Party. The peasantry had to contend with new taxes, 'voluntary' remissions, and the compulsory delivery of crops to the state grain monopoly. The seventy to eighty diverse ethnic groups of Ethiopia were once again subjected to centralization under Amharic leadership. With the introduction of forced recruitment, the peasantry began to withdraw its last support for the regime. Nationalist resistance groups and liberation movements were formed all over the country, and finally succeeded in demoralizing and defeating the 'largest army in Africa'.

The Eritrean People's Liberation Front (EPLF) took control in the newly independent Eritrea in 1991, while the Tigrayan Liberation Front (TPLF) became the leading political force in Ethiopia. The TPLF invited the other liberation movements to participate during the transition period, and submitted a Transitional Charter as a provisional constitution in which democracy and federalism were enshrined (Pausewang 1996; Leenco 1999).

A NEW FEDERAL GOVERNMENT FOR ETHIOPIA

Ethiopia has become a federal republic of eight regions coterminous with the largest ethnic groups (and in the southern region a conglomerate of ethnic groups, and in Gambela a region constituted of two competing groups) and three city-states (Addis Ababa, Harrar, Dire Dawa).

After the fall of the Mengistu regime, the TPLF had little choice but to promise self-determination and democratic participation in the new government to all ethnic groups. After the first year in office it was already becoming clear, however, that the TPLF would make no concessions on its leadership role in the coalition of different political groupings, and would in practice tolerate no deviation from its policy.

Tensions have developed particularly in the relationship with the OLF, the liberation movement of the Oromo people (the largest ethnic group representing between one-third and one-half of the population). They have been fuelled by the TPLF strategy of fostering client parties (polemically known as 'Quisling' or 'condom' parties') among all ethnic groups, which in return for implementing the EPRDF policy at local level are granted favours and privileges in their competition with political opposition movements. During the local government elections of 1992, the OLF was subjected to such a level of discrimination and persecution that the party boycotted the election, and resigned from the government. The militias were disarmed and the OLF pushed into exile. From there, it has been conducting a guerrilla war, which has been an irritant to the regime, but not a serious threat. The OLF has been insisting on the return to the principles of 1991 as a condition for suspending the armed struggle and participating in policy-making on the basis of equality and partnership (Leenco 1999). But the TPLF has refused to make any concessions in spite of its power being based on the Tigrayan people, a mere 7–8 per cent of the total population, and prefers to rely on the time-tested methods of 'divide and rule'.

The pressure on recalcitrant parties and ethnic movements refusing to subordinate themselves to the assertion of dominance by the TPLF has therefore been growing. All over the country, the leading positions in government and administration have been handed over to the client parties, which can then draw upon the material benefits and the infrastructure of the state, while the opposition parties have been starved of funds, and systematically discriminated against in any election process. Where this has still not been sufficient for delivering the desired electoral result, the heat has been turned up on the population (Pausewang and Tronvoll 2000; Pausewang 2001).

THE EXPERIMENT WITH DEMOCRACY AND GOOD GOVERNANCE

Taken at face value, the constitution that was adopted in 1994 and came into force in 1995 has left Ethiopia a model of democracy and good governance. The constitution contains a vigorous charter of rights, which guarantees individual rights including free speech, the right to assembly, the right to personal safety and the right to the protection of the law (art. 10, paras 13–44). Crimes against humanity are governed by article 28. Ethiopia has integrated all international conventions and treaties that have been ratified (art. 9.4) into its body of law. This includes all the major human rights conventions (art. 13.2), while the rights of the family, of women, children, ethnic and cultural minorities are all upheld by discrete articles (arts 34–36, 39) (Paul 2000; Pausewang 1996).

In reality, these constitutional rights play only a minor role, when the interests of the state – or, better phrased, of the ruling party – are touched upon. At the same time it should not be ignored that the Meles Zenawi regime has introduced a number of tangible improvements over the nakedly brutal system of repression under the Mengistu dictatorship. Addis Ababa now has a number of independent, private newspapers, which, within certain limits, can and do criticize the regime. But the lines of press freedom are not clearly drawn, leading to the constant arrest of journalists. Some may even find themselves convicted of offences against the press law, which prohibits among other things the incitement to racial hatred and the spread of false accusations against the government.

There are also several legal and registered opposition parties. Wherever these manage to build up a local organization, posing a threat to the position of the ruling party, they suffer the full force of repressive intervention. In theory the administration is decentralized, but the party tightly controls it. Moreover, is has become standard practice that when complaints are lodged the central government refers to the decentralized responsibility of the regions and zones. However, where its own political interests are concerned, it intervenes swiftly and without scruples.

The judiciary is formally independent and a few judges have indeed succeeded in passing independent judgments against the government that the press has immediately made public. But the government has found ways of neutralizing such judgments. In at least one case, the judge concerned has been replaced. In the rural areas, the conditions of the judiciary beggar belief. People have ceased availing themselves of the judicial system, which because of the long waiting times has simply become impractical. The independence of the judges remains on paper only, as they know they have to follow the instructions of the administration to keep their positions (EHRCO 1996a, 1996b).

A number of non-governmental organizations have been working against these trends. Often supported by foreign donors, they are tolerated by the government as long as they do not become too effective. The Ethiopian Human Rights Council (EHRCO), for one, exposes, documents and makes public the human rights violations of the regime. Apart from occasional harassment, EHRCO has been allowed to operate by the authorities, not least in consideration of the international reputation of the regime. Under the current government the founder and former general secretary of EHRCO has been released on bail and could avail himself of the *habeas corpus* (the right to an appearance in court). Under the Mengistu regime this would have been unthinkable, and liquidation more likely. The difference between the regimes is unmistakable, but how far does such generosity go? And can a state continue to justify its actions by claiming that its predecessor was worse?

The rural population has been benefiting from the abolition in 1991 of the government monopoly on grain marketing and compulsory deliveries. The peasant associations, the most important control systems in the countryside since 1978, have been retained under the new name of *kebele*. But new cadres have been formed, which are developing the control and repressive functions of the *kebele* (Tronvoll and Aadland 1995; Aspen 1995; Ege 1998).

In the run-up to every election, and in the speeches of the leading politicians, much praise is bestowed on the ostensible democratic system. But the elections of 2000 and 2001 have demonstrated that the government will stand by idly when loyalist forces, at local level, take extreme measures to thwart the electoral successes of opposition groups. Moreover, some local groups have been guilty of electoral fraud or murder (Pausewang and Tronvoll 2000). Up to now no single perpetrator has been brought to justice for these offences (Pausewang 2001).

The final conclusion, after close observation of the Ethiopian electoral process and a scientific analysis of the human rights and democratic development over the past ten years, is that there is no actual democracy in Ethiopia. It cannot exist as long as the leadership prioritizes the retention of power, and all resources are mobilized to secure the power of the incumbent leaders of the state (Pausewang 2001).

ARROGANCE OF STATE POWER AND THE FAILURE OF DEMOCRACY

Can these developments be described by the contemporary term of state failure? Is this not rather a failure of democracy in the face of arrogant state power? The question is how democracy can prevail in a state that, while proclaiming democratic values, stifles any development that might go beyond the formal demonstration of democratic processes.

A historical understanding of the origins of the state in Africa and the conceptualization of the state is illuminating. The modern Ethiopian state evolved in the mid-nineteenth century, during the period of colonial expansion. Although Ethiopia was the sole African country to avoid being colonized by the European powers, the process of colonization largely determined the formation of the Ethiopian state (Markakis 1994, 220; Marcus 1969).

State power has always revolved around the control of resources and power. These sentiments were expressed repeatedly by the representatives of Ethiopia's governing parties before the elections of 2000 and 2001, and according to one party officer: 'We have been fighting for 17 years – do you really expect us to hand over power to a party that was only born yesterday?' A very similar comment was reported by an election observer: 'We have delivered you democracy with our blood. Do these people think they can take it from us with paper?' (Pausewang and Aalen 2001). The naïve equation of democracy with state power is as symptomatic as the parallel between blood and ballot. The TPLF veterans felt betrayed when the electorate did not express gratitude 'for the liberation' with a vote for the TPLF. Although this attitude is difficult to reconcile with democracy, it is firmly established even in the highest government circles, as a Norwegian researcher discovered in a series of interviews with high-ranking TPLF officials (Tekeste Negash and Tronvoll 2000).

The problem does not lie in the weakness of the state, or even in state failure, but in the state itself. Within the colonial context the state in Africa always functioned as a system of repression. It served the maintenance of power, and guaranteed the supply of raw materials and colonial produce. This is not the only parallel between the Ethiopian state and the role of the colonial states.

Maintaining a colonial presence became militarily and economically untenable in the latter part of the twentieth century. The colonial powers, contemplating the transfer of power, had to identify suitable African rulers who could prevent a descent into chaos. In the event, they opted for those sections of the population who had become familiar with the colonial mode of administration, who had become culturally assimilated, and who had been trained.

Yet the very people who had been to Europe and had worked in the colonial administration had become detached from their own cultural background. They were left alone with an administrative machinery created for the exploitation of their people and a military trained to discipline the population, which was made up of diverse ethnic groups, clans and peoples who had no gratitude towards the state and expected little other than violence. Was it to be expected that the new rulers would build a democracy on this basis? (Davidson 1992).

The best among them (such as Julius Nyerere and Jomo Kenyatta) sought to build a nation and to unify the population into a new people, or tried alternatively to develop a collective sense of pan-African identity (for instance Kwame Nkrumah and Leopold Senghor). But such lofty projects were bound to fail. And where democratic governments did emerge they were quickly removed by coups. The military, created to secure power, were not prepared to give up the instruments of power. Where the new leaders had not turned into despots, they were soon replaced by military dictatorships. These had even fewer scruples in abusing the power of the state for their own gain (Davidson 1992; Chabal and Daloz 1999).

In spite of Ethiopia's history of independent statehood, the people regard the state not as theirs, but as an oppressive authority, which demands obedience. In this regard, contemporary Africa is reminiscent of medieval Europe, when the identity of the lord was of less significance to the peasant than the level of taxes and services. It took Europe over a thousand years before the division of labour, the Enlightenment, the beginning of industrialization, the French Revolution, the nationalist project of Napoleon and not least the workers' movement had secured the necessary concessions that alone could make democracy possible.

THE SECURITY SECTOR AND THE JUDICIARY IN ETHIOPIA

Like almost all armies on the continent, the Ethiopian army is more an instrument for maintaining internal control than for safeguarding external security. Although this fact was temporarily forgotten during the border war with Eritrea, reality has quickly returned, leaving the peasantry to expect nothing other of the state and its institutions than to concentrate power, exert control and secure access to resources. Intellectuals in the cities demand their human rights and appeal to the international community to obtain civil rights from their state.

Disarmament as rearmament After 1991 the army was allegedly disarmed with much fanfare and international support. As Günter Schröder has extensively documented, however, while Mengistu's troops were disarmed and demobilized, the TPLF troops became the national army, which built up and took over central positions from 1994 onwards. This provided them with complete control over the newly formed, multi-ethnic forces. While the army was reduced, local police forces were beefed up, and supported by various forces at regional and zonal level. The police and the local militia act as control organs of the party at local level. In practice, their main priority is not to maintain law and order, but to carry out the bidding of their Tigrayan supervisors and cadres. And with the 1998 border war the loathsome practice of forced recruitment has returned to many villages. Army ranks have been swelling to full levels, possibly even exceeding those of the Mengistu era in total numbers.

According to Schröder, the total of all the security forces is approximately the same as during the Mengistu regime. Although the defence budget has registered an impressive decline, the costs of the military forces have been spread across the budgets of the Ministry of the Interior, the budgets of the regional states, in administration and transport costs, and as investments. If these items are totalled up, the benefits of disarmament are seen to be negligible (Schröder 2001).

The police as an instrument of repression The police are part of the state's machinery of repression, and are rarely seen – with the exception of the traffic police and urban police patrols – as friends and helpers, or as the guardians of public order. The actual role of the police has been demonstrated by the assassination of the deputy spokesman of the human rights institute EHRCO, Assefa Maru, using vehicles provided by British development assistance (EHRCO 1997).[3] The police are even less restrained in rural areas, away from the paved roads and urban centres. During the elections of 2000 and 2001 office-holders were again responsible for deploying the police to arrest and incarcerate unwanted opposition candidates, to beat up their followers, and to influence or even deceive older voters into voting for the government party (Pausewang and Aalen 2001).

A group of teachers, all members of NGOs working on education on human rights and democracy, have been holding courses in police stations and academies since 1999. Over and over again the instructors hear from the beat officers: 'We know that we should not beat and injure people. You should teach this to our superiors though, who demand it of us.' An obvious excuse, perhaps, but also a reflection on reality.

The precarious position of the judiciary The Ethiopian judiciary has still not come out of the deep crisis into which it fell at the end of the Mengistu regime. While there is in Ethiopia no lack of ability and well-trained judges, trying their utmost to create conditions in which the rule of law can flourish, they are inhibited by different factors. Most judges who trained during the time of the student protest movements and the political activism at the university embraced the 1974 revolution as the way forward for their country and supported the Derg at least for a time. Many then became instruments of political justice, and became responsible for the injustice of the regime. Most, though not all, were removed from office in 1991, and are still awaiting trial as part of the Derg Trial.[4] These events decimated the ranks of the judiciary at a time when the decentralization of the administration created an even greater need for courts and judges. The gap was filled by training, in three- to four-month crash courses, teachers and high school leavers who may now be in charge of the courts of a region or zone (EHRCO 1997: 2 u.14). How can a young man emerging from such a fast-track training course retain his independence against a powerful local party chief or bureaucrat?

One example to illustrate the dilemma was published by EHRCO in 1996. In a community of the southern province a warrant was issued against a local murderer. The local administrator (and party chief, as is customary) sent the police to arrest the brother of the suspect. The judge released him on account of mistaken identity, very much to the chagrin of the party chief. He ambushed the released man on his way home, and kidnapped him in his car. The man's body was found the next day; he had been shot. Next, the uncommonly courageous judge issued a warrant against the party chief, and sent the police to have him arrested. When the policeman, his knees shaking from fear, read out the arrest warrant to the party chief, he became the object of general mirth: 'The judge seems to have a sense of humour, let us teach him a lesson. Go and arrest the judge,' the policeman was told. Knowing who was in charge, he hurried to carry out his orders. The judge, however, had been warned, and fled in the nick of time to the provincial capital of Awasa, where he sought the protection of the regional parliament. He was turned away and send to Addis Ababa, where he was told that this matter came under the jurisdiction of the regional government, not the central government ministries. In the meantime his wife had been arrested and maltreated in prison, leaving her arm permanently paralysed. The judge was dismissed by the local authorities and did not dare to return. Not even the attention of EHRCO could move the national authorities to intervene (EHRCO 1996a: 5–7, 1996b).[5]

The political dependence of the judges particularly in rural areas is becoming ever more apparent – not that it is to be expected that judges will muster the courage to defy the will of the administrator in their judgments, as this could cost them their office. The specially trained young people are almost without exception local party members; they know that without conformity, party book and loyalty, there will be no work.

More important still is the fact that the population expects nothing better from the judiciary. Popular knowledge in the southern region distinguishes between two different types of custodial punishments: those imposed by a court of law, and those imposed by administrative fiat. While the former provide, at least theoretically, for appeal, no such option exists for the latter (Pausewang 2001).

The justice system in Addis Ababa is of a higher quality, as several judges have the backbone to ensure that the rule of law prevails. Though undermanned and overworked, the courts do at least dare to challenge, when necessary, the government administration. One example is the court decisions in relation to the student demonstrations of April 2001. Professor Mesfin Wolde Mariam, founder of EHRCO, and the well-known economist Professor Berhanu Negua were arrested and charged with inciting the students to violence. The defence could prove with tape-recordings that the two academics had in the incriminating lecture indeed challenged the students to defend their rights – but had emphatically renounced all violent means.

The authorities took advantage of these events to arrest the leaders of several opposition parties. They were taken to a prison in Shoarobit in Oromia, 300 kilometres from Addis. In response to the demand for *habeas corpus* by relatives, the court in Addis Ababa released unconditionally one of the most popular party leaders, Lidetu Ayelew and some of his friends, as no charges had been brought against them. Mesfin and Berhanu were released on bail at the same time. At the third court hearing the minister of justice was called up and served a one-month prison sentence for having failed to allow a prisoner to appear in court. At the request of the government he was granted an amnesty to allow him to carry out his official duties.

In the meantime the government criticized the Addis Ababa court for ordering the release of Lidetu Ayelew, when it had no jurisdiction in Shoarobit. Even though the defendants, all residents of the capital, had been arrested in Addis Ababa for offences allegedly committed there, a Shoarobit court was set up to try the case. Lidetu was re-arrested and taken to Shoarobit, where a newly appointed judge set excessively high bail, before releasing him once more. The case against Mesfin Wolde Mariam was adjourned to December 2001, with the other cases to follow.

The power invested in the local administration is primarily manipulated in the pursuit of self-interest. Bureaucrats and administrators instruct the police to interfere with the rights and freedoms of individuals. Protest or resistance is not tolerated, as became manifest during the 2000 and 2001 elections. Candidates for the opposition were thrown into gaol on trumped-up charges, members of the opposition party's electoral teams were excluded, and sections of the electorate favouring the opposition cunningly prevented from casting their vote. Once supporters of the opposition had been identified, mocked and sent off, gifts were distributed. Peasants were reminded that: 'According to the constitution all land belongs to the state, and we will not allow those who betray us at the ballot boxes to own any.' Peasants, for whom land ownership is a matter of life and death, take such threats seriously.[6]

THE EQUIVALENCE OF PARTY AND STATE: THE STATE BELONGS TO THE POWER-HOLDERS

Where government can neither be called to account, nor ousted through the ballot box, democracy cannot prevail. But the TPLF and its partners in the governing coalition believe that they are protecting the true interests of the rural majority against the urban minority. Since most peasants belong to different ethnic groups, and the TPLF regards itself as the champion of pluralism against Amharic hegemony, electoral dissent is considered treachery, and not treated lightly. Comprising some 85 per cent of the population, the support of the peasantry is decisive in Ethiopian elections.

With the TPLF employing violence against any deviation, the coalition partners, recruited largely among the unemployed and the semi-educated school-leavers, adopt the same methods. Party leaders will readily resort to violence and have opponents imprisoned, especially if scrutiny by foreign observers can be evaded.

All levels of the state are quite openly made to serve as instruments of the party, as one example from the Norwegian team of election observers illustrates. The team would introduce themselves first to the head of the local government, and subsequently visit the offices of the different parties, including those of the opposition. But each time, two of these courtesy calls could be rolled into one, as leaders of local government and of the ruling party were invariably one and the same person. All the instruments of government, be they the fully equipped office, the vehicles or the staff, were all deployed during the campaign.

The current system is premised upon this merging of party and state administration. Without revenue of its own, the party depends on government finance. More insidious still is the fact that the party retains the loyalty of its members through the distribution of government posts. Candidates put themselves forward to run for regional or local councils because victory promises the automatic acquisition of a government job at regional, zonal or local level. Office-holders are therefore defending not only their party and seat in parliament or local council, but also their position in society, their income and their very existence.

For the TPLF – and even more the satellites in the EPRDF coalition – losing even one seat in parliament or the local council is simply intolerable. Allowing the opposition access to office would enable them to distribute positions and resources at the expense of party supporters, whose loyalty would be put to the test. The victory imperative is also manifest in matters of internal party discipline. Incumbents who lose their seats are dropped by the party, as happened to the head of the administration and party of the Endeber constituency in the southern province. He had earned notoriety during the border war with Eritrea by accusing the local Gurage people, who had resisted forced recruitment, of cowardice and femininity. When campaigning for a seat in the National Assembly, the locals translated their outrage at the defamation into political action by supporting a rival candidate. The latter, though unknown and up against official harassment, won the seat by a large majority, as a result of which the former incumbent was relieved of his party posts (Pausewang 2001).

The local and regional parties, their personnel, organization and finances are totally dependent on their access to the resources of the government. Such structures are hardly compatible with the constitutional guarantees of the rule of law, a transparent administration and institutions accountable to the citizenry.

CONCLUSIONS AND FUTURE PERSPECTIVES

At the heart of the problem of the Ethiopian state lies the fact that it serves the interests of the power-holders; it does not function as a democracy, does not serve free citizens, and does not safeguard human rights. Hence the crisis of state is caused not by state failure, but by the inherent contradictions between the claims to a constitutional democracy and actual diversion of state resources and powers to the ruling party.

The questions are: how long can Ethiopia continue to play at being a democracy? How long will Meles Zenawi be able to straddle the chasm between party and people, between constitutional democracy and control and repression? How long will the diplomats of the donor community allow themselves to be lulled into an illusion of democracy, when the state is really running it into the ground?

The border war with Eritrea has been a temporary setback for Meles. After his victory over the party hawks, he can now present himself on the international stage, however incongruously, as the liberal-democratic alternative. Critical observers are concerned that he may find fresh openings in the new US crusade against international terrorism. Manoeuvring himself on to the right side he may, in return, gain a free hand for his dealings with internal enemies and 'terrorists'.

According to recent reports, Meles Zenawi has succeeded in asserting his control over both party and government. It would seem that the crisis will have to deepen before he accepts the impossibility of reconciling the principles of the constitution and the existing reality. He would be well advised to grasp the still extended hand of the opposition and call for a conference of reconciliation. Such reconciliation would follow on from where the promise of 1991 left off, if the ideals of the Provisional Charter are to be realized.

(Translation: Axel Klein)

NOTES

1. 'Derg' is an Amharic term for committee or council. The term 'Derg' refers to the military council constituted of representatives from all garrisons in the spring of 1974, which seized power in September 1974.

2. All employees participate in assemblies for the evaluation of their functionaries. But usually, the outcome has been prepared in advance by the party leadership, instructing the employees as to what criticism is to be brought against whom. As the final vote is pre-determined, this process has lost all its democratic potential, and serves simply to discipline the workforce and to approve the decisions of the party.

3. The UK government issued protests against this abuse of assistance and froze the police assistance programme for half a year, after which it continued unchanged.

4. Several thousand officers and officials of the Derg regime were arrested in 1991. A tribunal was set up under the special prosecutor Girma Wakjira to bring charges of genocide and crimes against humanity. With insufficient evidence a large number of the three thousand or so arrested were released in subsequent years. Other suspects were arrested later or charged in absentia. Other suspects spend many years in pre-trial detention, without ever facing charges. The process is likely to drag on for years to come, partly in order to meet its two objectives: to punish and to document the crimes of the regime (Elgesem 1998; Pausewang 1996; Special Prosecutor's Office 1994).

5. The presentation by EHRCO (1996b) is slightly at variance with the version I heard in the southern region. According to EHRCO it was the party chief who dismissed the judge in a letter to the president of the court. The president, instead of reminding the party chief that he had overstepped his competence, informed the judge of his dismissal, whereupon he flew to Awasa, leaving his wife to be arrested and tortured in his stead.

6. The gravity of these allegations against the severity of local government administration is confirmed by personal experience and interviews with victims.

REFERENCES

Note: Ethiopian names are inverted; it is customary to address Ethiopians by their first names, the second name is the first name of the father; the first name is listed alphabetically.

Aspen, Harald (1995) *The 1995 National and Regional Elections in Ethiopia: Local Perspectives*, Norway: University of Trondheim, Centre for Environment and Development.

Bahru, Zewdie (1991) *A History of Modern Ethiopia, 1855–1974*, Athens: Ohio University Press/London: James Currey.

Balsvik, Randi Rønning (1985) *Haile Selassie's Students: Intellectual and Social Background to Revolution*, East Lansing: Michigan State University.

Chabal, Patrick and Jean-Pascal Daloz (1999) *Africa Works, Disorder as Political Instrument*, Oxford and Bloomington, IN: International African Institute and James Currey.

Cooper, A., with R. Dinsey, P. Gilkes, R. Murray and R. Pankhurst (1975) 'Class, state and the world economy: a case study of Ethiopia', paper given at the conference on *New Approaches to Trade*, Sussex, September, mimeo.

Davidson, B. (1992) *The Black Man's Burden: Africa and the Curse of the Nation State*, London: James Currey.

Ege, S. (1998) *The Promised Land: The Amhara Land Redistribution of 1997*, Norway: University of Trondheim, Centre for Environment and Development.

EHRCO (Ethiopian Human Rights Council) (1996a) 'The administration of justice in Ethiopia', Addis Ababa, EHRCO 9th Report (January).

— (1996b) 'A special urgent report', Addis Ababa (January).

— (1997) 'Extra-judicial killing', Special Report No. 14, Addis Ababa.

— (2000) EHRCO's 1st Report on the May General Election, 'Problems of the registration process', Addis Ababa, 10 March.

Elgesem, F. (1998) 'The Dergue trials in context. A study of some aspects of the Ethiopian judiciary', Human Rights Report, Oslo: Norwegian Institute of Human Rights.

Fukui, K. and J. Markakis (eds) (1994), *Ethnicity and Conflict in the Horn of Africa*, London: James Currey.

Gann, L. H. and Peter Duignan (eds) (1969) *The History and Politics of Colonialism, 1870 – 1914*, Cambridge: Cambridge University Press.

Ghai, Yash (ed.) (2000) *Autonomy and Ethnicity: Negotiating Competing Claims in Multi-ethnic States*, Cambridge: Cambridge University Press.

Leenco, Lata (1999) *The Ethiopian State at the Crossroad: Decolonisation and Democratisation or Disintegration?*, Lawrenceville, NJ and Asmara: Red Sea Press.

Marcus, H. G. (1969) 'Imperialism and expansionism in Ethiopia from 1865 to 1900', in L. H. Gann and Peter Duignan (eds), *The History and Politics of Colonialism, 1870–1914*, Cambridge, pp. 420–61.

Markakis, J. (1994) 'Ethnic conflict and the state in the Horn of Africa', in K. Fukui and J. Markakis (eds), *Ethnicity and Conflict in the Horn of Africa*, London: James Currey, pp. 217–37.

Mesfin Wolde Mariam (1995) 'Democracy, rule of law and human rights in Ethiopia. Rhetoric and practice', Addis Ababa: EHRCO.

Paul, James C. N. (2000) 'Ethnicity and the new constitutional orders of Ethiopia and Eritrea', in Yash Ghai (ed.), *Autonomy and Ethnicity: Negotiating Competing Claims in Multi-ethnic States*, Cambridge: Cambridge University Press, pp. 173–96.

Pausewang, S. (1996) 'Ethiopia', in *Human Rights in Developing Countries*, Yearbook 1996, The Hague: Kluwer Law International, pp. 195–247.

— (2001) 'In between elections in Southern region', Working Paper, Oslo: Norwegian Institute of Human Rights, p. 14.

Pausewang, S. and K. Tronvoll (eds) (2000) *The Ethiopian 2000 Elections: Democracy Advanced or Restricted?*, Oslo: Norwegian Institute of Human Rights.

Pausewang, S. and L. Aalen (2001) 'Withering democracy: local elections in Ethiopia, February/March', Working Paper, Oslo: Norwegian Institute of Human Rights, p. 7.

Rubenson, S. (1966), *King of Kings Tewodros of Ethiopia*, Addis Ababa and Nairobi: Addis Ababa University Press and Oxford University Press.

— (1976) *The Survival of Ethiopian Independence*, Lund: Scandinavian University Books (reprinted 1991), Addis Ababa: Kuraz.

Schröder, G. (2001) 'Demobilisation and Remobilisation in Ethiopia 1991–2000 in a Historical Perspective and its Contemporary Political Context', Frankfurt/M: preliminary draft (unpublished).

Special Prosecutor's Office (SPO) (1994), 'Genocide and crimes against humanity' (unofficial translation of the indictment), Addis Ababa: Government Printers.

Tekeste Negash and K. Tronvoll (2000), *Brothers at War: Making Sense of the Eritrean–Ethiopian War*, Oxford: James Currey.

Tronvoll, K. and Øyvind Aadland (1995) 'The process of democratisation in Ethiopia: an expression of popular participation or political resistance?', Oslo, Norwegian Institute of Human Rights.

PART THREE

Regional Conflict Management in
the Light of September 11

'Privatized Violence' and the Terror of September 11: Challenges to Foreign, Security and Development Policy

TOBIAS DEBIEL

§ It is already becoming clear that the events of 11 September 2001 are having profound implications for peace and security arrangements at regional level. The question then arises whether the global policy consequences will remain confined to a small number of countries in the Central Asian region and the Arab countries, or whether we are witnessing a fundamental change in the structure of global policy. Much speaks for the latter hypothesis, because the events of 11 September have evoked a new dimension of war and dangers of a different magnitude: an opponent operating transnationally and organized into clandestine networks has to be countered appropriately and effectively. At the same time, the horror of the attacks on New York and Washington pushes the significance of privatized forms of violence as a political challenge ever more into the foreground.

In the current situation of radical change, the metaphor of a 'watershed' (or we could also speak of a 'bifurcation') is most apt: 'a defining moment at which the players are faced with several options. Depending on what they decide, global policy will develop in different directions' (Müller 2001: 8). A number of states are experiencing the present developments as a foreign policy caesura. Nevertheless, a political sea change, affecting the underlying balance of international power, bringing central humanitarian problems closer to resolution, or transforming intractable conflicts in the world's crisis regions, remains unlikely. Even so, from a geopolitical and world-order viewpoint, 11 September 2001 represents probably the most significant event since the fall of the Berlin Wall. It will, according to Erhard Eppler (2001: 56), not entirely

determine the twenty-first century, but will certainly make its mark on
the beginning of the new millennium:

> Although it is most doubtful that this century will be one only of terror,
> its first few decades could well be characterized by the denationalized,
> privatized, commercialized and, in many cases, also criminal use of
> violence. 11 September 2001 stands for this since one form of such vio-
> lence is terror, the definition of which can be excellently disputed.

Does the task of overcoming structures of violence in regions torn
apart by civil war now appear in a different light? I shall approach this
question by looking at four selected aspects of the issue: redefining
conventional concepts of security and self-defence; the correlation between geopolitics and multilateralism in reacting to transnational threats;
the changed perception of selected crisis regions; and finally, the need
to respond by setting priorities in foreign, security and development
policy that are adequate to deal with the problems in the face of the
threat posed by 'privatized violence'.[1]

SECURITY, SELF-DEFENCE AND 'PRIVATIZED VIOLENCE'

In the aftermath of September 11, Western states are waking up to
the concept of 'extended security' in very concrete terms. They recognize that there are new dangers beyond the security dilemma. To take
the image put forward by Ernst-Otto Czempiel (2001), globalization is
no longer a one-way street running from North to South; there is
oncoming traffic, some of it dangerous. Since increasing interdependence means growing vulnerability, security must be redefined in this
context. New threats and forms of armed aggression also raise the
question about which framework and with what means self-defence is
legitimate and effective.

September 11 was a shocking defining moment for the USA, in
particular: 'It had slipped everybody's minds that the Americans are also
vulnerable to terror, and not only through nuclear war' (Augstein 2001:
24).[2] However, this defining moment does not only concern the 'vulnerability of the superpower' (Offe 2001: 1444). In Western countries – and
beyond – the state's core function as the guarantor of security is coming
to the fore once again. Seen against the backdrop of September 11, it is
appropriate – from an alienated viewpoint, so to speak – to quote from

David Darchiashvili's chapter on Georgia, in which he pleads in his fundamental deliberations for a complex concept of security:

> Security is one of the most important foundations for political power. However, it is also true that individual rights and the security of the state and/or society pervade each other ... If one area or the other becomes predominant, they will both be harmed, thus calling the stability of society and the security of its members into question. (Chapter 5, this volume)

Following September 11, it is becoming ever less possible to separate external and internal security – a virtually self-evident conclusion for crisis countries in the South and East with their simultaneous internal and regionalized conflicts, but a new insight for the industrialized countries in the West. At the same time, however, counter-measures are often taken as if one were faced with 'classic' threats. Sight is lost of the fact that the new terrorists can be dealt with only to a limited extent through massive military strikes externally or general control and monitoring arrangements internally. Although training camps and places of refuge can be eliminated, groups of persons monitored to a certain extent and, not least, the ability to act demonstrated in the sense of political symbolism in this way, such measures are no answer to the flagrant failure of the intelligence services in the run-up to September 11. What should be supported, on the other hand, are well-aimed concepts directed at tackling the sources of finance, the institutional structures, the training centres, the sympathizers and, of course, the leaders and manipulators of organizations prepared to use violence. It is not the quantity but the quality and evaluation of information that are crucial in preparing for political action. It is clear that the intelligence services – frequently blocked by mutual rivalries – and the criminal prosecution authorities were barely prepared for the tasks referred to in terms of prevention.

The new terrorists act not only with diabolical precision, but also with camouflage, which makes them very difficult to apprehend using loose-knit actions or conventional means in the area of external or internal security:

> the greatest deception was that they even used the banality of American everyday life as a mask and camouflage – as sleepy suburban residents,

as well-behaved college students, domesticated, hard-working and un-
obtrusive, awaking as time bombs from one day to the next. The perfect
mastering of this clandestine existence almost equates with the spectacular actions of September 11 in its terrorist content since it casts
suspicion on just about any and every individual: isn't every harmless
person or other a potential terrorist? (Baudrillard 2001: 16)[3]

The transnational terrorism of the twenty-first century has a new
quality compared with its predecessors. It is the 'expression of a de-
nationalization, deterritorialization and privatization of the use of
violence that has been taking place for some considerable time, as well
as of a global expansion of terrorism previously locally and regionally
confined within the context of specific conflicts that can be localized'
(Matthies 2001: 1). The new form of terrorism knows no borders or
bounds – in virtually every respect (that is to say geographically, ideo-
logically and morally), for instance in its economic reproduction via
transnationally linked markets of violence and financial networks, its
recruitment of assassins, its worldwide range of action, the proclamation
of its targets (challenging the USA as a world power)[4] and, not least,
its choice of means and victims. Portraying it in (cheap) enemy terms
does not help, however, and only leads to crusade mentalities.

Transnational terrorism also confronts international law with new
challenges because it is still primarily oriented towards international
conflicts between states. The UN Security Council has responded to
this with Resolution 1368 of 12 September 2001 and Resolution 1373
adopted on 28 September 2001. What is remarkable is that, for terror
attacks to be classified as a threat to world peace under international law
according to these resolutions, it is 'no longer a matter of the involvement in any form whatsoever of states or *de facto* regimes: in designating
the terror attacks in themselves as endangering peace, the private players
and organisers involved in such attacks are consequently deemed to
have passive legal capacity under international law within the context
of Chapter VII' (Bruha and Bortfeld 2001: 163).

It is a matter of controversy in the interpretation of the above-
mentioned resolutions within what framework the Security Council
acknowledged the right to self-defence. A further striking fact is that
the Security Council has not clearly defined its competence in relation
to states exerting the right to self-defence. Nevertheless, as Bruha and

Bortfeld (2001: 164) rightly point out, 'the cautious allusion to the right of self-defence in Resolutions 1368 and 1373 can certainly be inferred as a recognition, hedged in by clauses, of the self-defence situation and thus, necessarily, of the existence of an armed attack'. Up to now, it was deemed necessary for this situation that a state or *de facto* regime be substantially involved in terrorist actions,[5] whereas it would now appear possible to speak of an armed attack within the meaning of Art. 51 without this prerequisite. The law on self-defence resulting from this does not, however, mean that carte blanche be given for military retaliation or the pursuance of other political aims, and can therefore not be equated with a right to taking the law into one's own hands.[6]

One further point is also important for the change in the understanding of security. September 11 has served to increase attentiveness with regard to national and transnational networks of violence, from organized crime to warlordism and terrorism: phenomena that can contribute much towards explaining 'state failure', the ineffectiveness of development aid or the breakdown of transformation processes, but are still underexposed in the field of peace and development research. If the mildest form of these distortions, namely widespread corruption, can sometimes be described with concern but also with the wink of an eye as a way of life, the grave effects of the disintegration of state authority are immediately menacing, inasmuch as state crises enable organizations of violence and terror to reproduce themselves through 'markets of violence' (as already defined in the Introduction), and to do so worldwide:

> Robbery, protection rackets, taking hostages and smuggling are all part of this just as much as the trading of ideological wares. This trade in violence with ideological symbols entails selling a sacrifice to wealthy donors. In Europe, the IRA and its rivals had developed this into a fine art. The sacrifice of one's own fighters and/or the sacrifice to the person in the enemy camp were staged with great media effect. Donations then flow out of compassion for the victims or pride for the success of one's own cause. (Elwert 2001: III)

The consequences for foreign, security and development policy have so far not been thought through to any great extent – not by politicians or by the secret services, scientists or the general public. However, answers are now required more than ever before. An understanding of the logic of the highly professional specialists in violence and the way they see themselves in political terms is a prerequisite for combating them effectively. Georg Elwert (2001) has shown using the example of al-Qaida that such networks are highly rational and adaptive. Numerous tentacles of Bin Laden's octopus-like organization have formed in those countries in which the state's monopoly of violence has broken down completely or partially, such as Afghanistan, Sudan and Somalia.[7] There are also links to other Central Asian and African countries, as well as the Caucasus. To what degree the al-Qaida network encircles the globe is also illustrated by the fact that Osama bin Laden and his mujaheddin had a 'Bosnia connection'[8] and provided the Kosovo-Albanian UÇK, Ushtria Çlirimtare e Kosoves (Kosovo Liberation Army – KLA), with both financial and military assistance in exchange for the distribution of drugs from Central and Southern Asia (Oschlies 2001: 1301–2).

RECOURSE TO MULTILATERALISM OR A RENAISSANCE OF GEOPOLITICS?

The terror attacks and the response of the only remaining and, at the same time, 'wounded' world power are having repercussions on the West's priorities and commitment in all regions of the globe. As paradoxical as it may sound, a renaissance of geopolitics *and* recourse to (selective and hegemonic) multilateralism can be observed simultaneously on the part of the USA. US policy in the 'Eurasian region', in particular, appears at the moment to be influenced by geopolitical patterns of thought, for which Brzezinski's book, *The Grand Chessboard* (1997), together with Huntington's article 'The Clash of Civilizations' (1993), have developed a blueprint. Within the framework of forming international alliances, states that were considered in the preceding years to be 'pariahs' (such as Pakistan) or 'rogue states' (such as Syria) are now becoming 'presentable'. Furthermore, authoritarian-dictatorial regimes in Central Asia, in particular, are being granted huge levels of support – the very states that were previously avoided because of their dreadful human rights records (for instance Uzbekistan).[9]

In the choice of their coalition partner in Afghanistan, the USA and Britain have selected an ally that can perform military clearing-up operations but has also committed – in the past as well as the present – blatant violations of humanitarian international law. Behind all this is the power and equilibrium policy thinking – perfected by Henry Kissinger – that does not consider moral criteria to be particularly helpful in matters of war and peace and regards 'any enemy of theirs as a friend of ours'. This strategy has, of course, often been doomed to failure. The USA experienced this first hand with regard to the 11 September attacks, which, according to investigations, were supported and carried out by precisely those players – the Taliban and Osama bin Laden's mujaheddin – who were nurtured via the Pakistani Secret Service in the 1980s. Moscow had similar experiences in its support of Caucasian separatists, who did not bring any greater stability to the South Caucasus or the Russian Federation.

This type of geopolitical logic is different from that concerning human rights or crisis prevention, which supports democratically oriented forces in society, politics and the media and seeks to strengthen its voice. An example of this situation can currently be observed in Afghanistan: the Afghan war economies, which are substantially supported by the drug trade on all sides and guarantee the continued existence of structures of violence, are also likely to flourish further after the Northern Alliance's victory. For example Stratfor, a private intelligence service, in a background analysis stated as early as November 2001 that opium cultivation is being forced in the regions captured by the Northern Alliance and that the Central Asian route, co-controlled by the Russian mafia, is likely to become increasingly important for the drug trade.[10] For a large number of local warlords, the guarantee of the opportunity to cultivate drugs is seen as reward for their commitment or for changing sides in the war against the Taliban regime. An Afghan proverb could prove to be well founded: 'If you let a snake live in your sleeve, it will bite you one day.'

The hypothesis of a renaissance of geopolitics is supported by the fact that the major powers of Russia and China have evidently reached a tacit or explicit agreement to subject their respective actions in Chechnya and Tibet to 'reappraisal'. Claus Offe (2001: 1448–9) – from both a foreign and a domestic policy viewpoint – states cogently that 'the new type of international conflict situation has created an occasional structure that offers the prospect of an abundant yield of windfall profits for economically and, even more so, politically interested parties'. John Le Carré (2001) expressed a similar sentiment in less academic terms in his essay entitled 'A war we cannot win':

Until September 11, the United States was only too happy to plug away at Vladimir Putin about his butchery in Chechnya. Russia's abuse of human rights in the North Caucasus, he was told – we are speaking of wholesale torture, and murder amounting to genocide, it was generally agreed – was an obstruction to closer relations with NATO and the United States ... Well, goodbye to all that. In the making of the great new coalition, Putin will look a saint by comparison with some of his bedfellows.

Nevertheless, there is also evidence of recourse to multilateral action, which certainly serves geopolitics and is of a hegemonic nature. The change is especially noticeable in the case of the Bush administration, which had been steering a strongly unilateralist, even isolationist course since taking office. The tendency towards unilateralism had, however, already started under the Clinton administration, which moved away from its concept of *assertive multilateralism* after the Somalia débâcle of autumn 1993 and from then on inclined more to block rather than support decisions taken by the United Nations in relation to securing peace. The events of 11 September have resulted in a change in the relationship of the US administration and – equally important – of the US Congress with the world organization. At the time of creating its global alliance against terror, the only remaining world power considered using the UN as a forum and an instrument.[11] In light of this, the US Congress approved on 25 September 2001 a sum of $582 million to be paid to the world organization – an appreciable part of the total debts of $862 million still outstanding at that time.[12] It would appear that the USA is, in its own estimation, not in a position to assert its global policy ideas and ideals unilaterally in the long term and will need allies as well as a multilateral framework to achieve this aim (Nuscheler 2001a). In this context, the support or toleration of a further development of the UN is only logical for the foreseeable future – both in relation to safeguarding its own actions under international law and forming international consensus, as well as relieving the USA from obligations that it does not wish to carry out itself or alone in the world's geostrategically more insignificant regions, in particular.

CONSEQUENCES FOR SELECTED CRISIS REGIONS

A further consequence of September 11 is that conflict constellations localized in different regions of the world are being reinterpreted by globally oriented players. Whether this will have positive or negative repercussions on the possibilities for settling such conflicts remains an open question for the time being. What is certain, however, is that such selectivity will be subject to changed perceptions. Conflicts in the Islamic World (especially the Arab states, Iran, Pakistan, Indonesia) and the Israel–Palestine conflict will be observed to less extent with regard to their local causes and more in relation to global conflict formations (in the sense of Huntington's West versus Islam dichotomy). The Israel–Palestine conflict has a key function in this context. Even though the cause or reason for Islamic terrorism does not lie here, this conflict and the suffering of the Palestinian people do form a 'catalyst' or symbolic and almost iconic point of reference for Islamic terrorists and their spectrum of sympathizers. Solving this conflict is therefore more urgent than ever in the light of September 11 – not least because the Arab public is extremely sensitized to the West practising double standards. At the same time, the brutal attacks on Israeli civilians and the ruthless response of the Sharon government, which places its action in the context of a global fight against terrorism, have further blocked any possible approaches for a solution in the months following September 11.

I will now examine, in particular, the consequences of geopolitical and security policy reorientation for the systems of conflict dealt with in greater detail in this volume (South Caucasus, Central America, the Horn of Africa). The Caucasus is especially growing in significance as an interface between Europe and Central Asia. This is all the more relevant in view of the fact that politics and the economy in the region are being co-manipulated by organized crime, and Islamic terror networks also have groups in the region. Nevertheless, the Caucasus could – for some limited time – take a back seat to the region of Central Asia in the list of geopolitical priorities to which limited resources and (likewise increasingly limited) political attention are now being directed (Peuch 2001).

In their new willingness to cooperate with Russia, the USA and other Western states are evidently letting Moscow have an extensively free hand in Chechnya – thus tolerating what is an equally brutal and failed policy for 'pacifying' this republic in the North Caucasus. In the South Caucasus region, Georgia, which is, by virtue of its bordering on Chechnya, both a reception centre and place of refuge for the civilian population – as well as for rebels – is particularly affected by the consensus of the major powers on the fight against terror (Appelbaum 2001). Russia will be able to put forward and assert its demands more offensively in the future with regard to possible border violations by Chechnyan rebels. Moscow has already capitalized on this opportunity by using its enhanced freedom of action militarily: in November 2001, Russian fighter jets bombed villages in the Pankisi Gorge – Georgian territory where since 1999 thousands of Chechnyans have sought refuge and which, because of widespread lawlessness in this spot, has also served as a base for rebel attacks.

At the same time, Moscow's backing of the Abkhazian secession endeavour (which was, by the way, at the beginning of the 1990s supported by Chechnyan rebels) should prove more difficult to maintain. Accordingly, Moscow signalled in December 2001 its preparedness to acknowledge Abkhazia as a sovereign entity with the rule of law *within* the state of Georgia. In the other Southern Caucasian conflicts – not least in Nagorno Karabakh – the 'new common ground' between the USA and the Russian Federation may possibly defuse rivalries surrounded by power politics. The possibility that the security sector, which is distorted in many places, could take advantage of the new challenge to evade the increasing demand by a critical public for transparency and democratic control is likely to be a problem for the region overall.

Latin America is affected by the consequences of September 11 in an indirect manner, with the attacks raising the question of what stance should be adopted towards terrorism and the solidarity demanded by the USA and whether – similar to NATO – alliance should be proclaimed within the framework of the Inter-American Treaty of Reciprocal Assistance. Despite individual cases of resistance, the so-called Rio Treaty has indeed been activated, although this initially and primarily implies cooperation in the area of information (Kurtenbach 2001: 203). In Central America, the presidents of the region agreed on 19 September 2001 to intensify their monitoring of border traffic and migration and provide reciprocal information concerning any findings related to the fight against terror. The governments of Latin America are under pressure to adjust their relationship with the USA in view of the officially declared 'war against terrorism' – an undertaking that is met with scepticism among some sections of the population, as Kurtenbach (2001: 201) points out: 'Although there is sympathy for the victims of the terror attacks, voices can be heard everywhere to the effect that the US was at least partly to blame for such action through its policy towards the developing countries.' In the Central American countries of Nicaragua and El Salvador, the terrorism issue provides a special opportunity for conservative and right-wing parties to drive the left-wing opposition parties (with their guerrilla pasts and corresponding international contacts) into an ideological corner. The terrorism issue was most recently also used as propaganda by the USA in the Nicaraguan election campaign.[13] This pushes a far more important problem, namely the hesitant curbing of the military in the area of internal security (see Chapter 7, this volume), into the background. This could even be counteracted by the (problematic) argument that the army must continue to have comprehensive responsibility for a country's security in the face of the change in the threatening situation (Kurtenbach 2001: 207).

The attention paid to sub-Saharan Africa is likely to decrease in view of the change in geopolitical priorities – with one important exception, namely Eastern Africa (Horn of Africa and East Africa). This subregion not only has a high proportion of Muslim inhabitants, but also has links with the transnational drugs and arms trades as well as with crime syndicates and terror networks. It was not by chance that Islamically oriented terrorism demonstrated its new type of terrorism for the first time in Nairobi and Dar es Salaam on 7 August 1998 with the attacks on the US embassies, in which 224 people – including twelve US citizens – lost their lives.

US policy has viewed this conflict system – which it refers to as the 'Greater Horn of Africa' – against the backdrop of Islamic danger for some considerable time. This interest has increased further very recently with the awareness of the growing significance of Tanzania, Uganda and Kenya as a turntable for drugs directed to Europe and North America along the South and South-East Asia routes. The pressure on governments in the region to act against possible terror networks is becoming greater. Raids in November 2001 carried out by the Kenyan police in the extensively Muslim port of Mombassa confirmed this impression. This will presumably result in the already tense relationship between the Muslim and Christian communities being strained even further.[14] The

Horn of Africa could become an alternative route for the drug trade and is in some places also being troubled by Islamic terror groups. Politically adroit national leaders, such as the head of the Ethiopian government, Meles Zenawi, have offered their services as allies in the fight against terrorism and the drug trade (Ottaway and Ricks 2001; see also Chapter 9, this volume). This helps the regime to justify interventions (already a matter of course in the preceding years) in the neighbouring country of Somalia, while also presenting it with the possibility, as a partner in an anti-terror coalition, to avoid any application of human rights conditionality in relation to development aid. September 11 could have very tangible consequences for Somalia. Intelligence services not only see here a place of refuge for al-Itihaad al-Islamiya, a radical Islamic organization that was allegedly involved in the attacks of 7 August 1998, but also claim to have localized al-Qaida training camps in the region. So far, very little verifiable information has been published in this regard. There were various rumours and speculations in winter 2001–02 that US troops – flanked by the German navy – were going to wage battle against selected targets in Somalia from Somaliland. Berbera, a coast town, has both a deep-sea port and an airport that would enable Somaliland, which declared its independence ten years ago, to receive the international recognition it longs for. Whether the high-level presence of international troops would be good for the model of a traditional mediation of disputes pursued in this case or of state-building according to the bottom-up principle (see Chapters 2 and 8, this volume) must, however, be questioned.

REORIENTATION OF FOREIGN, SECURITY AND DEVELOPMENT POLICY

One of the central realizations of September 11 is that 'entités chaotiques ingouvernables' are 'contagious' (Eppler 2001: 56). Political wisdom therefore demands, especially in crisis regions characterized by a fragile peace, that a collapse into complete lawlessness be prevented. Where such countries have indeed become ungovernable, external players often see themselves as being between Scylla and Charybdis – unavoidable dangers that can hardly be 'circumnavigated': one either endeavours to contain, isolate or simply ignore crisis zones; or one attempts to establish an international protectorate. The former option is scarcely feasible in view of porous borders; neglecting ungovernable regions is, in particular, avenged more quickly than one would expect. Although the latter option may facilitate a certain degree of stabilization in small regions or states and where there is sustained strategic interest (such as in Kosovo), it is doomed to failure in countries of a certain geographical size or ones that (usually) find themselves on the periphery of world politics (such as Afghanistan). The US and UN operation in Somalia (1992–95) – a country that was at times in the global public eye but sank into oblivion in subsequent years – offers a range of sobering lessons.

The danger of politicians and the general public responding to the newly discovered threats to security with a knee-jerk reaction is great. Reference has already been made to the limitations (not to mention the dangers) of massive military strikes as an effective means of foreign and security policy. Up to now, development policy has also responded all too often along the same well-worn tracks. The impression gained sometimes is that old or new recipes are taken out of the drawer and revamped to suit the new challenge. However, their significance for the specific problem at hand is frequently very limited. Attempting to legitimize claims that are meaningful in other contexts solely through the aim of fighting terrorism therefore does no one any favours.

One example of this is that however much blatant poverty and the ever-widening gap between North and South in terms of prosperity and opportunity can form a breeding ground for the support of terrorism, these factors serve just as little to explain such a phenomenon directly. For it is not usually the poor that rebel, but, rather, the 'high priests' of violence being recruited from the affluent and well-educated strata of the business world as well as from the technical and academic intelligentsia (Nuscheler 2001b). The combating of poverty and a fair foreign trade policy have an original value and can contribute towards the just distribution required in both moral and political terms in the global society that is forming, thus enabling everyday crime and the decay of social cohesion to be countered. However, there are other factors that are more relevant to the problem of terrorism.[15] The socio-psychological aspect of humiliation, in particular, should not be underestimated in relation to the emergence of acts of terror – and it also plays a role in the 'clandestine joy' that has been observed in the aftermath of September 11, not only in some parts of the Islamic world, but also in other world regions (for instance, Latin America). Counter-strategies must amount to more than a 'dialogue among civilizations' between social élites; it is essential to reach the circles of sympathizers capable of discussion and their entourage – since it is this milieu that will finally decide whether potential perpetrators follow the erroneous path of violence (with all the consequences of self-isolation, resistance to reality and inhuman acts of violence) or remain within the legal structures. The everyday and implicit symbols and signals sent out by politicians in their day-to-day decisions and declarations are also of crucial importance. Empathy thus proves itself less in fundamental debates than in practical politics. Just how great and serious the difference between humiliating gestures and expressions of respect by political leaders is, can be seen from examples of the behaviour of leading politicians in the Israeli–Palestinian conflict.

It appears highly important to identify the immediate and truly critical points relating to the emergence of transnational terrorism. They lie to a very substantial part in the internal social situations of the countries in which it originated as well as in the chances of it developing its own socio-economic infrastructure. Political violence emerges above all in places where repression and a lack of prospects in life are no longer accepted and the possibilities for articulating oneself politically are denied. This is currently the case in very particular Islamic countries from which al-Qaida recruits its members: primarily Saudi Arabia, but also Egypt.

> Anyone who knows about everyday life and experience in these countries holds the key to the attacks in his hand. There is a desperate desire to exert influence: 'action' is called for. Terror creates a surrogate for the powerless. (Elwert 2001: II)

It is a very interesting fact that criminal financial networks come together precisely in the banks and investment funds of the states bordering on the Gulf. The diverse financial institutions have excellent relations with Western politicians and business circles. This raises the question of who would want to pick up a fight with the political and economic élites of the rich oil states.

An important response to the most recent variety of transnational terror is to drain such sources of finance – a course pursued by the UN

Security Council in Resolution 1373. Clause 1b obliges all states to 'Criminalize the wilful provision or collection, by any means, directly or indirectly, of funds by their nationals or in their territories with the intention that the funds should be used, or in the knowledge that they are to be used, in order to carry out terrorist acts.' It is now a matter of implementation, although this alone will not suffice. Unfortunately, there is evidence that double standards have been applied so far: while banking houses in Europe and in the wealthy oil states were requested in a more friendly and diplomatic way by the USA to prevent an abuse by terrorists, the Somali Al-Barakaat Group was closed down immediately – despite the fact that the owners of the bank had asked US authorities for assistance in order not to be used as a channel for the transfer and laundry of terrorists' money.

If the fight against terror is to be conducted within the framework of effective multilateralism, a regulated procedure supported by the UN Security Council is required for the indictment, apprehension and handing over of top terrorists, as well as for juridical punishment of their deeds. The decision taken in the summer of 1998 by an international interstate conference in Rome to create an International Criminal Court would provide a suitable forum to this end (Hamm et al. 2002: 13). The fact that criminal acts by terrorists are not referred to in its statutes need not be an obstacle. Crimes on the scale represented by the September 11 attacks can also be classified under the existing headings of 'war crimes' or 'crimes against humanity'. The setting up of an *ad hoc* tribunal by the UN Security Council could also be organized quickly as another possibility. Those who do not explore such options or even sabotage them leave themselves open to the accusation of not wishing to fight the new form of terrorism with clearly established legal rules and standards but, rather, according to political opportunism and geopolitical deliberateness.

An effective and, at the same time, practicable possibility in the foreseeable future for countering transnational terrorism would be political reforms in those countries from which the perpetrators come, as well as global measures to counteract state failure. Development policy has been sensitized to such political issues in recent years through the model of crisis prevention – a point that can also provide the basis for measures to counter the privatization of violence (see the Foreword to this volume). The chapters in this volume spell out options for *institution-*

building and international support, both in terms of content and in relation to specific regions and countries. One important lesson is that the establishment of a state monopoly of violence and the protection of individuals against the many varied forms of violence is a top-priority task. However, this must entail more than merely making the security sector effective, since this sector is abused all too often, as the wealthy Gulf States show. The specific contribution of Western-oriented democracies must therefore also include promoting and supporting the rule of law and political participation within the context of a (potentially critical) general public. This requires a peace and development policy commitment for an independent judiciary and for those sections of society (media, lobbies, non-governmental organizations) that stand up for the assertion of democracy and human rights – often risking their own freedom and physical well-being. If new means are now incorporated into the fight against terror in the light of changing priorities, this area – besides developing alternatives to economies of violence – would be of special significance. Establishing a solid and consistent foreign, security and development policy is, of course, more important than another change in development cooperation, which constantly seeks new legitimation and areas of responsibility. Such a policy should not get involved with dubious allies, but, rather, it needs courageously and resolutely to confront those who are responsible for and/or benefit from repression, violence, corruption and illegal profiteering.

(*Translation: Barry Stone*)

NOTES

1. Privatized forms of violence comprise, among others, organized crime, vigilantes, para-military groups associated with particular political factions, and terrorists. In addition to the 'privatization of violence', a 'privatization of security' can also be observed, with affluent individuals, companies and governments availing themselves of private service providers for security matters. This trend contributes in many cases, as does privatized violence, to the (further) erosion of the state's monopoly of violence; see the Introduction in this volume, and in greater detail Kaldor 1999, 2000.

2. The previous (semi-unsuccessful) attack on the World Trade Center in 1993 had already illustrated the vulnerability of US society to a certain extent. However, the scale, staging, coordination and selection of targets of the 11 September attacks displayed – also symbolically – an individual and new type of terrorism.

3. Baudrillard (2001: 16) cannot be quoted without mentioning a further

hypothesis (not shared by myself). According to this psychologizing–moralizing hypothesis, the US superpower is itself partly responsible for its 'self-destruction' or its 'suicide as a work of art' as 'it has itself, through its unbearable superior might, stirred up not only all the violence that presently fills the world, but also – without knowing it – the terrorist fantasy that we all harbour inside ourselves'.

4. Elwert (2001: I) states: 'It cannot be ruled out that the planners of the attacks hoped to liquidate the top echelon of the USA with one strike, thus giving the signal for a major international rebellion movement.'

5. Cf. Resolution 2625 (XXV) adopted on 24 October 1970 by the UN General Assembly (Declaration on Principles of International Law concerning Friendly Relations and Cooperation among States in accordance with the Charter of the United Nations); Resolution 3314 (XXIX) adopted by the UN General Assembly on 14 December 1974 on the Definition of Aggression (Art. 3 in particular). The Nicaragua ruling handed down by the International Court on 27 June 1986 is also an important point of reference. The judgment on 'Military and Paramilitary Activities in and against Nicaragua (*Nicaragua* v *United States of America*) (1984–1991)' is available on the Internet under: <http://www.icj-cij.org/icjwww/idecisions.htm> (accessed 4 September 2001).

6. In concrete terms, the military battle against al-Qaida and its affiliated organizations should be covered under international law if there is sufficient proof for involvement in the 11 September attacks. Such a battle may also take place on foreign territory if it can be proven that the government or *de facto* regime grants protection to a terrorist organization. It is contentious whether such measures may also directly target persons or institutions of the government or *de facto* regime (Bruha and Bortfeld 2001: 166). In the end, self-defence must also be subjected to the principle of commensurability and to humanitarian international law. Seen against this background, the objective (overthrowing the Taliban regime) of the war fought in Afghanistan through the late autumn of 2001 and winter of 2001–02 and the type of warfare (deployment of cluster bombs, supporting a local warring party that flagrantly violates humanitarian international law) are very problematic. Any extension of the war objectives that entails the fight against terror increasingly assuming the nature of 'preventive strikes' must also be assessed in critical terms.

7. However, terrorist organizations or activities do not emerge only in states that are breaking down; they also occur in countries where the state acts repressively with a certain degree of effectiveness and does not allow sections of the population to participate fairly in political or socio-economic matters. Examples of this are Saudi Arabia, Egypt, Israel/Palestine/Lebanon, Pakistan, Uzbekistan, Ethiopia, Eritrea, Northern Ireland, Columbia and the Philippines.

8. Both the Al Mujahed volunteer brigade active in the war in Bosnia and the 'Roubaix Group' recruited mainly from the Maghreb are said to have had links with Islamic terrorists. Many observers criticized the official and, in some cases, unofficial naturalization of Arab militiamen in Bosnia. The president at the time, Alija Izetbegovic, is suspected of having been involved in this. At the same time, excessive importance should not be attached to these facts, for they should rather be seen in historical terms in the light of the desperate situation of the Bosnian

Muslims. A general suspicion that there was a favourable environment for Muslims in Bosnia would be misleading in this respect. (Cf. *Neue Zürcher Zeitung*, 24 November 2001, No. 274: 7).

9. The situation in Tajikistan is somewhat different. The authoritarian regime of President Imamali Rahmanov does grant certain freedoms, and parties are allowed. The opposition occupies around 30 per cent of all government posts – in contrast to Uzbekistan.

10. Cf. Stratfor.Com (Strategic Forecasting – the Global Intelligence Company), 30 November 2001, ('US war on terror may undermine war on drugs'), <http://www.stratfor.com/northamerica/commentary/ 0111301800.htm> (accessed 1 December 2001).

11. See Kubbig 2001 with regard to (selective) recourse to instruments of multilateralism.

12. Cf. Julit Eilperin, 'House approves UN payment', *Washington Post*, 25 September 2001, <http://www.globalpolicy.org/finance/2001/0925delay.htm> (accessed 13 October 2001); 'US to make second dues payment to UN', *Associated Press*, 6 October 2001, <http://www.globalpolicy.org/finance/unitedstates/2001/1006bush.htm> (accessed 13 October 2001).

13. 'Honduras this week', Online Edition 45 (Monday, 19 November 2001) and Online Edition 44 (Monday, 5 November 2001), Central American Weekly Review. Member of the Inter-American Press Association, <http://www.marder.com/htw/central.htm> (accessed 3 December 2001).

14. Cf. Stratfor.Com (Strategic Forecasting – the Global Intelligence Company) from 20 November 2001 ('Kenya Crackdown Inflaming Religious Tensions'), <http://www.stratfor.com/africa/commentary/ 0111202040.htm> (accessed 21 November 2001).

15. Walter Laqueur (2001) argues firmly against the thesis that poverty spawns terrorism, since it occurs both in poorer regions of a country (such as Peru) as well as in more wealthy regions (such as Punjab/India, North-East Sri Lanka/Tamil). His principal argument (the empirical soundness and validity of which would admittedly have to be examined in critical terms) is that: 'Among the 49 countries designated by the UN as being the poorest of the poor, terrorism has played a certain role in only two of them, that is: in the Sudan and Afghanistan, and in neither case was it an indigenous product but, rather, a foreign import. Terrorists bought themselves a country.'

REFERENCES

Appelbaum, A. (2001) 'Crackdowns, confusion ahead for central Asia and Caucasus', in David Johnson (ed.), *Johnson's Russia List* (Eurasianet.org, 13/18 September 2001) <http://www.cdi.org/russia/johnson/5448-12.cfm> (accessed 3 December 2001).

Augstein, R. (2001) 'Abenteurer und Strategen', in *Der Spiegel*, 47: 24 (Kommentar).

Baudrillard, J. (2001) 'Der Geist des Terrorismus. Das Abendland, das die Stelle

Gottes eingenommen hat, wird selbstmörderisch und erklärt sich selbst den Krieg', *Süddeutsche Zeitung*, 12 November, p. 16.

Bruha, T. and M. Bortfeld (2001) 'Terrorismus und Selbstverteidigung. Voraussetzungen und Umfang erlaubter Selbstverteidigungsmaßnahmen nach den Anschlägen vom 11 September', *Vereinte Nationen*, 49 (5) (October): 161–7.

Brzezinski, Z. (1997) *The Grand Chessboard: American Primacy and its Geostrategic Imperatives*, New York: Basic Books.

Czempiel, E.-O. (2001) 'Die Globalisierung schlägt zurück. Die Terrorakte in den USA zeigen: Außenwirtschafts- und Entwicklungspolitik müssen einem Paradigmenwechsel unterzogen werden', *Frankfurter Rundschau*, 5 November 2001, p. 6 (documentation; abridged version of a talk given by the Frankfurt peace and conflict researcher on 3 November 2001 at the Römerberg talks in Frankfurt/Main).

Elwert, G. (2001) 'Rational und lernfähig: Wer die Terroristen des 11 September bekämpfen will, muss zunächst ihre Logik begreifen', *Der Überblick*, 37 (3) (September): I–VIII.

Eppler, E. (2001) 'Weder Krieg noch Frieden', *Der Spiegel*, 41 (8 October): 56–9.

Hamm, B., J. Hippler, D. Messner and C. Weller (2002) 'World Politics at the Crossroads: The 11th of September 2001 and the Aftermath', Policy Paper 19, March, Bonn: Development and Peace Foundation.

Huntington, S.P. (1993) 'The clash of civilizations?', *Foreign Affairs*, New York, 72 (3) (Summer): 22–49.

Kaldor, M. (1999) *New and Old Wars: Organised Violence in a Global Era*, Cambridge: Polity Press.

—— (2000) 'Cosmopolitanism and organised violence', paper prepared for the conference *Conceiving Cosmopolitanism*, Warwick, 27–29 April 2000, London, Centre for the Study of Global Governance, London School of Economics, <http://www.theglobalsite.ac.uk/press/010kaldor.htm> (accessed 27 January 2002).

Kubbig, B. W. (2001) 'Ein Crash-Surs in Schen Multilateralismus. Über den aussenpolitischen Schwenk der USA und die Brüchigkeit der Ein-Punkt-Allianz gegen dan Terror', *Frankfurter Rundschau*, 12 October 2001, p. 18 (documentation).

Kurtenbach, S. (2001) 'Lateinamerika nach dem 11 September 2001', *Brennpunkt Lateinamerika*, 19 (17 October): 201–8, Hamburg, Institute for Ibero-American Studies.

Laqueur, W. (2001) 'Ist Armut ein Grund für den Hass der Moslems? Ursachen des Terrors: Mythos und Realität. Eine Spurensuche nach den Motiven der Anschläge vom 11. September', *Die Welt*, 4 December.

Le Carré, J. (2001) ' A war we cannot win', *Nation*, 19 November. <http://www.globalpolicy.org/wtc/analysis/ 1119carre.htm> (accessed 10 November 2001).

Matthies, V. (2001) 'Thesen zum internationalen Terrorismus: Zur Bedeutung des terroristischen Anschlags vom 11. September 2001', unpublished manuscript, Hamburg (November).

Müller, H. (2001) 'Verbrecher sind keine Krieger. Die zwei Ebenen der Terrorismus-bekämpfung', *Frankfurter Rundschau*, 11 October, p. 8 (documentation).

Nuscheler, F. (2001a) 'Multilateralism vs. unilateralism, cooperation vs. hegemony in transatlantic relations', Policy Paper 16, January, Bonn: Development and Peace Foundation.

— (2001b) 'Die Armen rebellieren nicht', a *ZEIT* interview with development researcher Franz Nuscheler, in *DIE ZEIT*, 11 October, No. 41 (Wirtschaft), <http://www.zeit.de/2001/41/Wirtschaft/print_200141_interv._nuschele. html> (accessed 21 November 2001).

Offe, C. (2001) 'Die Neudefinition der Sicherheit', *Blätter für deutsche und internationale Politik*, 46 (12) (December): 1442–50, Bonn.

Oschlies, W. (2001) 'Die Bosnien-Connection des Osama bin Laden', *Blätter für deutsche und internationale Politik*, Vol. 46 (11) (November): 1301–4, Bonn.

Ottaway, D. B. and E. R. Thomas (2001) 'Somalia draws anti-terrorist focus', *Washington Post*, 4 November, p. A01. <http://www.washingtonpost. com/ wp-dyn/articles/A36231–2001Nov3.html> (accessed 3 December 2001).

Peuch, J.-C. (2001) 'Caucasus: Russia may benefit from 11 September fallout', Radio Free Europe, Radio Liberty, <http://www.rferl.org/nca/features/2001/10/ 30102001085301.asp> (accessed 3 December 2001).

'New Realism' or 'New Development': Meeting the Challenges of Identity Conflicts, Organized Crime and Transnational Terrorism

AXEL KLEIN AND JAMES OPORIA-EKWARO

§ There is a sense that following the events of September 11 international relations have arrived at a policy crossroads. With the most spectacular act of terrorism in history, and the first violent attack on the American mainland since the Civil War, the world, so goes the media refrain, will never be the same. Since then we have witnessed the US–UK campaign against the Taliban regime in Afghanistan and the occupation of Palestine by Israeli forces. The subsequent entanglement of the USA and to a lesser degree the European Union in these regional conflagrations, and their impact on the global economy manifest already in volatile oil markets, only serve to underline the importance of the contributions in this volume, dedicated to the identification of conditions and methodologies for the construction of durable peace. Without wishing to revisit the ground covered so comprehensively by Debiel in Chapter 10, we would like to add to the argument that global security is best served by a redoubled commitment to a new development co-operation strategy, however alluring the promise of military interventionism. We seek to enrich the contributions to *Fragile Peace* with selected case studies from Africa. These are particularly pertinent because of the continent's unparalleled experience of state decay, development stagnation and spreading webs of conflict.

THE COMPLEX CAUSALITY OF CONFLICT

The discussions of conflict in the Caucasus, Central America and the Horn of Africa bring out clearly that it takes a composite of factors to 'heat up' latent conflicts. The intermesh between external interests in, for example, the Caspian Sea, the oil reserves, and resurgent group identities can erupt in irredentist or secessionist demands formulated in the idiom of nationalism. Freitag-Wirminghaus (Chapter 4) does emphasize the importance of external nations organized in the Minsk group, and touches on the role of private corporations engaging in a Great Game as well as historic Russian dominance as important framing conditions. The importance of external agents varies between the conflict theatres, between direct intervention, covert operations, active destabilization, the tacit support of particular factions, the promise of financial reward, the supply of arms, and so on. One thing remains common: external agents are usually driven to a crisis region by self-interest, and may easily accelerate the spiral of conflict. This self-interest has conventionally been a matter of material gain or strategic access. Debiel (Chapter 10) and Holtz (Foreword) point out, however, that it is no longer possible to confine conflicts to regional theatres in an era of globalization. Hence the Western powers at the centre of the global system have to begin to view conflict resolution, peace-making, peace-building and the pursuit of classical development aspirations as measures that strengthen their long-term security.

To that end we need to develop an understanding of the dynamics of conflicts. There are general conditions fuelling the propensity to resort to violence by corporate groups, including the defence of traditional rights and assertion of legitimate claims, a deeply rooted suspicion of existing power structures, a list of grievances and a sense of immediate threat to the conditions of the communal way of life. It is instructive to note that in most crisis situations each of the antagonists explains the use of violence as responsive and corrective. Even pre-emptive strikes can be fitted into this ideological concept of victimization.

While a shared faith and nationhood can be active agents for cementing a people to the state, nothing works more effectively at consolidating state power than the threat posed by culturally different neighbours. The importance of warfare in the construction of nationalisms and the rise of the state is well recorded in European history. Whether war has a similar 'constructive' function in the developing countries in general, and the crisis regions in particular, is open to question, especially as the lines of division are often so vaguely defined, and interpretation of status can be so fluid. Conflict across state boundaries is made all the more volatile by the presence of sizeable minority communities within, who can be abused as scapegoats for the martial exertions of makeshift militias and gangs of thugs. The danger then is that political posturing by government representatives at home can put into jeopardy the fate of minority communities abroad. The repercussions suffered by the diaspora can then be used to justify an escalation of hostilities at state level. While India and Pakistan have not yet crossed the Rubicon, the politics of brinkmanship yield considerable political dividends to nationalist politicians and the manipulators of the mob in either country.

IDENTITY AND JUSTICE

Group identities that come to the fore in a prolonged violent conflict are melded in the cauldron of economic deprivation, dislocation, political oppression and existential threat. The crucial ingredient, however, is the subsequent recording and representation of the concrete experience of collective victimization. Writing on the impact of particular historic atrocities on group formation, Levene and Roberts argue that 'once embedded in the collective memory of a group or nation ... the past victimization can become a legitimate ingredient in one's self image' (1999: 27). This means that the sense of collective self is defined partly by reflection in the antithesis of a hostile other, a power dedicated to the destruction of collective self. Violent conflict is therefore a logical consequence of the order of being, rooted in the presuppositions of social existence.

The description of group identity conflict as primordial is less useful when taken as a reference to a retro-stage in the evolution of warfare or to the means by which the conflicts may be conducted. This is a line of interpretation popularized in the mid-1990s by the 'New Barbarism' school, which has been instrumental in preparing the field for some specious distinctions between different types of violence and has enjoyed considerable influence in the USA.[1] We agree with Richards that 'there is little if any analytical value in distinguishing between cheap wars based on killing with knives and cutlasses, and expensive wars in which civilians are maimed or destroyed with sophisticated laser-guided weapons' (1996: xx). In the final analysis, the distinctions between acts of barbarism and civilized warfare have less to do with the identification of targets, concern for civilian casualties or efforts to contain collateral damage than with the identity of the perpetrator.

It could be argued that the fight against barbarism is something that, in one form or another, runs through US military history, be this in the conquest and 'pacification' of the West, the expulsion of Spain from its remaining colonies, and the wars against the Kaiser, the Nazis, Japanese militarism or communist expansion. In each case the military fervour was whipped up not by the sense of immediate danger, but by a moral purpose and pre-destiny: each war a crusade, embarked on for the greater good of humanity at large, including the enemies, who once conquered could then be saved. As the motto of Church schools in the Western reservations clearly set out, the task was to 'kill the Indian to save the child' (French 2000).

For groups or nations facing an opponent with overwhelming power, neither willing nor compelled to negotiate, the response is indeed primordial. The victims worry precisely about their chances of survival and the preservation of society itself. For peoples caught in situations of state collapse, foreign occupation or exile, the term primordial signifies a sense of existential threat, calling for extreme and desperate measures, including the Ghost Dance[2] and suicide bombers. When this situation drags on with no resolution in sight, the line between cause and struggle becomes blurred until fighting becomes a self-perpetuating series of tit-for-tat killings, seasonal campaigning and tactical engagements. Not only have all attempts to address the underlying preconditions of violence been abandoned by this stage, but also violent struggle becomes assimilated into the social norm, thereby guaranteeing a ready supply of fighters.

No conflict will ever be short of opportunists, including such modern-day mercenaries as the Ukrainian pilots flying for Eritrean and Ethiopian air forces in the border war. Much more important for the endless spiral of retributions, however, is the generation of martyrs who embrace the conflict as sacred, and death and sacrifice as ends in themselves. Interestingly, the destruction of a usually rural and agrarian way of life and the diversity of culture it supports can in the course of shared suffering and struggle lead to ethnogenesis – the formation of new, larger identities. This provides a further example of the instrumental power warfare has in transforming human society. We think, for instance, of the Nuba in Sudan, or the Palestinians: where these identities are forged in liberated zones or refugee camps, this is portentous of cycles of violence to come. As Kelly acutely observes, 'substantial cultural elaboration is required to make the killing of an unsuspecting and uninvolved individual "count" as reciprocity for an earlier death, to make it morally appropriate and socially meaningful' (Kelly 2000).

Yet deprivation is neither a necessary nor automatic precondition for violent conflict. In sub-Saharan Africa the responses to development failure have varied: Congo, for example, has fragmented, while Nigeria preserves its integrity. The divergence can be found among neighbouring states elsewhere: Guatemala remains mired in systemic violence, while Costa Rica prospers peacefully; Peru, Colombia and Algeria are still caught in the throes of a civil war, while Ecuador, Venezuela and Morocco are not.

In the polarization of the world into Islamic and non-Islamic nations, the adherents of the movement lend credence to a Huntingdon-type fragmentation of the world into blocs of clashing civilizations. By defining itself first as Islamic, and secondarily as Arab, the terror network identifies with the injustice being committed against the Palestinian peoples, symbolic of the vulnerability and the impotence of the entire Islamic world. A sense of shame is mixed into the emotional cocktail by Israeli triumphalism and the relentless advance of US culture and consumerism.

Religion, nation and ethnicity provide ready holdalls for collective identities, big enough to meld tribes into countries and match the nation with a state. Conflicts are then fought between different nations and their respective countries, or over the ethnic identity or religious outlook of the country. Violence is projected outwards from the in-group against the enemy, which provides an opportunity to combine self-interest with collective endeavour.

The difficulty in reining in the forces of violence once unleashed are illustrated by the Central American studies included in this volume. Peace talks are hampered by the vacillation of the political élite, wishing for the return to barracks of the military guardians without risking the economic privileges, which the soldiers were called out to defend in the first place. The result of the botched peace process is a chronic state of insecurity with a record homicide rate of 156 per 100,000 inhabitants in 1995 (see Chapter 6) – an actual increase in the number of violent deaths since the end of the war.

How then to ensure that the peace process stays on course and the different sides negotiate with goodwill and integrity? How can a restless military (Chapter 7), an authoritarian government (Chapter 9), or a predominant executive (Chapter 4) be contained?

STATE FAILURE AND RESPONSES

There is a prolific growth of questions that can be pruned back to a single issue – the state. Development theory has long struggled with the role of the state in former African and Asian colonies. Emerging from an era with an iron-fisted and unaccountable executive, the state in most developing countries assumed the role of engine of modernization, social development and economic growth upon independence. It delivered only rarely and partially on these promises, and came into some disrepute during the 1980s. With the entrenchment of the neoliberal paradigm in the key international financial institutions, the assault on the state in developing and later in transition countries was on the way. Structural adjustment programmes conducted in developing countries across the globe significantly changed the power relations between the national governments and the private sector. Only with the crisis spinning out of control in a number of African countries was the function and regulatory role of the state rediscovered and reviewed. It was suddenly realized that, short of direct intervention, functioning governments were the sole guarantee for preventing territories from being used by terrorists, drug smugglers and other forms of organized crime.

This is a far cry from the 1980s, when the state was widely perceived as holding back economic progress with the deadening hand of over-regulation and control. Acknowledging the tenacious problems facing developing countries, economists such as de Soto advocated the reduction and minimization of the state, to allow the private sector to flourish. In this view, civil society was inherently creative and productive, while governments and states were obstacles to growth. The structural adjustment programmes that were rolled out in one developing country after another accordingly cut down the size of bureaucracies, retrenched workers in parastatal concerns, and sold nationalized assets to private investors in the pursuit of efficiency and economic growth. The hardship that followed and the collapse of state services in health, education and infrastructures were all seen as part of the bitter but necessary medicine. A series of incremental changes did, however, effect a more fundamental shift. The state lost both its capacity to drive forward the development process and its remaining patrimonial function as redistributor of wealth, and this also undermined its capacity to maintain law and order.

Where violent crime becomes endemic the role of the law enforcement agencies begins to assume the role of an occupation force. In many urban conglomerations in developing countries many neighbourhoods are quasi outside the state in the sense that there are no state services, and the writ of the court can be enforced only by a massive incursion. In some of the 'garrisons' of Kingston, the *favelas* of Rio de Janeiro or neighbourhoods of Lagos, for example, the police can only enter in force, and have no function in maintaining law and order internally. Many of the post-colonial constabularies have adapted the concept of the riotous masses to one of the 'dangerous classes', who have to be controlled by force (Harriott 2000: 105). The upshot is a withdrawal from the inner city, collusive relationship with informers and gang leaders, and a cycle of impunity that is episodically interrupted by paramilitary actions.

Yet to many political philosophers the upkeep of personal safety and the guarantee of property are not only the most important functions of the state, but also the pillars of legitimacy. According to Adam Smith: 'The obligation of the subjects of the Sovereign is understood to last as long, and no longer, than the power lasteth, by which he is able to protect them.' Failure to guarantee fundamental freedoms therefore releases the subject of the need to abide by rules, regulation and duties that tie a polity together. They cease, in other words, being citizens and become defined by membership of other corporate groups. And the state has simply failed, or, as in Somalia in 1991, collapsed.

State failure has been one of the unintended outcomes of the end of the Cold War. Prior to that, states were liberated from colonial oppressors or Marxist regimes, depending on the ideological position. Partisan observers may try to employ the euphemism 'liberated zones' for rebel-held territory in some conflict areas. But the administrations set up by the National Union for the Total Independence of Angola (UNITA) in Angola, the Sudanese People's Liberation Army (SPLA) in southern Sudan, and the Revolutionary United Front (RUF) in Sierra Leone are too rudimentary and exploitative to merit any suggestion either of reflecting popular will or of carrying the responsibility of government.

The turmoil enveloping a number of African countries has since given rise to extensive theories and taxonomies. Criteria have been identified to distinguish between anarchic, phantom, anaemic, captured or aborted states, and efforts have gone into finding the main drivers: extreme income disparity, authoritarianism, militarism, affliction by 'Malthusian phenomena', and so on (Gross). The focus on such a crisis region occludes the wider picture of changing state–society relations in a series of processes loosely known as 'globalization', which have eroded what Amin (1994) identified as the three pillars of post-Second World War international orders: Fordism and the welfare state, Sovietism and developmentism. Today the explanatory power of these three grand narratives is exhausted, as the 'integration and fragmentation' (Kaldor 1999) of globalization ring in a paradigm shift.

In the West the role of the welfare state as the 'management framework for social compromises' (Amin 1994) between capital, labour and the state has been steadily eroded. We maintain that this very same assault has been levied against the South, triggering a structural crisis in the process, which in some cases has been termed 'state failure'. The new classification succeeds in obscuring the causal interrelationship between terms of trade, investment flows and aid conditionality, by placing the onus and responsibility on the shoulders of the nations and societies affected. At the risk of inviting a cynical Western response, dismissing such critiques as an African litany of woes caused by colonialism and slavery long after independence, we would like to argue that state failure can be attributed in large part to three factors:

- The structural adjustment programmes (SAP) of the international financial institutions (IFIs) aimed at 'reining in the states' (Mkandawire 1998).
- The triumph of the SAPs was a consequence (and cause) of the shift in the balance of forces between capital on the one hand, and organized labour and popular movements on the other, including the demise of African nationalism.
- The shift from a bipolar to a multipolar world dominated by one military superpower wiped out the political space that a number of state-centred international alliances had created, among them the

Non Aligned Movement, Group of 77, Afro-Asian Solidarity, and so on.

Having spearheaded the assault on the state, the IFIs have belatedly recognized the need for governments to carry out the regulatory functions for capital to flow in. Neighbouring governments, and since 9/11 many further afield, have also rushed into crisis regions with the sense that 'something needs to be done' to prevent to gradual decline of countries into chaos.

Refugees and the economic-knock on effects of lost markets already affect neighbouring countries. Clandestine trading networks in guns, drugs, diamonds, precious metals and tropical hardwoods develop outside the formal economy and usually outside the law. These negative incentives further undermine the rule of law and the development efforts of national government, and can easily degenerate into conflict spillover, from banditry to bush war. These may be, in part at least, characterized as another byproduct of globalization and the integration of markets: rebel groups can easily obtain the hardware, especially small arms, in turn for raw materials. It is important to remember that the horrific acts of violence are not simply random or casual, but calculated to expose the weakness of government, to draw in an already overstretched enemy, to send waves of refugees, and simply to conquer land. We must also measure it against the atrocities committed by way of collateral damage in the conduct of 'conventional war', and ask if the differences are as categorical as is claimed.

Since 'new wars' rarely enjoy the backing that liberation movements could once attract from vying superpowers, they are increasingly locked in with enclave economies. These often use extra economic modes of exploitation including forced labour and forms of slavery. They are reminiscent, in a sense, of the grosser episodes of colonialism, perhaps most hideously of the Congo Free State (Hochschild 1998). One of the epiphenomena of these new wars are the roving bands of factions of rebel soldiers, described as 'nomad economic units' (Douma and Lebillon 2001). Even more curious is the spectacle of barter trade between enemy soldiers, especially of essential items.

The attempt at managing such conflicts and resurrecting states runs into a web of interests, which is frequently upheld by force of arms. But the international community is bound to pursue the reconstruction of governments and countries in order to eliminate potential havens for outlaws, and contain the potential contagion of unsettlement. It is important, therefore, to equip a state with the instruments of governance – including a judicial system (Chapter 2), regional and local levels of government (Chapter 3) and conflict resolution mechanisms (Chapter 8) to render it stable and sustainable. Many of the conflict resolution activities organized by Western partners designed to support this development are open to criticism, particularly the depoliticization of eminently political relations (all technique and no politics) under the false claim of neutrality, with endless process seminars and workshops (all process and no solution), compounded by the lack of attention given to economics, for fear of upsetting the investors.

Critical observers of the post-conflict reconstruction in the Balkans are increasingly beginning to suggest that the inappropriate application of imported methods is in fact counter-productive. Attempts at foisting liberal institutions textbook fashion on divided communities may indeed undermine the state and undermine local autonomy. Chandler suggests that 'Democratization provides the perfect form for this ongoing process of international cooperation because there is no end point' (1999: 193). Like the *mission civilisastrice* parading as a justification for late-nineteenth-century colonialism, democratization provides both alibi and programme for an ongoing presence. In the long term it also provides a pretext for intervention. The removal of democratically elected government, however fake, could attract the attentions of external powers with pretensions of being a 'force for good in the world'.[3]

MEETING THE TERRORIST THREAT: NEW REALISM OR NEW DEVELOPMENT

The willingness of Western powers to deploy in trouble-spots or attack perceived enemies has risen dramatically since the end of the Cold War. For the comity of nations this appears to be a critical moment, where the nature of international relations lies in the balance as the repercussions of the September attack wash across the entire spectrum of foreign policy concerns. The direction of these changes depends largely on the analysis of the attack. In their initial responses American politicians ascribed the motives to jealousy of US greatness and hatred of the values it stood for. This was a visceral reaction, partly aimed at nursing the wounded sense of national pride. Yet it was also deeply fallacious. Understanding the dynamic of violence is not facilitated by the rhetorical depiction of suicide bombers as criminals, and the mis-interpretation of their motivation as one of hatred of American freedom.

With the highest in-migration rate of any region of the world, and the phenomenal export of lifestyle products from fashion to films to fast food (Schlosser 2001), and the highest number of university students from overseas, the global popularity of the US 'way of life' is beyond a doubt. The object of the terrorist hatred is not primarily the USA, but the power projection of US foreign policy (Blum 2000) and its align-ment with repressive regimes. It is not the USA *per se* that has offended the adherents of al-Qaida, but the military presence of US troops in Saudi Arabia, on 'sacred Islamic soil'. The symbolic rejection of the icons of American culture as emblematic of materialism or sexual immodesty is largely reactive, and derived from a politically defined antagonism.

Moreover, the perpetrators were motivated by an idealism quite removed from their personal experience. What consumed them was a sense of chronic injustice needing to be rectified. Their identity was stretched between two poles, with the victims of this chronic injustice by virtue of shared religion, race or humanity, and with the oppressors by reason of economic privilege. Unprecedented is the reach of the al-Qaida network, launching operations from Eastern Africa, to the Philip-pines and the USA itself. They have a strong sense of what they are fighting: the USA and the projections of Western capitalism. Objectives are manifold: direct demands reminiscent of the liberation wars such as the withdrawal of US troops from Mecca, a hoped-for uprising of the toiling masses, and retribution against the excesses of Western ex-pansionism.

The underlying dynamic is often ignored by politicians and political commentators on the right, who seek to use the attack on the twin towers as an opportunity to accelerate the new militarization, and to forgo the diplomatic niceties of coalition-building for a strident unilateralism. As Gerard Baker of the *Financial Times* observes: 'Mr Cheney and his fellow conservatives argue that in the post-cold war world, the US has the military wherewithal to take care of the threats posed by its enemies, if only it would break free of the illusory multilateralism.'[4] It has the backing of a powerful constituency, in the numerous arms of the security and law enforcement service that regard operational constraints as a source of US vulnerability. There are complaints about the self-imposed restraint on overseas security missions because 'political correctness has taken deep root at Langley and in Washington' (Baer 2002). The spy-turned-story-teller Robert Baer has argued that with a few well-targeted assassinations in the 1980s the suicide bombings could have been averted, if Washington had accepted that the USA was at war with the terrorists and taken the moral authority to order killings (2002). President Bush has already widened the operational powers of the secret services.

One of the assumptions of this 'new realism' is that the more liberal approaches have failed, particularly in the field of development. They point to an unimpressive record of development assistance, which has neither won the USA friends overseas, nor succeeded in kick-starting development. According to some, much development assistance has even been counterproductive, creating negative incentives, corruption and dependency. According to Edward Jaycox, former vice-president of the World Bank:

> After thirty years of technical assistance, and so much money spent, Africa's weak institutions, lack of expertise, and current need for more – rather than less – assistance tells us we have failed badly in our efforts … the donors have done a disservice to Africa, and many African governments have participated blindly.

One of the most prominent proponents is US Treasury Secretary Paul O'Neill, who is seeking to make US contributions to the IFIs conditional on evidence of success. The Washington institutions, who have long been the whipping boys of the left for spearheading the capitalist assault on the developing world, are suddenly left out in the political cold. The main theatre of global politics is not the World Trade Organization, less concerned with developing countries, than the conditions of trade among the large trading blocs.

The justified critique of much development assistance does not account, however, for the considerable stock of experience and the lessons learned by what we call new development. Increasingly the development interventions by some of the leading agencies, including the Scandinavian organization Noraid, the German Gesellschaft für Technische Zusammenarbeit (GTZ), the European Commission-administered European Development Fund and the UK Department for International Development are subject to clear principles: they are free from procurement requirements, they aim at recipient benefit, and concentrate upon poverty alleviation and institution-building. Moreover, the close monitoring and evaluation of the outcomes of the development partnership provide the insights and the data for forging new development paths in the future, including a more equitable trading relationship. Access restrictions to agricultural and textile products in the main European and North American markets remain some of the most formidable development obstacles to date.

There is a real danger that if development cooperation is traded for security, state failure will spread across ever greater areas of the developing world, creating new empty spaces for terrorist groups to take root in, spawning new shoals of recruits, and giving rise to new causes. A mainly military response has the danger of locking the West into a mirage war, without a clearly identified enemy, defined war aims, and no end in sight. The emotional responses that have found expression in the new 'war on terror' have borrowed heavily from the rhetoric of the decade-old 'war on drugs'. The growing consonance of the discourses of drug and terror warriors should give pause for thought, as supporters of the controversial Plan Colombia are seeking to redefine US military assistance as a war on economic and political terrorism.[5] This crusade first embarked upon by the Nixon administration has delivered none of the hoped-for results in spite of significant resource mobilization and collateral damage.

An equally heavy-handed approach to terrorism, ignoring the realities that fuel conflict, may, far from enhancing the security of the West, only serve to jeopardize it. It is now well known that the Islamist militants who have become the embodiment of the terrorist threat to Western security were at their inception trained and armed by Western intelligence agencies. In the security service parlance this has become known as 'blowback', 'shorthand for saying that a nation reaps what it sows, even if it does not fully know or understand what is has sown' (Johnson 2002).

Reliance on intelligence and security measures, then, contains fallacies: it is ignorant about the underlying causes of privatized violence, which lie in the experience of social injustice and poor governance in developing countries, often backed by the US government. There is a considerable discrepancy between the ethical values regulating domestic politics in the West, and a foreign policy governed by a narrow interpretation of national interest. Widespread and historic apathy concerning foreign policy on the part of the US electorate has for decades left politicians and bureaucracies much room for unscrutinized manoeuvre. The current mismatch between the global popularity of the American way of life on the one hand, and the deep-seated animosity towards Uncle Sam's interference on the other, bears testimony to the success of such policy.

It also misreads the nature of power, by assuming that military solutions lie in the hands of the one remaining superpower. Power, however, is too complex to be reduced to a single dimension. Joseph Nye uses the model of a three-dimensional chess game to describe the current global power balance – the military game is played on the top, and here the USA is predominant. In the middle an economic game is played, with North America, Europe and Japan presenting two-thirds and China catching up rapidly. 'The bottom chessboard is the realm of transnational relations that cross borders outside government control' (Nye 2002). Here power is widely dispersed, and talk of polarity is indicative of a wholly inadequate analysis.

And with the technological skills to harness instruments of mass destruction, and the organizational capacity to deliver them ever more widely available, a far-sighted security policy seeks not merely to combat external threats, but to tackle its root causes. This means redrafting the foreign relations agenda in favour of a renewed development commitment by the West. This must include not merely honouring existing commitments in terms of meeting the Millennium Development Goals and UN contributions. It must also include an invigorated 'horizontal' internationalism. While the transition processes in China, Eastern Europe and the former Soviet Union have been inspired largely by Western models, finance and political support, there is much to be gained from an East–South dialogue. The chapters in this volume illustrate the value of comparison and the exchange of experience. While each conflict has particular historical antecedents, structural conditions help explain both the outbreak and the resolution of violence.

Identifying the root causes of conflict, examples of good practice in conflict resolution, and successful institution-building processes from different theatres of conflict hold the promise of tangible benefits. The agenda for coming years should be to expand the East–South dialogue in order to enable stakeholders from countries unsettled by conflict to learn from perspectives across different crisis regions. This volume, by integrating studies on flashpoints in three different continents, provides a promising start.

NOTES

1. The most influential proponent of the new 'doctrine' is probably Robert D. Kaplan. See his 'The Coming Anarchy', *Atlantic Monthly*, February 1994.

2. The Ghost Dance was a cult among nineteenth-century Plains Indians in response to European intrusion, advocating violent resistance and accepting death.

3. Tony Blair on the global role of the UK.

4. G. Baker, 'Cheney's new realism runs into old constraints', *Financial Times*, 21 March 2002.

5. John Diamond, *Chicago Tribune*, 18 February 2002.

REFERENCES

Amin, S. (1994) *Re-reading the Post War Period: An Intellectual Itinerary*, New York: Monthly Review Press.

Baer R. (2002) *See No Evil: The True Story of a Ground Soldier in the CIA's War Against Terrorism*, London: Crown Publications.

Blum W. (2000) *Rogue State: A Guide to the World's Only Superpower*, Monroe, ME: Common Courage Press.

Chandler D. (1999) *Bosnia: Faking Democracy after Dayton*, London: Pluto.

Douma, P. and P. Lebillon (2001) 'Recent trends in the political economy of war', paper presented at London CODEP Conference, School of Oriental and African Studies.

French, L. A. (2000) *Addictions and Native Americans*, Westport, CT: Praeger.

Gross, J.-G. (1996) 'Towards a taxonomy of failed states in the New World Order: decaying Somalia, Liberia, Rwanda and Haiti', *Third World Quarterly*, 17 (3): 455–71.

Harriott, A. (2000) *Police and Crime Control in Jamaica: Problems of Reforming Ex-Colonial Constabularies*, Mona, Jamaica: University of West Indies Press.

Hochschild, A. (1998) *King Leopold's Ghost*, London: Macmillan.

Johnson, C. (2002) *Blowback: The Costs and Consequences of American Empire*, London: Little, Brown.

Kaldor, M. (1999) 'The structure of conflict', in Lennart Wohlgemuth, Samantha Gibson, Stephan Klasen and Emma Rothschild (eds), *Common Security and Civil Society in Africa*, Uppsala: Nordiska Afrikainstitutet.

Kelly, R. C. (2000) *Warless Societies and the Origin of War*, Ann Arbor: University of Michigan Press.

Levene, Mare and Penny Roberts (1999) *The Massacre in History*, New York: Berghahn.

Mkandawire, T. (1998) *Developmental States in Africa*, Geneva: United Nations.

— (2002) *Thinking about Development States in Africa*, Copenhagen Centre for Development Research.

Nye, J. (2002) *The Paradox of American Power: Why the World's only Superpower Can't Go it Alone*. Oxford: Oxford University Press.

Reno, W. (1998) *Warlord Politics and African States*, Boulder, CO and London: Lynne Rienner.

Richards, P. (1996) *Fighting for the Rain Forest: War, Youth and Resources in Sierra Leone*, Oxford: James Currey.

Schlosser, E. (2001) *Fast Food Nation: What the All-American Meal is Doing to the World*, London: Allen Lane Penguin Press.

Webb, G. (1998) *Dark Alliance: The CIA, the Contras and the Crack Cocaine Explosion*, New York: Seven Stories Press.

Index

national independence movements, 95–6
National Islamic Front (Sudan), 161, 164, 167
National Reconciliation Commissions, in Central America, 133
National Secretariat for Reconstruction (SRN) (El Salvador), 50
National Union for the Total Independence of Angola (UNITA), 217
nationalism, 16, 18, 110–28; separation from democracy, 125
Negua, Berhanu, 182
neopatrimonial state, 5–6
New Barbarism, 213–14
new realism, 211–26
Nicaragua, 19, 20, 129, 131, 132, 133–4, 136, 137, 138, 139, 141, 201
Nigeria, 215
Nixon, Richard, 223
Nkrumah, Kwame, 179
Non Aligned Movement, 219
non-governmental organizations (NGOs), 59, 62, 80, 153; performing state functions, 4
Noraid, 222
North Atlantic Treaty Organization (NATO), 89, 91, 103, 116, 121, 198, 200; Partnership for Peace, 116
North–South wealth divide, 203
Nye, Joseph, 224
Nyerere, Julius, 178

oil, in Caspian Sea, 89, 92, 212
O'Neill, Paul, 222
Operation Rachel (South Africa–Mozambique), 40
Organization for Economic Cooperation and Development (OECD) Development Assistance Committee (OECD/DAC), 9, 52
Organization for Security and Cooperation in Europe (OCSE), 92, 103, 104, 106, 116, 117; monitoring of elections, 99
Organization of African Unity (OAU), 163, 165

Organization of American States (OAS), 134; Verification Commission in Nicaragua, 137, 139
Oromo Liberation Front (OLF), 24, 158, 159, 164, 171, 172, 174
Ortega, Daniel, 133, 141
Ossetia: North, 111; South, 18, 91, 93, 111, 115, 118

Palestine and Palestinians, 51, 214, 215
participation, 82
Partido de Avanzada Nacional (PAN) (Guatemala), 152
partnerships, creation of, 42–6
patron, figure of, 5–6
Patten, Christopher, 12
Pausewang, Siegfried, 24
Peace and Reconciliation Committees (PRC), 166–8
peace missions, international, 61
peace-building, 8, 20, 45, 141–3; defining of, 35–6; enhancing effectiveness of, 46–8; personnel for, 52; tasks of, 36–9
peace-keeping operations, 45, 46, 65, 68, 163
People's Front for Democracy and Justice (PFDJ) (Eritrea), 160, 164
perestroika, 115
Peru, 151, 215
Plan Colombia, 223
police, 27, 65, 115, 217; in Ethiopia, 179–80; reform programmes, 51
political institutions, strengthening of, 35
Popular Front (Azerbaijan), 97
Portillo, Alfonso, 141, 150
poverty, 4, 20, 130, 203; combatting of, 27; reduction of, 33, 35–6, 39, 42
presidential rule, 98–101; boundaries of, 106–8
Primakov, Yevgeni, 104
privatization of violence, 191–210, 223
property rights, 33
public choice school, 75
Puntland, 15, 23, 78, 158, 160, 165
Putin, Vladimir, 102